Ross-of-Bladensburg

The Coldstream Guards in the Crimea

Ross-of-Bladensburg
The Coldstream Guards in the Crimea
ISBN/EAN: 9783743426313
Manufactured in Europe, USA, Canada, Australia, Japa
Cover: Foto ©ninafisch / pixelio.de

Ross-of-Bladensburg

The Coldstream Guards in the Crimea

THE COLDSTREAM GUARDS
IN THE CRIMEA

BY THE SAME AUTHOR.

Including an Account of the Political Events and Campaigns with which the Regiment has been associated.

A HISTORY OF THE COLDSTREAM GUARDS
From 1815 to 1885.

With numerous Coloured Plates, Drawings, and Maps, by Lieutenant NEVILE R. WILKINSON. Crown 4to, cloth, gilt top, 2 guineas net.

"Colonel Ross-of-Bladensburg may justly claim for this magnificent volume that it is something more than a regimental chronicle. . . . The book is full of interest. The reputation of any ordinary work of the kind would be made by the illustrations alone."—*Times.*

"The Coldstream Guards is fortunate in its chronicler. The book is a valuable contribution to military history."—*Spectator.*

"The book is invaluable alike to the soldier, the civilian, and the politician."—*Saturday Review.*

THE COLDSTREAM GUARDS IN THE CRIMEA

BY

LT.-COL. ROSS-OF-BLADENSBURG, C.B.

LONDON
A. D. INNES & CO.
BEDFORD STREET
1897

PREFACE.

THE following pages are a reproduction of the Crimean portion of a *History of the Coldstream Guards from* 1815 *to* 1885, which was published a few months ago. Such parts have been omitted that refer to matters, less interesting to the public generally than to the Officers past and present of the Regiment and to their friends. But otherwise the present volume contains all that was written in the larger work upon the hostilities conducted against Russia in the middle of the present century, and upon the action of the distinguished Corps, just mentioned, during that memorable period.

The struggle for Sevastopol forms the main feature of the one great European war, in which we have been engaged, since the defeat of Napoleon I. at the battle of Waterloo. Though obscured by other events, it is still fresh in the minds of all thoughtful Englishmen ; and while a great deal has already been written about it, we cannot say that the subject has yet been exhausted. Indeed, this is far from being the case ; and it is possible that only in the present day—when the leading actors of the great drama have all disappeared—will historical criticism sufficiently elucidate many of the important points, connected with events in the East between 1853 and 1856, which up to now have scarcely been weighed and considered as they deserve.

As a slight and very imperfect contribution to the history of this war, I now venture to present this small book to my readers. I do so with no little diffidence, being well aware of its many shortcomings. But I have the conviction that few modern episodes in the annals of our country are more worthy of their attention than this one is; while I also have the pleasant assurance that the brave deeds and the heroic endurance of our splendid Crimean soldiers must always excite a warm and enthusiastic interest among all classes of Englishmen.

I desire again to express my grateful thanks to General Sir Frederick Stephenson, G.C.B. (now Colonel of the Coldstream Guards), and to General Hon. Sir Percy Feilding, K.C.B. (late of the Coldstream), both of whom served throughout the war with Russia, for the interest they showed in my work when I was preparing the larger book,—of which the following pages form a part, as has been mentioned above,—and for the trouble they took to enable me to carry it out; also to Major Goulbourn, Grenadier Guards, who kindly lent me the very interesting Crimean diary of the late Colonel Tower.

Lastly, I also beg to offer my acknowledgments to Messrs. Blackwood & Sons, and to Messrs. Seeley & Co., for their courteous permission to use the maps in Mr. Kinglake's *Invasion of the Crimea*, and in Sir E. Hamley's *War in the Crimea;* as well as to Lieutenant Nevile Wilkinson, Coldstream Guards, whose maps, drawn originally for the larger book, I have been allowed to reproduce here.

J. R.-OF-B.

August, 1897.

CONTENTS.

PART I.
BEGINNING OF THE WAR IN THE EAST.

CHAPTER I.
HOW ENGLAND AND FRANCE WERE DRAWN INTO THE WAR.

Position of Russia in Europe—General attitude of the Western Powers—State of the Continent in 1853—Of France—Friendly feeling towards England—Alliance between the two nations—Condition of Austria, Prussia, and Germany—The Tsar's quarrel with the Sultan—Commencement of the war—The Vienna Note—Its failure—Turkish successes on the Danube—The affair of Sinope—Events that caused it—And how it involved England and France in the struggle 1

CHAPTER II.
THE ALLIES IN THE EAST.

Three Battalions of the Brigade of Guards ordered on Foreign Service—Departure of the Coldstream from London—Arrival in Malta—Concentration of the Allies in the Mediterranean—Occupation of Scutari—General Lord Raglan assumes command—The British Army begins to form—Want of transport—The Allies move to Varna—Women at the seat of war—Good feeling between the British and French troops 19

CHAPTER III.
OPERATIONS IN BULGARIA.

Course of the war on the Danube—Siege of Silistria—Bravery of the garrison—The Russians fail to take it—Other failures, and their retreat from Turkish territory into Bessarabia—Intervention of Austria—Importance of this event; and how it affected the war—The Allies in Bulgaria—Their inaction—Sickness among the troops—Return to Varna—Preparations for the invasion of the Crimea—The organization and strength of the Allies ... 31

PART II.

THE INVASION OF THE CRIMEA.

CHAPTER IV.

DETERMINATION TO ATTACK SEVASTOPOL.

Small results gained by the Allies—Embarrassment of the British Government—Sudden determination to attack Sevastopol—Inconveniences of this resolution—Russian position in the Trans-Caucasian provinces—Conditions under which the Crimea was invaded—The object of the expedition not kept secret—The isolation of the Peninsula not attempted—Lateness of the season—No provision made for a lengthened operation ... 51

CHAPTER V.

LANDING IN THE CRIMEA.

The allied Armada sails from Varna to Eupatoria—Landing effected at "Old Fort"—How the troops were equipped—Serious deficiency of transport—The move to Sevastopol—Strength of the invaders—Their order of march—Skirmish on the Bulganak—The enemy on the Alma river opposes the advance of the Allies—Preparations made to dislodge him—Description of the field of battle—Strength and position of the Russians 64

CHAPTER VI.

BATTLE OF THE ALMA.

Commencement of the battle—Advance of the Light and Second Divisions—Deployment of the First Division—Advance of the Guards and Highland Brigades—Defeat and flight of the Russians—No pursuit—Losses—Bravery and steadiness of the British troops—The Allies lose valuable time after the battle—Arriving at last before their objective, Sevastopol, they refuse to attack it—General description of Sevastopol 76

PART III.

BEFORE SEVASTOPOL.

CHAPTER VII.

FLANK MARCH ROUND SEVASTOPOL.

Predicament of the Allies—Determination to attack the south side—Flank march—Strange meeting with the rear of Menshikoff's army—Occupation of Balaklava by the British and of Kamiesh Bay by the French—The Allies refuse to assault Sevastopol; they prefer to bombard it—Depression of the Russian garrison, who fear a prompt assault—Their strength and the state of their defences—Successful efforts to strengthen the latter 97

CONTENTS.

CHAPTER VIII.
A REGULAR SIEGE UNCONSCIOUSLY BEGUN.

Description of the upland of the Chersonese occupied by the Allies —Position of Menshikoff's army—Of the French—Of the British —Weakness of the right flank of the allied line—Nothing done to defend it—Supply of tents to the troops—Preparation for the projected bombardment—Official confidence in an immediate success—Severe duties—How the enemy utilized the unexpected respite accorded to him 109

CHAPTER IX.
THE FIRST BOMBARDMENT.

Importance and magnitude of the operation—Results of the first day's fire—No attack—Continuation of the bombardment—No better result—The insecurity of the British right flank—Augmentation of the Coldstream for the purposes of the war—Russian reinforcements begin to arrive—Battle of Balaklava—Cavalry charges—Consequences of the battle—*Sortie* against our right flank—Its failure—Its object—Another bombardment projected early in November 122

PART IV.
BATTLE OF INKERMAN.

CHAPTER X.
CONDITIONS UNDER WHICH THE BATTLE TOOK PLACE.

Large Russian reinforcements reach the Crimea —Menshikoff determines to drive the invaders into the sea—Position and strength of the enemy—Numerical strength of the Allies—Length of the line to be defended by them—Plan of attack—Prospects of the Russians—Their confidence of victory—Description of the field of Inkerman—Position of the Allies opposing the attack—Hearing the sound of fire, the Guards move quickly to the front ... 143

CHAPTER XI.
EARLY STAGES OF THE FIGHT.

Events of the morning — Unexpected approach of the enemy — Confusion in the Russian arrangements for the attack—First struggle with the British outposts—The Second Division soon involved— Arrival of General Buller's Brigade—Inequality of the numbers engaged—Arrival of the Guards' Brigade; their strength and composition—Situation on the field at that moment —The Guards move to the Kitspur, and join the rest already engaged there 153

CHAPTER XII.

STRUGGLE ON THE KITSPUR.

The Sandbag battery on the Kitspur, the central point of the main attack—A contest against very superior forces—A confused but exceedingly fierce struggle—Impossibility to describe accurately the exact details as they occurred—Arrival of the Fourth Division under General Cathcart — His manœuvre and its failure — Arrival of the French—Exhaustion of the Guards—They withdraw to Home Ridge... 166

CHAPTER XIII.

REPULSE OF THE RUSSIANS.

Operations of the French — Successes of the British artillery — Repulse of the Russian attack — Retreat of the enemy — No pursuit—What the garrison of Sevastopol did during the day —Operations of the Russian forces in the valley of the Tchernaya—Their unaccountable inactivity—Great losses incurred on both sides—Those among the Coldstream Officers abnormally large — Reaction after the struggle — A scene of carnage—Extraordinary gallantry of the British troops 179

PART V.

THE WINTER OF 1854-55 IN THE CRIMEA.

CHAPTER XIV.

DISTRESS OF THE ARMY.

Prostration of both sides after the battle of Inkerman—Sevastopol not to be taken in 1854—Tardy arrangements made for the winter—Depletion of the ranks—The right flank is at last secured —Violent hurricane of the 14th of November; stores scattered and destroyed—The winter begins in earnest—Causes of the sufferings that overwhelmed the army—How Government attended to its wants—No road between the base and front— Miserable plight to which the army was reduced... 195

CHAPTER XV.

OPERATIONS DURING THE WINTER.

Indignation in England, and the measures taken to relieve the army—Admirable manner in which the misfortunes were borne by the British soldiers—Testimony of the commission of inquiry —The Russians quiescent during the winter—Operations of the Allies—The French extend their siege-works—The Turks brought to the Crimea and occupy Eupatoria—Their successes at the battle there—The Guards brigade are sent to Balaklava ... 215

CONTENTS.

PART VI.
THE FALL OF SEVASTOPOL.

CHAPTER XVI.
EVENTS OF THE SPRING OF 1855.

Stay of the Brigade at Balaklava—Improvement in the condition of the men—Return of the Guards to the front, June 16th—Changed aspect of affairs before Sevastopol—Review of events during the time spent at Balaklava—Interference by Napoleon III. in the course of the war—Second bombardment—Operations paralysed—General Canrobert resigns, and is succeeded by General Pélissier—Energy displayed by the latter—Third bombardment 229

CHAPTER XVII.
END OF THE SIEGE.

Fourth bombardment; assault on Sevastopol—Its failure—Death of Lord Raglan; succeeded by General Simpson—Siege operations continued—Battle of the Tchernaya—Fifth bombardment —Sixth bombardment; the second assault—The Malakoff is captured—Failure of the assault on the Redan—Fall of the south side of Sevastopol—The Russians evacuate the town, and retreat to the north side—State in which the Allies found Sevastopol ... 241

PART VII.
THE END OF THE RUSSIAN WAR.

CHAPTER XVIII.
HOW THE UNFINISHED WAR LANGUISHED.

Home events during the war—Sympathy of Her Majesty with her Crimean soldiers—Badges of distinction added to the Colours —Inactivity of the Allies after the fall of the south side of Sevastopol — Causes for this — Small expeditions against the Russian coast—The fall of Kars—Sir W. Codrington succeeds as Commander of the Forces—The winter 1855-56—Negotiations for a peace, which is concluded, March 30th, 1856 ... 263

CHAPTER XIX.
RETURN OF THE TROOPS, AND SUMMARY.

Events after the cessation of hostilities—A British cemetery in the Crimea—Embarkation and return home—Regimental Crimean statistics—British losses during the war—Computation of Russian losses—The Crimean Guards Brigade at Aldershot; visit of Her Majesty the Queen — Move to London, and cordial reception there—Distribution of the Victoria Cross—Summary of events connected with the war 281

APPENDIX A.
GENERAL ORDER, NO. 1, CONSTANTINOPLE, APRIL 30, 1854 ... 297

APPENDIX B.
DEATH OF FIELD-MARSHAL LORD RAGLAN, G.C.B. 299

APPENDIX C.
AGES AND PREVIOUS OCCUPATIONS OF THE NON-COMMISSIONED OFFICERS AND MEN OF THE 1ST BATTALION COLDSTREAM GUARDS, AND DRAFTS SENT TO THE EAST, ENGAGED IN THE WAR WITH RUSSIA 302

APPENDIX D.
DEATHS IN THE 1ST BATTALION COLDSTREAM GUARDS BY MONTHS DURING THE WAR WITH RUSSIA 304

APPENDIX E.
1. RETURN OF THE NUMBERS KILLED IN THE CRIMEA ... 306
2. RETURN OF THE NUMBERS WOUNDED IN THE CRIMEA, DEAD, INVALIDED, ETC. 307

MAPS.

No. 1.—THE BLACK SEA REGION	*To face*	31
,, 2.—THE CRIMEA FROM EUPATORIA TO SEVASTOPOL	,,	65
,, 3.—THE BATTLE OF THE ALMA	,,	86
,, 4.—THE COUNTRY NEAR SEVASTOPOL	,,	102
,, 5.—SEVASTOPOL	,,	124
,, 6.—THE BATTLE OF INKERMAN	,,	166

PART I.

BEGINNING OF THE WAR IN THE EAST.

THE COLDSTREAM GUARDS IN THE CRIMEA.

CHAPTER I.

HOW ENGLAND AND FRANCE WERE DRAWN INTO THE WAR.

Position of Russia in Europe—General attitude of the Western Powers—State of the Continent in 1853—Of France—Friendly feeling towards England—Alliance between the two nations—Condition of Austria, Prussia, and Germany—The Tsar's quarrel with the Sultan—Commencement of the war—The Vienna Note—Its failure—Turkish successes on the Danube—The affair of Sinope—Events that caused it—And how it involved England and France in the struggle.

THE Empire of Russia—except for the great expansion in Central Asia which has taken place during the last forty years, and which has now brought its frontiers close to India—was scarcely less vast and formidable in 1853 than it is at present. Stretching from Germany on the west, to the Pacific Ocean on the east, bordering the Black Sea, and pressing on Turkey, Persia, and China, it occupies an immense and continuous territory, both in Europe and in Asia, and exercises many and important influences over the civilization of the world. Inhabited generally, by a docile agricultural population who live in the plains, and whose liberties and property are at the mercy of a strong executive power, it is ruled by an Autocrat both in name and in reality, and is governed by a trained army of ubiquitous administrators and officials, who enforce his decrees, and coerce the whole people to spend their existence in the service of the Tsar. The organization of Russia, less adapted, perhaps, to secure the welfare of her subjects than to accomplish the will of her rulers, is skilfully constructed; and the sagacity she displays in the conduct of her affairs, is as conspicuous in the manner she brings fresh conquests within her grasp, as in that by which she controls and assimilates the numerous and heterogeneous nationalities, that are to be found within her borders.

But here her advantages end. Russia has no seaboard, and her foreign commerce, incommensurate to her size and importance, is not sufficient to enable her to develop her vast resources, or to consolidate the stupendous forces with which her disciplined intelligence, large possessions, and teeming population should endow her. A glance at the map reveals the disability under which she labours. Fettered in the north by an ice-bound ocean, she has but two outlets through which to reveal her strength, and these are blocked by the narrow channels of the Sound and the Bosphorus.

That Russia is ambitious and greedy of power, few will deny; but her encroachments are not altogether due to the mere love of extending her territories. Her existence, as a nation of the first rank, is menaced by her maritime weakness, and until she frees herself from the shackles that cripple her commercial activity on the sea, she is the ready and easy victim of the Power that holds, and has strength to use, the keys of her house. But, added to this, her statesmen have long perceived that, as soon as they shall have gained the Bosphorus, they will win a commanding supremacy over the destinies of the world. While, therefore, they are impelled to a system of aggrandisement, in order to force their way to the sea and to preserve the life of their Imperial structure, they by no means despise the glorious goal of wide dominion, to which the success of this policy must infallibly conduct them. This, then, is, and has been for many generations, ever since their genius conceived the design, the reason which has urged them relentlessly to enlarge their possessions in Poland, Persia, and in Central Asia, and to exhibit undying hostility towards the Turkish Empire.

The Western Powers have not failed to recognize the danger to which they are exposed by this active and aggressive policy, and Great Britain, having vital interests of her own in the far East, has never been able to view with unconcern the absorption of Turkey by her Northern rival. Hence, it has come about that, when the Sultan has been threatened, many nations of the West have endeavoured to go to his assistance, and to ward off the disaster that seemed to be imminent. But their efforts have been badly directed. For, divided among themselves, pursuing divergent interests, interfering without wisdom, or led away by false conceptions of the real situation, they too often manacled the defensive power of Turkey, and gave victory to the Russians, when the latter had not won it by their own strength. In this way Russia advanced and prospered,—by the ascendency that organized intelligence will ever command over a policy of mere sentimental or unreflective expediency,—until 1853, when another crisis was impending in the East, which produced a great European war, and terminated the long peace that had existed since 1815.

It is not necessary to dwell upon the origin of the war. It arose from a trivial incident—the possession of the keys of the Holy Places in Palestine. The Emperor Nicholas I. reigned at St. Petersburg at that time, and he claimed these emblems of superiority as head of the Greek Church; so also did the French, in virtue of an old Treaty made in the sixteenth century, which, they affirmed, constituted them protectors of the Latin Church in the East. The Sultan adjusted the petty cause of dispute, and thereupon the Tsar made fresh demands, which the Porte resisted. These will be adverted to presently, but a word will be necessary here to describe briefly the position of affairs, that existed on the continent of Europe.

France did not long maintain the Republic set up by the Revolution of 1848. Louis Napoleon, nephew and political heir of Napoleon I.—in spite of the old decree banishing the family of that great Emperor,—was elected President for four years by a large majority (December 20th). Strengthening his position with the army, by appeals to past glory, and with the people generally, by the maintenance of order in troublous times, he resolved to revive the Empire, and succeeded in December, 1851, in constituting himself President for ten years, with largely increased powers, and with the title of Prince. Twelve months later (December 2, 1852), he was proclaimed Emperor under the name of Napoleon III., and was so acknowledged by Europe.

The new Sovereign was not blind to the advantages which a friendship with England would confer upon him; he was even anxious to conciliate a people he had known and respected in the days of his exile. The defect in his title, moreover, was best obliterated by the adoption of a policy of adventure. The appearance of the Eastern cloud furnished him with an opportunity he was glad to seize; and, as it became darker, so did he, the more readily, co-operate with the British Cabinet, in their attempt to disperse it. When it was determined that peace could no longer be maintained, an alliance was cemented between the two countries, and England and France, so often in the past unhappily opposed in war, were at length found side by side in the strife, combating the same foe and loyally supporting each other in the field of battle —rivals only in the honour and glory to be derived therefrom.

And yet this union was not without serious drawbacks. Seldom can a confederacy of independent States be satisfactory; for each has different interests to serve, and conflicting opinions too frequently weaken the efforts of those who have banded themselves together to accomplish an object avowedly dear to all. In 1854 the alliance was definitely established; it became *l'entente cordiale*, as it was felicitously termed, and, when the war was in progress, harmony and mutual respect and confidence reigned between the armies engaged. But, as a price, to please Napoleon, England gave up some of her most cherished customs of naval warfare—a sacrifice which the armed forces of Europe had in vain sought to wring from her,—

and hostilities assumed a direction which, as will be seen, did the least damage to the enemy, and effected injury to the cause which the British nation had most at heart.

The popular explosion in France in 1848, affected not only that country, but produced widespread results, and its consequences were felt, like the Revolution of 1830, all over the continent of Europe. In Austria the crisis had been peculiarly acute, and the Hungarians and Italians rose in rebellion against the authority of their Sovereign. The latter was able to re-assert his power in Lombardy by his own resources; but in Hungary the resistance was so strong that, when the Tsar offered the assistance of his troops, the proposal was accepted, and Russian bayonets reduced the Magyars to obedience, and placed them once more under the Austrian Emperor (1849).

In Prussia and in the petty States of Germany less difficulties had been experienced; but the temper of the people had been aroused, and they clamoured for reform and a greater control over their own affairs. The German Princes were alarmed; they distrusted their subjects, and relied for counsel and aid upon Russia—the only Power whose government, like theirs, was despotic, but who, unlike them, had no fear of a popular ebullition.

In truth, the credit of the Tsar was in the

ascendant in Central Europe: he ostensibly saved Austria from disaster, if not from dissolution; he intervened in the question of the Danish Duchies,* which then agitated the whole of Germany; and he mediated successfully between Austria and Prussia, when they became rivals and jealous of each other, on account of the efforts of the latter to restore in her own favour the Imperial Constitution of Germany, which had come to an end in 1806. In short, the Emperor Nicholas controlled the German nations; he arbitrated in their differences; and could involve them in serious trouble should they see fit to dispute his pleasure.

When Russia, therefore, not content with the settlement effected with respect to the Holy Places, determined still to provoke a quarrel with Turkey, the Western Powers were not united upon the problem that invited their attention. England and France alone resolved to resist her pretensions, while the others—Austria, Prussia, and the minor States of Germany—practically ranged themselves on her side. The demands made upon the Porte are of little importance; any pretext is good, where an object is to be gained. The Sultan was required to accept the protection of Russia over his Christian subjects, and he refused to submit (May 23, 1853).

In this determination England agreed; indeed, it

* Schleswig and Holstein, torn from Denmark in 1864.

is clear that it would have been impossible for him to deliver over a very considerable section of his people into the hands of his hereditary enemy. Thereupon a Russian force, under Prince Michael Gortchakoff, crossed the Pruth (July 2nd), occupied the Principalities (now the kingdom of Roumania), and established itself upon the Danube. The Turks immediately made great efforts to meet the emergency, by collecting troops and despatching them both into Asia Minor, and into Bulgaria. But no declaration of war took place, for the Western Powers persuaded the aggrieved party to have patience, while they sent representatives to Vienna to try to avert hostilities by the arts of diplomacy.

These endeavours failed entirely, not to say ridiculously. An Instrument was drafted, called the Vienna Note, to which both the Tsar and the Sultan were to consent, as a basis for a future arrangement. The former did so readily, but the latter peremptorily refused his adhesion to it. That he was right, is shown by the fact that the Note was so loosely drawn, as to be capable of an interpretation, whereby the full demands of Russia would have been agreed to by Turkey; and in the negotiations which followed, it became apparent that this was the only interpretation which the Emperor Nicholas had adopted! So the intervention projected at this centre of Russian intrigue, came to an end with the full concurrence of the

British and French Governments, who were obliged to recognize that they had been duped.

In October, the Porte formally called upon General Gortchakoff to evacuate the Danubian Principalities, and ordered Omar Pasha, the Turkish Commander-in-chief in Bulgaria, "to commence hostilities if, after fifteen days from the arrival of his despatch at the Russian head-quarters, an answer in the negative should be returned." After the stated interval, towards the end of the month, the war commenced, not only on the Danube, but also on the Armenian frontier in Asia.

Interesting as is the campaign that now began, to the student of military history, it will be impossible to describe it at any length in these pages. It must suffice to say that, at the end of the year, the results in Asia were unimportant. There were victories on both sides, but no great progress was achieved by either of the combatants. It was different in Europe, for there, thanks to the skill and energy of Omar Pasha, and to the gallantry of his troops, the Turks gained many and considerable advantages. Crossing the Danube at Turtukai, they secured a position on the northern bank of the river at Oltenitza, in the face of superior forces, and repulsed every attempt to dislodge them. Again, having established themselves firmly at Kalafat, opposite Widin, they attacked and dealt a crushing defeat (early in January, 1854) on a strong corps, which had entrenched itself in their vicinity near Citate. The Ottoman troops were everywhere victorious in this theatre of operations; the Russians, on the other hand, were beaten and disorganized, their *morale* shaken, and their losses, on their own admission, amounted to 35,000 men.

While these successes were being won, an incident occurred which caused the war to spread, and drew England and France into its meshes. A small Turkish squadron of a few frigates and smaller vessels lay at anchor at Sinope; whereupon, a far more powerful Russian fleet, consisting of heavily armed and large ships, approached under cover of a fog, surprised them, and completely destroyed them (November 30th). The attack was conducted under circumstances of considerable barbarity; no quarter was given, the ships were sunk, the wounded and the helpless were not spared, and 4000 men were slaughtered or drowned. When the news of this action reached Europe, indignation, already aroused by previous events, could not be restrained in England, and so strong was the feeling evoked in the country, that war could no longer be avoided.

At first sight it may appear strange, that the story of useless butchery, perpetrated in war time, should produce so violent a resentment; but when events are reviewed, the reasons for it will be perceived. It is necessary to glance at these events, in order to understand some features connected with subsequent operations.

The guiding line of thought that influenced the statesmen of the two Powers, interested in curbing the aggression of St. Petersburg, was the conviction that Russia was at that time overwhelmingly powerful, and that the Ottoman Empire was in the last gasp of impotence and decrepitude. The Emperor Nicholas had for long fostered this idea, and had carefully instilled it into our Government. With this object, he made a journey to this country as early as 1844, and he pressed it upon our Ambassador at his Court, in secret communications held in the spring of 1853, before the actual crisis had taken place. We were then told that Turkey was "a sick man—a very sick man" who might at any moment "die upon our hands," and that it was therefore advisable to divide his inheritance; and our cupidity was tempted by the offer of Egypt, and even of the island of Crete, if we would take these bribes, and give Russia a free hand. We believed these assertions of omnipotence on the one hand, and of prostration on the other, though needless to say we had no desire to share in the spoils. Our minds instantly recurred to the campaigns of 1828-29, when the Russians crossed the Balkans, and forced a disastrous treaty upon the Sultan at Adrianople. We dwelt upon these results, showing only Russian victories and Turkish defeat, and we drew our conclusions therefrom. But we forgot a few historical facts connected with that war. We forgot that the Russians could only undertake a successful invasion of Turkey, when they had the command of the Black Sea, and that we ourselves had secured this for them, in 1828, by annihilating the Turkish fleet the year before (August, 1827), at the unfortunate victory of Navarino. We forgot, also, that the Balkans do not form the last line of defence, but that the difficulties of an invader increase materially as he approaches the Sea of Marmora. In 1829, the Russian army had achieved a great deal, but it had not attained to victory. It was exhausted, and unable to maintain itself at the end of a long line of communications; while Turkey, on the other hand, was gathering her forces together. We surely, then, failed to recollect, that we seized the opportunity at that very critical moment to force the Sultan to make a shameful peace; thereby saving the aggressor from disaster, and securing to him advantages which otherwise he could never have hoped to gain.

As a consequence of the exaggerated dread inspired by the great Northern Power, the Turks were not allowed to act in their own defence in 1853; they were obstructed by severe diplomatic pressure, and harassed by vexatious interference. At last, after the *fiasco* at Vienna, they could no longer be restrained by their timid friends, and, in spite of them, they at length declared war, in the autumn of 1853.

Now, when the Emperor Nicholas ordered an advance into the Ottoman Empire (viz. the Danubian Principalities) in July, and when the Porte, dissuaded from using force to repel the invasion, was obliged to allow her enemy quietly to consolidate himself therein, Russia, to appease Europe, made an announcement that she intended only to seize a material guarantee, and would engage in no further offensive operations. She would only meet any assault directed against her. England and France had sent their ships to a port near the Dardanelles (September 11th), and, as soon as the Sultan commenced hostilities, they ordered them up to Constantinople, to protect Turkey from Russian aggression (October 22nd).

Conscious of the dangers surrounding the small Turkish squadron in the Black Sea, very urgent requests were made, that the friendly fleets should pass through the Bosphorus, to prevent its falling into the power of the enemy. But these applications were all peremptorily refused.* To make the matter very much worse, and, indeed, to render the

---

* "Our last information from St. Petersburg, still represents Russia as desirous to treat, and as determined, above all, to assume the offensive in no quarter. This confidence explained why our fleets did not move" (*M. Drouyn de Lhuys to Count Walewski*, Paris, Dec. 15, 1853).

whole course of action unintelligible, *the Turkish fleet itself*, by the strong representations of the Sultan's Western advisers, was also kept back idly in the Bosphorus, and was prevented from sailing to the support of the exposed squadron ! *

Hence the disaster at Sinope became inevitable. When this state of affairs was realized in England, —when it was seen that our diplomatic skill was again at fault, that the assurances of Russia were not to be relied upon, and that our naval demonstrations were held in contempt,—then the natural consequences followed, and the British people, their Government notwithstanding, determined that the disturber of the peace of Europe should be punished.

Early in 1854, the English, French, and Turkish fleets entered the Black Sea, but the Russian flag had everywhere disappeared. The victorious Admiral at Sinope,—never dreaming that our extreme caution and fear of giving offence to his Imperial Master would prevent us from taking some prompt action, or from giving the Sultan leave immediately to pursue and capture him,—had betaken himself back to Sevastopol with the

---

* See *Correspondence respecting the Rights and Privileges of the Latin and Greek Churches in Turkey*, part ii., pp. 248-258. Writing from Therapia, November 5, 1853, to Lord Clarendon, Lord Stratford de Redcliffe, the British Ambassador at Constantinople, says, "I have succeeded in dissuading the Porte from sending a detachment of line-of-battle ships and sailing frigates into the Black Sea at this moment" (*ibid.*, p. 250).

C

utmost speed ; he only waited to make the necessary repairs to secure a safe passage, for "the Russian squadron had suffered considerably."

Nor was the Emperor Nicholas cast down by recent events, except for the fact that Omar Pasha was steadily destroying his military prestige on the Danube, and was revealing to the world the real weakness of his supposed power in the field. He ordered his Ambassadors in London and Paris to demand their passports, and they left those capitals on the 6th of February. Meanwhile the tedious and fruitless negotiations continued at Vienna, and Russia, far from showing any conciliatory disposition, increased her demands. But these conferences came to nothing, and on the 13th the British Ambassador was invited to quit St. Petersburg.* An Ultimatum followed, calling upon the Tsar to evacuate the Principalities, and the formal declaration of war was issued on the 28th of March.

* The French Ambassador in Russia thereupon applied for his passports.

CHAPTER II.

THE ALLIES IN THE EAST.

Three Battalions of the Brigade of Guards ordered on Foreign Service—Departure of the Coldstream from London—Arrival in Malta—Concentration of the Allies in the Mediterranean—Occupation of Scutari—General Lord Raglan assumes command—The British Army begins to form—Want of transport—The Allies move to Varna—Women at the seat of war—Good feeling between the British and French troops.

BEFORE hostilities were officially proclaimed, preparations for the coming strife had already been made. Treaties of alliance were concluded with France and Turkey, and an expeditionary force was sent to Malta. On the 10th of February a Brigade Order was issued, whereby a Brigade of Foot Guards, consisting of the 3rd Battalion Grenadiers and the 1st Battalions Coldstream and Scots Fusilier (now Scots) Guards, were to be held in readiness to proceed on foreign service by the 18th, each Battalion to be completed to 40 sergeants, besides the usual Staff-sergeants, and 850 rank and file. The 1st Coldstream, then quartered at St. George's barracks, London, were sent on the 14th of February to Chichester, where the 2nd Battalion were stationed, there to be made up to field strength, and to transfer weakly or unfit men to the latter. This was the first movement of the troops in London, and the people, eager for war to commence, and ever ready to welcome their brave defenders, hailed the appearance of the men with unbounded enthusiasm. A contemporary writer thus describes the scene:—

"It was just noon when the Battalion left, . . . the whole line of streets, from the barracks, along the Strand, over Waterloo Bridge, to the terminus of the South Western Railway, was literally blocked by multitudes, all eager to show some token of sympathy. Many a hand was stretched out to the brave fellows as they passed, which they had never clasped before—men of the humblest station grasped hands in which the best blood of England flowed. 'Fair women and brave men' waved their parting adieus. The windows and even the housetops were peopled with spectators, whose cheers, and waving of hats, and kerchiefs, testified their interest in the scene. Many of the Officers were young-looking men, and the rank and file seemed to be in the very bloom of youth and manhood, and to have attained that soldierly bearing which only a perfect discipline, united to professional pride, ever thoroughly forms."*

The Battalion, having been inspected at Chichester on the 17th, proceeded to Southampton, and, amid the hearty cheers of a dense crowd, embarked on board the steamship *Orinoco* (22nd) for

* Nolan, *History of the War against Russia*, i. 92.

Malta. Arriving there after a prosperous voyage, on the 4th of March, they were stationed at Fort Manoel (4 companies), Fort Tigne (1 company), and in the Lazarette (3 companies). The strength was 35 Officers, 919 men, and 32 women, the average age and service of the men being twenty-nine and seven years respectively.*

The three Guards Battalions reached Malta about the same time, and were commanded by Colonel Bentinck (Coldstream Guards), who was appointed Brigadier-General, February 21st. There they remained for about seven weeks, awaiting events; while other troops, all infantry, poured into the island, without General Officers, Staffs, or Departments, wherewith to form an army. At first it seemed somewhat doubtful whether they would go further. Our Government at home still dreamt of peace, and could not make up their minds that war was upon them; they even seemed to have thought that, though a naval demonstration had signally failed at Constantinople, a military display in the Mediterranean might frighten the Russians!

The interval, however, was not misspent; it was utilized in preparing the men for active service, principally in the exercise of musketry, which was practised without interruption. With reference to

* John Wyatt, Battalion-Surgeon, *History of the 1st Battalion Coldstream Guards during the Eastern Campaign, from February*, 1854, *to June*, 1856, p. 1 (1858).

this important subject, the following, written by a Coldstream Officer (Colonel Wilson), who was present with the Battalion, will be of interest :—

"When the Household Brigade was ordered abroad, the military Court of Chancery had come to no decision relative to the suitableness of the Minié rifle for the general use of infantry. As yet that amazing tool was in the possession of only a few *select* men in every regiment.* Hence, Lord Hardinge, who, it must be confessed, did much for the improvement of English small arms, judged it expedient that the Guards should take 'Brown Bess' to Malta; but, at the same time, he despatched thither cases of Miniés, under the charge of a competent instructor of musketry, Captain Lane-Fox [now General Pitt-Rivers, late Grenadier Guards]. . . Thanks to Captain Fox's exertions in favour of modern betterment, and a few experiments, a right verdict was at length delivered. At Scutari, old Brown Bess was marched off ignominiously to the Ordnance stores, and the Minié maiden became the faithful consort of every foot soldier. How completely have subsequent events substantiated the truth of Fox's arguments!" †

Towards the end of March our French allies,

---

* The Battalions of the Brigade proceeding on foreign service, started with 200 stand of Minié rifles and 650 percussion muskets (*Brigade Order*, Feb. 21st). Even as late as February, 1854, the respective merits of these two firearms were so little determined, that we find parties from each Regiment of the Brigade, ordered to fire 100 rounds "of the common balls out of the old musket," and to report upon the comparative accuracy of the fire (*ibid.*, Feb. 8th).

† "A Regimental Officer" (Colonel C. T. Wilson, late Coldstream Guards), *Our Veterans of* 1854, *in Camp and before the Enemy*, p. 15 (London, 1859). The exchange of these firearms was not effected in the Battalion till the end of May, 1854.

already formed into fighting units, began to appear in Malta on their way to Gallipoli, when they fraternized freely and cordially with their British friends. A few days later, Lieut.-General Sir George Brown reached the island, and started for the same destination, where he was joined by five battalions of infantry. Shortly afterwards, Scutari, opposite Constantinople on the Asiatic side of the Bosphorus, was occupied by our troops, and the British forces in the East began to collect there. The Guards Brigade left Malta on the 21st of April, in three ships, and, landing at Scutari on the 29th, they encamped there.

Next day a General Order was issued, which announced to the troops the arrival and appointment of General Lord Raglan, to the command of the army in Turkey,* whose composition into divisions and brigades, "to replace the provisional arrangement hitherto made by Lieut.-General Sir G. Brown," was also notified. The organization and strength of the Allies will be given later, when they were more complete, but it may be stated here, that five Officers belonging to the Coldstream (eventually five more) were placed upon the Staff; among them, Lieut.-Colonel T. M. Steele was appointed Military Secretary to Lord Raglan.

"The army, or rather the infantry element of an army," writes Colonel Wilson, "accumulated apace.

* See Appendix A.

Most mornings saw leviathan steamers letting go anchor in the Bosphorus; and an evening seldom passed without a fresh uprising of tents. But cavalry, artillery, military stores of all sorts, were yet afar off, tossing somewhere in sailing transports. In too many quarters, indeed, there were indications that the administration still clung to the fatal hallucination of peace, when there could be no peace,—still tried to believe that a demonstration within a mile of Constantinople, must be successful. 'Floriana and its parades failed,' some said, 'because Malta is so distant from the Pruth; but this concentration of ours at Scutari has a real business look, which *must* tell!' Unluckily, the Tsar knew that the government of England was built up of incoherent materials. He had faith in his old familiar friend, '*ce cher* Aberdeen.' His Greek spies informed him, how on the heights of Chalcedon stood no army ready to combat, only a stout corps of the unrivalled British Foot; therefore, he stayed not his hand. Old birds are not to be caught with chaff." *

The six weeks spent at Scutari passed pleasantly enough. The scenes around them were new to the rank and file, and many, in the Household Brigade certainly, had never dreamt of the East and its marvels. There was much to excite the interest of the men, and little to mar their enjoyment. British sports and pastimes were freely indulged in; the food was good; stores of groceries and other material comforts were provided; no hardships were endured; the heat was not too oppressive. The military authorities even relaxed some of their

* *Our Veterans, etc.*, p. 20.

old-fashioned and most cherished regulations, and the dog collar, called the stock, which then throttled our soldiers, was happily discarded. Cavalry and artillery began, moreover, to arrive in camp, and we seemed at length to be consolidating into a field army.

The troops were turned out on the Queen's birthday, and again on the 31st of May, for the inspection of the Sultan ; and, as usual, they presented a splendid appearance, both in physique and discipline ; moreover, they also began to look like an organized force. Still there was no transport, and the medical service left much to be desired. With no efficiency in these departments, how was war to be conducted ? And as the deficiency was absolute, did our Government really mean that we should take the field ? At last a makeshift was proposed, which is best described in Colonel Wilson's words :—

"The utter insufficiency of means of land-transport greatly perplexed the authorities, and, judging from the ever-varying complexion of the memoranda, orders, and notifications on the subject, which issued continually from the bureaux of Selimnieh, it was unlikely a satisfactory solution of the problem would be promptly reached. At one moment, we were assured that the commissariat (hapless institution ! doomed from the very beginning to be the scape-goat of every administrative failure or short-coming) would provide for the conveyance of tents, sick, baggage, and the like ; an hour afterwards, it was noised abroad that that department declined to engage in such duties, that the poor Treasury camel, starved and cuffed about as it was, had quite enough to do to provide the troops with daily bread, without undertaking any fresh burdens. Then did a public-spirited man in authority, hit upon the policy of making the Captains responsible for the carriage of the *impedimenta* of their respective companies; naturally enough, this scheme was unfavourably received by those so seriously menaced in that delicate point—the pocket. The intended victims remonstrated, inquiring whence the purchase-money of so many horses and mules was to be derived? how losses were to be indemnified? meekly adding, that the project was unprecedented in military finance. These objections silenced the prescriber of the nostrum. The alarmed centurions heard no further about the matter." *

After this, orders were issued to all Officers to provide themselves with bât-horses.† Twenty-one were allotted to each battalion, of which two belonged to every company for the transport of tents (*General Order*, June 1, 1854). Baggage parades frequently took place, to instruct the men how to pack the loads, and to accustom the animals to carry them.

During the stay at Scutari, the question arose as to what further should be done, and, to resolve it, the British and French Commanders-in-chief

---

* *Our Veterans, etc.*, p. 23.

† *Battalion Order*, May 25, 1854: "Officers are to provide themselves with animals for the conveyance of their baggage without delay."

proceeded to visit Omar Pasha in Bulgaria. The latter naturally desired to have the Allies at his back, and he urged that they should occupy Varna. This was agreed to, and the armies of England and France were at last to be transferred to the seat of war. On the 29th of May, Sir G. Brown's division began to move, and a fortnight later (June 13th), the Guards and Highland Brigades, forming the First Division, steamed up the Bosphorus for their new destination. The men started in light order; a reduced kit was carried in the knapsacks, the great coats, smock frocks, and blankets rolled on the top, but the rest of the clothing and necessaries were packed in the squad bags and left behind.*

It may strike the modern reader as strange, that a proportion of women were allowed to accompany their husbands belonging to the force destined for the East. In Scutari they were lodged in huts in the camp, and though inadequately provided for, badly housed, and subject to inconveniences which could not be permitted in the present day, their existence still was tolerable. But seeing how incomplete were the transport arrangements, our astonishment must be extreme, when we learn that the British army, about to take the field in a

* *General Order*, May 25th. "There will be no store of any kind at Varna. Everything not intended for the field must be left here in store" (*Battalion Order*, dated Scutari, 26th).

quarter where no depôt or base of operations existed, was to be accompanied by these women, whose presence under such circumstances, could not fail to be a misery to themselves, as well as a serious burden upon our defective military organization. Yet this was done, and we find two tents per battalion, making a total of ninety-six, allotted for their accommodation.

In the subsequent operations these unfortunate women, as might have been easily anticipated, suffered considerably. They remained in camp until the embarkation for the Crimea took place. A few were even allowed to sail with the army to that coast, and during the passage the wife of a sergeant of the Coldstream gave birth to a daughter, who was appropriately christened "Euxina." Fortunately they did not all land.* They were sent back to Scutari, where the main depôt and primary base of operations of the army in the East was formed, of which a Brevet Major of the 30th Regiment was appointed Commandant.†

* At least some of the men's wives (none belonging to the Brigade, as far as can be ascertained) accompanied their husbands into the Crimea, and remained there, during the course of the campaign. When we come to the winter of 1854-55 (Part V.), it will be seen what hardships they had to suffer. In mid-winter a letter, dated December 31st, was published in Orders, stating that some women's clothing had arrived, and would be issued upon the production of a certificate that the women applying, were fit persons to receive it.

† *General Order*, June 8, 1854. Subsequently a smaller depôt was also formed at Varna, under command of a Captain of the 50th Regiment (*General Order*, June 30, 1854).

Arriving at Varna (June 14th), the 1st Coldstream landed late in the evening, and had to pitch their camp in the dark. The site was unfortunately selected, both for the Brigade and for the rest of the British army, being situated on a slimy flat, close to a large lake of stagnant water, three-quarters of a mile from the town. Before a week elapsed, the intense heat, bad water, indifferent and insufficient food, and the monotony of inaction began to tell upon the men; they were afflicted with diarrhœa and other ailments, so that the health of the troops, hitherto entirely satisfactory, rapidly deteriorated. The French, on the other hand, had taken greater care of themselves; they occupied higher ground, and they suffered less.

During the stay there—about a fortnight, for, on the 1st of July, an advance was made to Aladyn, some ten miles in the interior—the masses of the allied soldiery met each other for the first time, and the warmest good-fellowship existed between them. The French Chiefs, Marshal St. Arnaud and General Canrobert, often rode through our camps, and the men invariably turned out and cheered them with the utmost heartiness and good will—a welcome which was always much appreciated.

In spite of the sickness that oppressed our troops, the Officers amused themselves, as they are always sure to do, in various ways, not least of which was a hunt, extemporized (but without hounds), after the wild mongrel dogs that were driven out of the town, and infested the district.

In the month of June, the armies continued their concentration in Bulgaria; and by the 21st the bulk had arrived there, when, in addition to the detachments of Turkish and Egyptian troops that were stationed in the neighbourhood, they mustered some 60,000 men.*

* Nolan, *History of the Russian War*, i. 201.

CHAPTER III.

OPERATIONS IN BULGARIA.

Course of the war on the Danube—Siege of Silistria—Bravery of the garrison—The Russians fail to take it—Other failures, and their retreat from Turkish territory into Bessarabia—Intervention of Austria—Importance of this event; and how it affected the war—The Allies in Bulgaria—Their inaction—Sickness among the troops—Return to Varna—Preparations for the invasion of the Crimea—The organization and strength of the Allies.

MEANWHILE the forces under Omar Pasha were seriously engaged with the enemy, and a few words will be necessary to explain briefly the military events that took place. After the victory at Citate, there was a pause in the operations till the middle of February, owing to the severity of the winter and to the temporary illness of the Turkish Commander. The Russians made strenuous efforts to repair their failures and their losses sustained in 1853, and they poured large reinforcements into the Principalities. In March, the Ottoman troops gained several successes. On the 4th, they crossed to the northern bank of the Danube and made a raid on Kalarashi; they repulsed an attack at Kalafat on the 11th, and on the 15th they prevented a passage at Turtukai, while a like attempt upon Rustchuk was also defeated. But the enemy, under General Luders, succeeded about the same time in crossing the river lower down, near its mouth, at Galatz, and invaded the Dobrudsha—an unhealthy district, full of swamps, and badly suited to military operations.

Overjoyed with this advantage, Gortchakoff now reinforced Luders. After a series of well-contested engagements, at the price of great losses, the principal fortresses of the province, as far as Trajan's wall (which extends from Rassova to Kustendji, on the Black Sea), were reduced; while Omar left them to their fate, and took no steps to retrieve the fortunes of the campaign in this quarter. These reverses, however, were partially compensated by another victory near Kalafat, and, as the Russians retired before the Turks in this direction, Krajova was occupied by the latter. This retreat was in reality a change of plan, for the enemy moved a portion of his forces to the east, and pressed on the right of Omar's line, with the design of establishing himself between Varna and Silistria.* His intention was now to lay siege to the latter place which interposed, and which he had to take, if he meant to try and secure a footing in Eastern Bulgaria.

The protracted siege of Silistria has become

* Nolan, *History of the Russian War*, i. 127, etc.

famous in the annals of the war, indeed in the history of military achievements. Space does not allow a proper description of the gallant and desperate resistance, which was then made by the Turks against overwhelming odds; but the principal points connected therewith may be glanced at in this work, if only because the British Officer, Major Butler, to whom, with Major Nasmyth, great glory is due for the defence, was transferred to the Coldstream Guards, as a reward for his brilliant services, though he never belonged to the Regiment, for his death occurred before he was actually gazetted.*

Silistria was attacked on the 14th of April, but it was three weeks later before a partial investment of the place was effected. The Russians were determined to take the place at any cost, and they made desperate efforts to accomplish their object; they brought up all their available forces, and placed their most renowned and capable Officers in command. During the siege, the war seemed almost everywhere else to stand still in Eastern Bulgaria, and all eyes were fixed on the memorable drama, that was being enacted in this part of the theatre of operations. The garrison was weak, and the indifferent works were only hastily repaired

* Captain J. A. Butler, from half-pay, Ceylon Rifles, was gazetted Lieutenant and Captain, Coldstream Guards, July 15, 1854; he was promoted Brevet-Major; and, on the 28th following, Lieutenant Ramsden was appointed Lieutenant and Captain, *vice* Brevet-Major Butler, "died of his wounds." His death took place on June 22nd, but his appointment was never cancelled.

and strengthened; but the defenders were well led, while the matchless bravery and the military virtues of the Turk were fully displayed. Among the leaders, Mussa Pasha, the Commander, stood pre-eminent for intrepidity and firmness. He was admirably supported by the two British Officers, Captain Butler and Lieutenant Nasmyth, whose scientific knowledge, ardent valour, and cool judgment made their services of the utmost value, and gained for them undying renown.

The enemy having drawn his lines as close as possible to the fortifications, resorted to every art to carry them. His principal efforts were directed against an open work, called Arab Tabia, whose fall would have disconcerted the whole defence. Time after time during the month of May, the besiegers bombarded the stronghold, sapped up to it, tried to mine it, and assaulted it both by day and by night. All to no purpose; every attempt was repulsed with slaughter and disgrace. The Turks held fast to their entrenchments, repaired them, met the enemy underground by countermines, and made continual sorties, which they always pressed home. Nowhere was a lodgment made; the troops of the Tsar gained no single advantage, but were harassed and beaten.

During this time Omar Pasha was at Shumla, only some fifty miles distant, at the head of a formidable corps. Contrary to his well-known character and to his previous conduct in the war, he unaccountably remained inactive, and his subordinates near him followed his example. But in the beginning of June, he broke loose from the fetters that seemed to numb his faculties, and once more began to display something of his wonted energy. He ordered attacks to be made on various points of the Danube, which were successful; and he pushed a brigade to Silistria, which entered it and reinforced it. The Russians were now thoroughly disheartened, and, under cover of a final assault, they raised the siege on the 23rd of June, and fled in disorder from the scene of their disaster. In the siege alone they lost as many as 12,000 men, and all their principal leaders were severely wounded. Of the Turks, 4000 to 5000 men fell, but among them were counted the brave Mussa and the heroic Butler, who succumbed to his wounds on the 22nd, the day before victory crowned his noble deeds.*

Nor was this the only success gained by the Ottoman troops. During May, the Turkish army based on Western Bulgaria, and operating from Kalafat, was not idle, and defeated the enemy in several engagements, pushing him back towards the east. By the end of the month, this advance began to have some effect on the fortunes of the

* Nolan, *History of the Russian War*, i. 214, etc.; Alexander W. Kinglake, *The Invasion of the Crimea*, ii. 48, etc.

siege, and to be inconvenient to the communications of the Russians. When, therefore, the latter gave up all hope of taking Silistria, and left it in despair, they also soon after evacuated all the strong places they had taken in the Dobrudsha, and, re-crossing the river, they abandoned that province. This event was followed by an attack on Giurgevo, opposite Rustchuk, where the Russians still endeavoured to maintain a position; but the Turks drove them out, and forced them to fall back towards Bucharest, in the middle of July. Shortly afterwards, the enemy made a disorderly retreat towards the Pruth, pursued by the victorious Turks, who entered the Roumanian capital in triumph on August 8th.

"The retreat of Gortchakoff was neither dignified nor skilful; his whining appeals to the inhabitants for mercy, and his haste to get his troops beyond the reach of their enemies, contrasted ludicrously with the braggart bulletins and proclamations which were so profusely scattered, when there was no armed foe to dispute the seizure of the 'material guarantee.'" *

About this time another element was introduced into the tangled web of Eastern affairs, which had great influence over the course of events, and over the future conduct of the Anglo-French Allies. Austria now intervened; and her action at this juncture led to important results. This action must

* Nolan, *History of the Russian War*, i. 236.

OPERATIONS IN BULGARIA. 37

be taken briefly into consideration before we can understand the causes that led to the invasion of the Crimea. The geographical position of this Empire necessarily exercises a deciding control over the communications of an army entering the Ottoman territory from the north. Austria, in short, commands the lid of the Turkish box ; she can open it, and she can shut it, and prevent the hand of Russia from trying to snatch the prize— Constantinople—which lies at the bottom.

In 1853, she held the lid wide open ; but in 1854 another course was adopted, more pleasing to the Allies, though not less gratifying to the Tsar. It would not have suited the Government of Vienna to run directly counter to the two maritime Powers of Europe, and to declare themselves openly on the side of Russia ; a diversion in Italy might have been serious to their prosperity. So the plain policy of opening the lid could no longer be maintained with safety. They therefore concentrated a force of observation on the south-eastern frontier early in spring, and, having prudently made an offensive and defensive treaty with Prussia, whom they did not trust, they calmly awaited events ; and nothing was done till the summer. Austria then prepared for future contingencies, by inducing the Porte to sign a convention (June 14, 1854), by which she undertook to make Russia evacuate the Principalities, and to occupy them herself while hostilities lasted. Still she avoided any dispute with the Emperor Nicholas. She remained inactive, until the fortunes of the war should decide which of the belligerents was going to win in the field.

On the 20th of August, however, when victory had declared itself entirely on the side of the Ottoman armies, then, and then only, her forces entered the Principalities, under the agreement that had been already signed, and thereby she rendered several important services to the Russians.

She protected their retreat, saved them from disaster, and enabled them to proceed undisturbed into the Crimea, by preventing the Turks from pressing upon them, during their unfortunate march to the Pruth. She became a barrier in the way of the Allies should they deem it necessary to invade Bessarabia, and take a "material guarantee" for the repression of future encroachments in Turkey. And, lastly, she upheld the false prestige of the Tsar's omnipotence, by making it appear that the Russians had evacuated the Danubian Principalities, not because they were forced to do so by the unaided valour of the Turks, but because the strategic position of the Austrian Empire had obliged them to retire.

Meanwhile, little or nothing had been done by the Allies. Their fleets, indeed, found no enemy to oppose them. Except, therefore, bombarding Odessa (April 22nd) to avenge an outrage on a flag of truce, and destroying batteries erected at the mouth of the Danube, there is nothing of interest to record. It is to be noted that we neither utilized, nor assisted the Turks to utilize, this great and important river—over which our naval superiority gave us considerable power—for the purpose of the war; but if our Ministry had the intention of remaining inactive in Bulgaria, the want of all enterprise is easily understood, and was the natural result of the policy pursued in London.

In the military sphere, a few squadrons, under Lord Cardigan, were sent, in the end of June, when the fighting was all but over, to reconnoitre towards the Dobrudsha, and returned about the 10th of July. They acquired no information that could be of service, but, owing to the heat, exposure, and insufficiency of food, many of the horses perished or were disabled, and our small body of cavalry was uselessly weakened. After their return, a large French force was pushed forward from Varna as far as Kustendji. There was obviously nothing to be done in this quarter at this period, so no advantage was or could be gained; but cholera attacked the expedition, causing enormous loss, and they, too, were needlessly weakened.*

We left the Guards Brigade at Aladyn, close to

---

* On August 8th it was computed that 10,000 lay dead or were stricken down by sickness (Kinglake, *Crimea*, ii. 133).

Varna, which they reached on July 1st. Here a halt was called, and the humdrum of camp life was resumed. In the morning, the men were drilled, they practised musketry, made fascines and gabions, or threw up earthworks; in the heat of the day they lay about and slept; in the evening, the more energetic endeavoured to obtain some addition to the ordinary scanty and insipid supper. The peasants were conciliated, and a bazaar was established, under the auspices of Colonel Gordon Drummond of the Coldstream, which was fairly successful. It may be also noted that, after some discussion, the old-fashioned regulations were further relaxed at this time, and, shaving being dispensed with, beards were at length allowed to be worn in the field.*

The Brigade was inspected by Omar Pasha on the 6th of July, and his presence inspired the men with genuine admiration. Here, at last, was a General who had really seen the Russians, who had fought against them, and who had beaten them. The sight of such a leader gladdened our gallant soldiers not a little; for they were sadly disappointed with their forced inaction in Bulgaria,— so close to scenes of martial glory. Now at last they buoyed themselves up with hope; they would

* This change had probably a wider bearing, if we may judge by the following Regimental Order (London, July 25, 1854): "The moustache will be taken into wear by the Coldstream, commencing to-morrow morning."

move to the front and take the field in earnest against the enemy. But this, alas! was not yet to be, and before their warlike ardour was to be satisfied, many trials were still to be endured.

Next day, the Brevet, dated June 20th, arrived in camp, and made considerable changes in the Coldstream. By this gazette, Brigadier-General Bentinck and Colonels Hay (commanding the Battalion) and Codrington were promoted Major-Generals. The first of these Officers continued to command the Guards Brigade in Turkey; the second, appointed to the Mauritius, returned home; while General Codrington remained at the seat of war, and shortly afterwards obtained a brigade there;* and before the peace, he became Commander-in-chief of the British army in the Crimea. Owing to these changes, Colonel Hon. G. Upton (the late General Viscount Templetown) was posted to the command of the 1st Battalion, *vice* Colonel Hay, and Colonel G. Drummond to the 2nd Battalion. The latter accordingly, as soon as he was relieved, was ordered to proceed to England, as also were four other Officers, who were transferred on promotion to the home Battalion. By Brigade Order (London, June 6th) a draft of 150 men for each Battalion in Turkey, was held in

* Vacant by the appointment of Major-General R. Airey as Quartermaster-General on Lord Raglan's Staff, *vice* Major-General Lord de Ros, invalided home.

readiness to proceed to the East on the 1st of July. The Coldstream detachment, under the command of Colonel Upton and nine Officers, including a Medical Officer, embarked in H.M.S. *Vulcan* on the 27th, and reached their destination at the seat of war on the 20th of July.

The camp at Aladyn was placed near the lake of Devna in a singularly beautiful spot, "the seventh heaven of the artist;" but it was terribly unhealthy, and entirely unsuited to a military station.* Sickness, in the shape of typhus, dysentery, and ague, was not long in appearing among the troops. It assumed increasing and alarming proportions, and it was found very difficult to restore the strength of those who were once attacked. During July, about a fifth of the Battalion were admitted into hospital; the men lost their elasticity, and their spirits drooped. On the 27th of the month, it was determined to move to a higher situation near Gevreklek, a village about three miles away. It was hoped that the change would produce an improvement, and everything was done to endeavour to stay the disorders that had broken out. But without avail, and cholera appearing, added its ghastly horrors to the general

* This remark does not apply only to this camp, but to every camp occupied by the British army in Bulgaria at this time. The evils that befell the Brigade of Guards were reproduced with greater or less intensity, at each of our military stations in this Turkish province.

distress. In spite of the efforts of the military authorities, and the devotion of the doctors, the medical department was unable to bear the strain thus suddenly put upon it, and the sick, placed in small bell tents, and unprotected from the scorching heat, suffered terribly. The rest, weakened by disease, awed by the plague that burst upon them, and doomed to passive inactivity, were depressed and nerveless.

"A heavy torpor hung about the camp, voices rarely to be heard, except when the sergeants warned the duties, or summoned a funeral party to turn out. The poor men lounged about, pallid, gloomy, depressed, and, worst of signs, their appetites were remarkably affected; not half of their daily portion of pork or beef could they consume; and yet, with strange perversity, the authorities chose this moment as the apt time for superadding an extra half pound of meat to the rations—the original allowance being overmuch for our feeble digestions, we were to get still more!" *

At length the stricken troops were moved out of the pestilential place in which they were stationed. A new decision was made, and the British army was to be taken back to Varna. The Brigade left Gevreklek early on the 16th of August; but such was the condition to which they were reduced, that three days were required to accomplish a distance of less than fifteen miles. The health of the men was so entirely broken down, that they were

* *Our Veterans, etc.*, 81.

even unable to carry their packs during the short stages of five miles each.

"Seldom has there been a more dismal march. The men, very ghosts of the rosy giants who, but six short months before, had stepped so cheerily across Waterloo Bridge, now plodded along in gloomy silence. Not the most tremulous version of a song, not the feeblest effort at a joke proceeded from the haggard ranks; and, worst sign of all, even tobacco had fallen to a discount; . . . and yet 'twas the flesh alone that ailed, the spirit was willing as ever; ay, that it was!" *

During the period the Battalion was stationed in Bulgaria, 57 men died in the camp hospital, 28 of them from cholera and 25 from typhus fever. The chief mortality occurred among the men lately arrived from England, who appear to have been very young, with an average age and service of $21\frac{3}{4}$ and less than 2 years respectively. Many Officers were also affected by the pestilence, and the Regiment had to mourn the loss of two among them — Colonel Trevelyan, and Lieut.-Colonel Hon. R. Boyle, M.P. Five others were invalided, and had to return home.†

Arrived at Varna, the sea breezes, the prospects of at last getting a glimpse of the enemy, and possibly the new site selected for encampment— away from the influence of the plague-breeding lake, in the position which Omar Pasha had originally advised before the British army left Scutari—

* *Our Veterans, etc.*, p. 91. † Wyatt, p. 15.

produced beneficial effects upon the men. Though they were still sickly and weak, and cholera lurked among them, their health improved, and their spirits revived.*

On the 29th of August, the Brigade embarked for the much-talked-of invasion of the Crimea, but the start was not made till some days later. The Coldstream, 26 Officers and 737 men, were divided into two wings; the left wing and head-quarters on board the *Tonning*, the right in the *Simoon* with the Grenadier Guards. From the latter, to prevent overcrowding, two companies, under Colonel Lord F. Paulet, were subsequently trans-shipped to the *Vengeance*, and, on the 4th of September, to H.M.S. *Bellerophon*.

The sick of the Battalion, 89 in number and 30 convalescents, were left behind in the camp hospital, in charge of Assistant-Surgeon Trotter; shortly afterwards they were sent to Scutari with the same Medical Officer, who rejoined the Battalion on the 9th of November. A Brigade detachment, moreover, consisting of three Officers (under a Captain and Lieutenant-Colonel), four sergeants, and 100 rank and file, selected from convalescents and those unfit for active service, were left behind at Varna; of these the Coldstream

* "At last the order to embark for the Crimea arrives. We are wild with delight at the prospect of being shot at instead of dying of cholera!" (Colonel Tower, late Coldstream Guards, *Diary*, Aug. 28, 1854).

furnished a sergeant and 33 rank and file, under Captain MacKinnon, who rejoined the Battalion in the Crimea, on the 4th of October.

The fleet weighed anchor on the 7th of September, and, getting into communication with our French and Turkish allies, the united armada started on its errand to the Crimea. The events that now took place will be described in the next and subsequent parts ; but, before concluding this one, it will be necessary to give some idea of the forces and organization of the Allied hosts that sailed on this memorable occasion to invade the Empire of the Tsar of All the Russias.

The British army, under the command of General Lord Raglan, consisted of five infantry divisions and of one cavalry division, each of two brigades.

The First Division, under Lieut.-General H.R.H. the Duke of Cambridge, consisted of the Guards (3rd Grenadiers, 1st Coldstream, and 1st Scots Fusilier Guards, Major-General Bentinck), and the Highland brigades (the 42nd, 79th, and 93rd Regiments, Major-General Sir Colin Campbell), and of two field batteries of artillery.

The Second Division, under Lieut.-General Sir de Lacy Evans, consisted of Major-General Pennefather's (30th, 55th, and 95th Regiments), and Brigadier-General Adams' brigades (41st, 47th, and 49th), and of two field batteries.

The Third Division, under Lieut.-General Sir

R. England, consisted of the brigades of Brigadier-Generals Sir J. Campbell, Bart. (1st, 38th, and 50th), and Eyre (4th, 28th, and 44th), and of two field batteries.

The Fourth Division, under Lieut.-General Hon. Sir G. Cathcart, was still incomplete, as two battalions had not yet arrived; the remainder was formed of the 20th, 21st, 63rd, 68th Regiments and the 1st Battalion Rifle Brigade, together with one field battery; the brigades being commanded by Major-Generals Arthur Torrens and Goldie.

The Fifth or Light Division, commanded by Lieut.-General Sir G. Brown, was formed of the brigades of Major-General Codrington (7th, 23rd, and 33rd), and of Major-General Buller (19th, 77th, and 88th), also of the 2nd Battalion Rifle Brigade, and of one troop horse artillery, and one field battery.

The Cavalry Division, under Lieut.-General Earl of Lucan, was formed of the Light (4th and 13th Light Dragoons, the 8th and 11th Hussars, and the 17th Lancers, Major-General Earl of Cardigan), and of the Heavy brigades (4th and 5th Dragoon Guards, and 1st Royal Dragoons, the Scots Greys, and 6th Inniskilling Dragoons, Major-General Hon. J. Scarlett), also of one troop of horse artillery. General Scarlett's brigade left Varna later than the rest of the army, and reached the Crimea in October.

A siege train had also been provided; but it was temporarily left behind.

Each division was about 5000 men strong, and the English army numbered altogether some 26,000 infantry, nearly 2000 cavalry, and 60 guns.*

The French, under the command of Marshal St. Arnaud, were formed into four infantry divisions, each about 7000 strong, commanded by:—Generals Canrobert, 1st Division; Bosquet, 2nd; Prince Napoleon, 3rd; and Forey, 4th Division. At first they brought no cavalry with them to the Crimea, but they had 68 guns. They were also accompanied by some 7000 Turks, who, commanded by Suleiman Pasha, were attached to the French Marshal's army.

* General Sir Edward Hamley, K.C.B., *The War in the Crimea*, pp. 31, 112 (London, 1892).

PART II.

THE INVASION OF THE CRIMEA.

CHAPTER IV.

DETERMINATION TO ATTACK SEVASTOPOL.

Small results gained by the Allies—Embarrassment of the British Government—Sudden determination to attack Sevastopol—Inconveniences of this resolution—Russian position in the Trans-Caucasian provinces—Conditions under which the Crimea was invaded—The object of the expedition not kept secret—The isolation of the Peninsula not attempted—Lateness of the season—No provision made for a lengthened operation.

HITHERTO the Anglo-French Allies had done nothing in the great struggle, which had been raging between Russia and Turkey since the autumn of 1853, though they had been officially at war with the former for more than five months, and were preparing for the strife before hostilities had been declared.) There was much cause for disappointment at this inglorious result; and it was humiliating to the gallant armies of the two foremost nations of Europe, to be sent to the East, merely to eat out their hearts in inactivity, when feats of valour against the enemy were performed almost within earshot of their camps. Nor was the excuse put forward for this apathy—the want of transport—of any value; for every member of the Government knew that transport is indispensable to an army's motion, and that without it no campaign is possible. That it could have been obtained is not to be denied; and the conclusion is irresistible, that the intention of taking the field in earnest, did not enter into the calculations of our Cabinet.

But now, when the enemy, driven out of the Principalities, effected his escape under the friendly cover of an Austrian force, when the Tsar, moreover, in no mood to sue for peace, still breathed defiance, our Government were placed in a difficulty. They had undertaken to make Russia submit; but their diplomacy was unsuccessful, and their demonstrations were disregarded; added to these failures, valuable time had slipped away, and the season was wasted. Something, then, had to be done at once to retrieve the past, for the country was losing its patience, and would brook no further vacillation. Hence a change in policy became inevitable.

The Government had been cautious, not to say timid; but they now entirely altered their demeanour. They suddenly became bold to the verge of rashness, and resolved at any price to take Sevastopol by a *coup de main*. It is true they were in complete ignorance of the strength, defences, armament, and capacity of that fortress; they knew little of its position, and nothing of the peninsula in which it is situated; and, while the transport of the army was more than defective, the commissariat and medical services were not in a much better condition. But these things seem to have pressed them lightly. Their opinion was strong, that Sevastopol was sure to fall, directly the Allied forces appeared before its ramparts; and its destruction, they doubted not, would bring about a peace, and cause the Tsar to relinquish his arrogant pretensions.

As soon, therefore, as the raising of the siege of Silistria put an end to the war on Ottoman territory, they hastened to frame a despatch to Lord Raglan, dated June 29th, directing that an expedition against Sevastopol should be prepared. The despatch was so worded, that it left the British Commander little option but to comply. He therefore accepted the arduous undertaking which was pressed upon him, though he did so very much against his better judgment, and he announced his intention to the Government in a letter, dated July 19th.* It was early in September, as we

* Kinglake, ii. 115, etc. It is not without interest to observe, that the draft of the despatch of June 29th, was submitted to the Cabinet the day before, and that it passed without modification or even comment. Mr. Kinglake tells us that the Ministers, upon whom devolved the momentous duty of directing the course of military operations at this critical time, "were overcome with sleep; . . . the despatch, though it bristled with sentences tending to provoke objection, received from the Cabinet the kind of approval which is often awarded to an unobjectionable sermon" (*Ibid.*, 94).

have seen, before the armada was ready to sail from Varna.

There can be no doubt, that it was anomalous and very inconvenient to send out a military expedition to check Russian aggression with no rational plan of action. In the beginning of the year, the terror which the supposed omnipotence of the Emperor Nicholas inspired, made us believe that all our efforts would be required to save Turkey from certain and swift destruction. We even imagined that Constantinople was in imminent danger; and the French rushed to Gallipoli, to take up a flanking position against the hostile columns, which were almost immediately expected to assault that city. This was our only plan, and we trusted to events to develop another for us, should it be required.

When, therefore, we found that the result of the war on the Danube had overturned all our preconceived ideas, we were unprepared for such an event; and we drifted towards the first plausible scheme put forward, irrespective of ways and means. Hence, the descent on Sevastopol was in the nature of an afterthought: a crude design, hastily proposed and rashly adopted, without reflection or calculation, and concerted without reference to the Commanders at the seat of war, who, nevertheless, were forced to accept it, and were held responsible for its execution.

After the collapse of the campaign in the Principalities, the urgent question naturally arose —where was Russia to be attacked, and how was she to be coerced by the Western Powers? There were vitally delicate joints in the armour of that Empire, not inaccessible to our resources, in Poland and in Finland. But the resuscitation of the oppressed northern nationalities formed no part of our policy; they were held to be beyond the scope of our aspirations. So we confined ourselves to a few inconclusive descents on the coast of the Baltic, and the enemy had no serious cause of disquietude in this important portion of his dominions. Our intervention, therefore, in these quarters need not further be discussed.* The army being in the Levant, principal operations were to be conducted there.†

The Crimea, no doubt, occupies an important position in the Black Sea, and its conquest would

---

* The overwhelming catastrophe that overtook Napoleon I. in 1812, when, in spite of his military genius, he lost his whole army of 500,000 and his great power in Europe, calmed the impetuosity of those who might have hoped to invade Russia, as if she were an ordinary European nation. Yet the object-lesson could have been, and it is feared was, pushed too far. Napoleon's disaster was due to his own perversity and to his military pride; for had he been content to re-organize and emancipate Poland, and avoid the snow-covered and barren steppes of the interior, his success, in destroying the sources of the power of Russia, could not have failed to be complete, and the tide of her encroachments must have rolled back for generations.

† See Map No. 1, p. 31.

necessarily cramp the future plans of Russian aggrandisement. But who was to hold it, if it were taken? Sevastopol, also, situated in the peninsula, is a land-locked harbour, and a base of naval operations, defended from the sea, and, in 1854, it was partially protected, on the land fronts, by some indifferent works. If there were a good prospect of rapidly capturing it, the design to do so had much to recommend it. Such an event would injure the prestige of Russia, on which she greatly relies for acquiring power; it would temporarily put an end to a secure harbour suitable to maintain her fleet in the Black Sea, and it would be one step towards the conquest of the Crimean Peninsula. But was the chance —the slender chance—of prompt success worth the risk? Why enchain our whole forces before the walls of a single and isolated fortress, if the *coup de main* were to miscarry, and a lengthened siege became necessary? Was not the Euxine in our sole possession, and, as long as this remained so, was not Sevastopol outside the sphere of military operations, and entirely innocuous?

Austria had been allowed to close the western theatre of operations against the belligerent Powers. But it never seemed to have occurred to them to cast a thought on that other theatre of war, which still lay open to their attack in Asia. During 1854, the Turks were in disorder there;

acrimonious quarrels broke out among the leaders of their forces, and, though the Russians made no great progress, the fortunes of the war were deciding against our allies, to the detriment of the cause we had undertaken to defend. In this quarter, moreover, we had every prospect of success; we should have exposed ourselves to the least risk, and, if victory crowned our efforts there, we should have secured the most brilliant results. This field of operations, not distant from the Crimea, offered ample scope for our energies; and, as we approached it in 1855, though we did not avail ourselves of its advantages, a brief allusion to it must here be made.

The Caspian Sea is connected with the Euxine by a chain of lofty mountains (the Caucasus), which runs from Baku, on the former, to near Poti, on the latter, and then, taking a north-westerly direction, skirts the shore as far as Anapa, close to the straits of Yeni-kale. The Caucasus forms the natural southern limit of Russia, but, in the course of years, by the incomparable ability and, perhaps, by the unscrupulous character of the policy pursued at St. Petersburg, the frontiers of the Empire have been pushed south of these mountains, pressing upon Persia on the Araxes, and on the Ottoman Empire in Armenia.

Now, communications with these Trans-Caucasian provinces (Mingrelia, Georgia, etc.) were insecure in 1854. For, inhabiting the northern slopes of the great range were vigorous, unsubdued races of hardy mountaineers, called by the general name Circassians, who for years had preserved their liberties and independence, in spite of the efforts of the Tsar to enthrall them. This eastern Switzerland had some claim upon our sympathy, if not because of the cause of freedom for which the people struggled, at least on account of the peculiar position they occupied on the Russian line of communications.

Nor should it be forgotten that the subjugation of these mountaineers affected, in no slight degree, the tranquillity and the future security of India; for, until they were overcome, the systematic advance of Russia into Central Asia was not easily accomplished. Operations to support the Circassians and the kindred tribes in the Caucasus, had the advantage, then, of directly protecting, in the far East, those interests, to secure which, we had embarked in the war; and, if they had been successful, as they could not fail to be successful, even by the employment of a moderate force, the enemy must have lost Trans-Caucasia.

The Russian Empire, considered to be safe from attack, was very vulnerable in this quarter, at a time when the mountain region was still unsubdued; and a blow struck there, making the Allies masters of the situation, would necessarily have enabled them to settle the Eastern Question as they thought best for the welfare of Europe. But the influence which was exercised over the Tsar's aggressions in Turkey, by the brave races, who for so long held the passes against tremendous odds in defence of their homes, was scarcely recognized and hardly noticed in the West in 1854.*

We have already seen that, owing to the benevolence displayed by Austria to the Russians, the latter were enabled to retire from the Danube into Bessarabia unmolested by the pursuing Turks. This act on the part of a Power regarded as a friend by Great Britain, cost us dear shortly after this time. Its immediate consequences were, however, not unnoticed, and it was plain both to the allied Governments and to the Commanders, that the enemy would push his forces into the Crimea, without delay, if he got an inkling that an attempt

* Major-General Sir Henry Rawlinson, K.C.B., *England and Russia in the East*, p. 272 (2nd. edit. ; London, 1875). The writer doubts if the fall of Circassia has ever been properly understood. He alludes to the great efforts made by Russia immediately after the Crimean war to subdue these tribes ; she practically accomplished this difficult task in 1859, when Shámil was taken prisoner. A year or two later, the extinction of the Circassian nationality was achieved. This " was the turning-point of Russian Empire in the East." The regular and successful advance in Central Asia took place after this event, beginning in 1863. Since then, but only since then, this advance has been rapid, and has proceeded without a check, until, in spite of "neutral zones" and "buffers," the present commanding position has been gained in Asia, almost within sight of our Indian frontiers.

on Sevastopol were imminent. Unfortunately the enemy got more than a hint as to our intentions.

In order to prepare for the success of a *coup de main* on a position, it is evident that one essential condition to be observed is secrecy; nor is it immaterial to mislead the enemy by false attacks, alarms, and reports. But exactly the reverse took place. No demonstrations were made, and we blazoned our real design to the whole world. The English press spoke of it freely and openly, since the end of June; and Marshal St. Arnaud had the imprudence to issue a vainglorious proclamation to his army, on the 25th of August, which ended with the following inflated words: "Bientôt nous saluerons ensemble les trois drapeaux réunis flottant sur les remparts de Sévastopol de notre cri national, Vive l'Empereur!"

A plan, previously concerted with the Officers who were to carry it out, upon so difficult a subject as the operation in hand, could not have been matured and adopted, unless the means of isolating the Crimea from the rest of Russia, had also been considered. There are two principal lines by which the peninsula is fed from the main land—the isthmus of Perekop and the Sea of Azof. The former, unconnected with the great river system of the Empire, was of service mainly to bring portions of the army of Bessarabia to the neighbourhood of Sevastopol. The latter, however, receiving the waters of the Don, served to take down reinforcements and supplies from the interior to the new seat of war. The despatch of the 29th of June already alluded to, contains a passage on this matter: "As all communications by sea are now in the hands of the Allied Powers, it becomes of importance to endeavour to cut off all communication by land, between the Crimea and the other parts of the Russian dominions." It would have been fortunate if, in accordance with these instructions, we could have seized the narrow isthmus of Perekop; but we did not do so, and it remained open to the enemy.

On the other hand, a small body of troops could have gained a footing near Kertch, and have maintained itself there; for, the Allied naval resources were more than ample to support it, to occupy and dominate the Sea of Azof, and to cut the Crimea off completely from the supplies sent down the river Don, from the large depôts and magazines established in its vicinity. Such an expedition, moreover, would have served to blind the enemy as to the intentions of the invaders with regard to Sevastopol, and have made him uncertain whether the ultimate aim was not to operate in the neighbourhood of the Caucasus. Having much to lose in this quarter, he was all the more sensitive to pressure there, and greater deception could thus have been practised on his fears.

That these expeditions did not take place at that time, is probably to be ascribed to the belief of the Commanders that the whole force was little enough, in order successfully to carry Sevastopol by storm. The orders they received from home did not contemplate a lengthy operation. Not for an instant did any one suppose, that it could last through the winter. It was late in the year; barely six weeks, or at least two months, of good weather could be expected to continue. It was known that the winter in the Black Sea region was intensely severe and cold; there was no provision made for the army against the terrible hardships which the snow, frost, and hurricanes of the Crimea must entail. The plan proposed to the allied Commanders was a short operation, and by them it was so accepted. It was a descent upon a coast, a march, and an assault. Fixing their eyes intently upon this plan, the importance of attacks on the enemy's communications, dwindled in their estimation, and lost much of its value. Expeditions of this nature were fitted rather to a regular siege, which might be expected to last for many months, and were scarcely deemed to be essential to carry out the object which was then in hand, viz. to bring up every available battalion to the point, where a ready-prepared and decisive victory was to be gained.

These preliminary observations are necessary as

an introduction to the events which are now to be recorded. For if they were not stated, it would be impossible for the reader to understand the reasons for the hardships, which our troops had soon to suffer, or to appreciate the glorious part they played in a calamitous war, where their fortitude and courage not only saved, but enhanced, the military greatness of Great Britain, and stood out in bright relief to so much that was unfortunate and damaging to our reputation as a nation of the first magnitude in Europe.

It may in truth be stated, that to the British soldiers, and to the Officers who led them, the country owes it that a national catastrophe did not occur. Their discipline and dogged resolution never wavered for an instant, and they carried England unscathed through the ordeal. A history dealing with the actions of a Regiment engaged on that memorable occasion, would be sadly incomplete, if it failed to show this truth, or to describe the false positions in which the vital interests of this country became unhappily involved, and from which it was extricated solely by the manly bearing, and unflinching self-sacrifice of the army.

CHAPTER V.

LANDING IN THE CRIMEA.

The allied Armada sails from Varna to Eupatoria—Landing effected at "Old Fort"—How the troops were equipped—Serious deficiency of transport—The move to Sevastopol—Strength of the invaders—Their order of march—Skirmish on the Bulganak—The enemy on the Alma river opposes the advance of the Allies—Preparations made to dislodge him—Description of the field of battle—Strength and position of the Russians.

THE armada, which left the shores of Bulgaria on the 7th of September, did not immediately sail to its destination; part of the Allied fleet had started before that date, but the whole met together on the 8th, and next day the British portion anchored in deep water some miles east of the Isle of Serpents. Lord Raglan now left to reconnoitre the coast, and to choose a landing-place. His French colleague was ill, and could not accompany him. Proceeding from Balaklava to Eupatoria, he finally selected a stretch of sandy beach, covered by lagoons, at a spot marked on the maps as "Old Fort," situated some twelve miles south of the latter town, and about twenty-five from Sevastopol.*

* See Map No. 2, p. 65.

A LANDING EFFECTED. 65

Meanwhile, the Allied flotilla again got into communication, the slower sailing ships coming up to the *rendezvous*. On the 12th, the magnificent and orderly array of the united fleets, occupying nearly nine miles of sea room, approached the Crimea, and converged on Old Fort; and then our men got a first welcome glimpse of the strange and unknown country they were about to invade. Next day, Eupatoria was summoned, and surrendered without a shot being fired; and on the 14th, exactly the forty-second anniversary of the triumphant entry of Napoleon I. into Moscow, the Allies began to land, the Turks on the right, then the French, and the British on the left.

The sea voyage braced up the health of the men; they were fast losing the lassitude and despondency that so lately oppressed them, and were regaining their usual strength, elasticity, and good spirits. "Notwithstanding there is no casting loose the foul fiend—cholera," and many casualties were reported; but the Coldstream seem to have been spared by the scourge during the passage, though eight sick were unable to disembark, and were sent to the *Simoon*. A foretaste of cold weather was also unexpectedly experienced, for on the 12th, there was a hail-storm "abundantly accompanied by snow." *

Before leaving their ships, the troops had the

† *Our Veterans*, etc., p. 102.

F

temporary character of the expedition brought strongly before their imagination. The bât-horses, collected with difficulty at Scutari, were left behind in Bulgaria; there was no transport for regimental baggage, except an animal to carry the medicine-panniers. Officers loaded their haversacks and their persons with three days' salt pork, biscuit, and such indispensable articles, that a short campaign required. Dressed in tight-fitting swallow-tailed coatees, resplendent with gold lace, now sadly tarnished, their clothing was scarcely adapted to the harsh trials of actual warfare; added to which, they were weighted and encumbered, and had the appearance of "animated lumps of undigested packages, all cloak, bundle, and hairy cap."

Nor did the men fare any better. It appears that the only heavy part of the knapsack was its wooden frame, and this had been discarded some weeks before. When this was done, it served as a light and fairly good valise in which to carry the necessary kit safely and secure from rain. At the last moment, however, it was feared that the men were still too weak to carry even their lightened packs. But, instead of reducing the articles to be taken therein to a *minimum*, this *minimum*, in the shape of a pair of boots, a pair of socks, a shirt, and a forage cap, was ordered to be wrapped in the blanket and great coat; while the knapsack itself, designed to hold them, was left behind on board ship, together with all other articles of private property brought from Varna. Thus an unsightly and most inconvenient bundle was formed, ill-adapted to its purpose, and a doubtful place for the safe keeping of the few articles that were considered indispensable to the soldier's welfare.* Three days' rations, some cooking utensils, wooden water-kegs, and sixty rounds of ammunition per man completed the personal equipment brought into the enemy's country.

From the 14th to the 18th, the disembarkation of the Allies continued, observed by Cossack horsemen until driven away, and interrupted only by the rolling waves, which, tumbling on the beach, made it sometimes unsafe to land the horses and guns. The Light and First Divisions were on shore on the 14th; the Guards Brigade, remaining in formation till the afternoon, marched inland for about three miles, after the Light Division had started, where they bivouacked for the night. The morning was fine, but the evening turned very cold, the wind rose, and the rain came down in torrents, drenching all ranks and conditions, from the Divisional Commander, H.R.H. the Duke of

* It appears that the two companies of the Coldstream which were on board H.M.S. *Bellerophon*, under the command of Colonel Lord F. Paulet, retained their lightened knapsacks (Wyatt, p. 19). The reader will be interested to learn that the men left Varna dressed in white trousers; the order to take cloth trousers into wear, is dated Sept. 15th.

Cambridge, to the youngest drummer. It was an inhospitable welcome that awaited our first night on the Crimean coast, but the men were in good heart, and made light of their misfortunes. On the 16th, a few tents were landed, but, for want of transport, they had to be returned on board the following day,—except one, which was retained for the sick, and was to be carried between the medicine-panniers on the hospital bât-horse.

The story of the halt near Old Fort, would not have been complete had there been no "scare" to record. Was it ever wanting among troops, who for the first time await the approach of an enemy? Here it took place about midnight on the 16th, when an alarm was raised of the approach of Cossacks, and the troops turned out hurriedly. Nor was it unlikely that the Russians would endeavour to attack the Allies, before they were ready to advance from the coast. Upon this occasion, however, a false report only had gained credence. There was no enemy in the vicinity, and the occurrence, though startling for the moment, doubtless, eventually served to steady the nerves of men who had never yet heard a shot fired in anger. In one way, things went smoothly enough, at all events in the camp of the Brigade, who, placed near a friendly Tartar village, bought small sheep at two shillings each, and fowls for fourpence or fivepence. But the dreaded cholera still hovered about, and one man of the Battalion died, after a few hours' sickness, on the 17th.

At last, early on the 19th, all arrangements being completed, the troops, horses, and guns landed, a small number (250) of country carts collected, and some cattle, sheep, and other supplies procured from the neighbourhood, the Allies began their march to Sevastopol, supported by the fleets that steamed slowly along the coast in the same direction. They numbered rather less than 60,000 men and 128 guns, and as the French and Turks had no cavalry with them, the united army had only one brigade (Lord Cardigan) to rely on. Marshal St. Arnaud marched near the sea; Bosquet's division was in front, followed by Prince Napoleon on the left, by Canrobert on the right, and by Forey in rear; and, lastly, the Turks and the baggage and reserve ammunition, were in the open space which was surrounded by these four divisions.

The British army moved on the left of the French, and were thus placed on the exposed flank; the Second and Light Divisions leading, the former nearest our allies, followed respectively by the Third and First Divisions, the Fourth marching after the First. The guns were on the right of their divisions; the infantry in double column of companies from the centre of battalions; and the cavalry divided, two regiments on the left flank, two covering the advance, and one in rear. This formation was adopted, because, the left of the Allies being undefended, it was not improbable that the enemy might venture to make an onslaught upon that flank from Simferopol. The weather was sultry, and the advance lay across a vast rolling plain, destitute of trees and shrubs, and swept bare of inhabitants and supplies by the Russian cavalry. After two hours, the heat affected some of the men, and, the ever-recurring plague of cholera still dogging their footsteps, victims to its ravages began to fall out.

"And now an astounding fact became patent to all—we had no ambulance! We had invaded an enemy's country without means of transporting the sick and wounded, beyond a few stretchers in the hands of bandsmen and drum-boys! The sick and wounded of 27,000 British soldiers were to be carried bodily over burning steppes, where water was not, by drummers and fifers! These lads being physically unequal to the duty expected of them, we endeavoured to supply their places with files of the heavy-weighted soldiery: but of course this hard expedient broke down too; the work could not be done by human muscle, in fact; hence, tall fellows, not a few, were left behind, to take their chance of being picked up—God help them!" *

But in the afternoon the attention of the troops was diverted from these scenes of suffering; shots

* *Our Veterans*, *etc.*, p. 122. Kinglake tells us that, in the evening, a force was sent to bring in the stragglers, who were very numerous during the march (*Invasion of the Crimea*, ii. 209).

A LANDING EFFECTED.

were heard in the front. The enemy was expected to take up a position near one of the rivers that flow at right angles across the Eupatoria post-road, on both sides of which the Allies were advancing; and here, at length, on the Bulganak, the divisions in rear thought that they were going to try conclusions with the enemy. In a very short time, however, the firing proved to be but a skirmish; for, after the expenditure of a few rounds, the Russians —6000 infantry, 2000 cavalry and two batteries— moved back, before they had made us deploy much of our force, and left us in possession of the stream without further resistance. There we bivouacked for the night, in the full assurance that a great action would be fought on the following day.

According to an estimate of the enemy's forces in the Crimea, made by the Foreign Office at home, it was computed that there were some 45,000 men near and in Sevastopol, excluding troops which might be drawn from the Caucasus and Bessarabia. Of this estimate Lord Raglan had been informed, but it seems he placed no great reliance upon it. He knew, however, that the Russians were relatively strong in cavalry, and that their army was commanded by Prince Menshikoff.

It was between nine and ten before the Allies moved from their bivouacs on the morning of the 20th, the British army bringing their left shoulders up, to get into closer communication with the French. On reaching the top of a grassy ridge which looks over the valley of the Alma, the position taken up by the enemy on the heights above that stream, first came into sight, and immediate preparations were made to dislodge him.

The field of battle is a sloping plain from the north to the river, which is fordable in summer, from whence springs abruptly on the south bank, to a height of 300 to 400 feet, a commanding range of hills overlooking the plain, and running from the sea, for a distance of five miles, to a bluff called Kurgané Hill.* The river makes a trifling bend, forming a slightly re-entering angle towards these heights, on the western side of the Kurgané; and here the post-road crosses the stream, close to the village of Burliuk, by a wooden bridge, which had not been destroyed. This point marked the junction of the English right and the French left.

On the French section of the field, the heights press close and cliff-like to the river, but they recede and become more accessible for a mile to the west of the angle mentioned. Roads available for guns ascend the hills at the mouth of the Alma, at the village of Almatamak, at a farm a mile further up, and again close to Burliuk, where, on the Russian side, the ground is more practicable; this last road leads to a height known as the

* See Map No. 3, p. 86.

Telegraph Hill. On the English section, the heights are further from the river, and the ascent is everywhere easy for all arms. But on that very account it was the more difficult to storm; for here the ground could be swept with fire, and the defenders had every facility for making counter-attacks. The tops of the hills form a wide plateau, stretching southwards towards the Katcha river, indented only near the angle, by a depression between the Kurgané and Telegraph Hills, through which the post-road rises, as it proceeds to Sevastopol.*

The Russian army, numerically weaker than the Allies, being 33,000 infantry, 3400 cavalry, and 120 guns, occupied the plateau. The main portion, 21,000 infantry, 3000 cavalry, and 84 guns, was placed on Kurgané and on the post-road, opposite the English section; the remainder, 12,000 infantry, 400 cavalry, and 36 guns, near the post-road and on Telegraph Hill, were opposed to the French. The cavalry took post on the enemy's right and rear, supported by horse artillery; but no troops were further to the west, where the ground was under fire from the war-ships. Menshikoff, however, forgot, though he had time at his disposal, to block the roads which ascend the cliff and the rough precipitous hillsides opposite the French position. Nor did he construct field-works on his front and

* Hamley, *War in the Crimea*, p. 47, etc.

right flank, contenting himself with only two gun-epaulments on Kurgané, one of which, about 300 yards from the river, was armed with 14 heavy guns of position.

There was a pause when the Allies approached the position they were about to assail, during which the troops refreshed themselves with cold pork and biscuits, after their march on a warm and glorious morning. In the interval, all eyes were turned to the heights that frowned in front, and saw in the distance the hostile sharpshooters extended along the river, in the vineyards and gardens, through which the advance was about to be made. Nor were we unconscious that the whole of our force was easily to be discerned, and our intentions to be divined by our antagonist; for we halted boldly on the sloping plain, in full view of the enemy, who, perched on the higher ground, was enabled to make his observations and to conceal much of his own order of battle from our anxious gaze. Meanwhile, the two Commanders-in-chief were concerting their plans. They had met before, but this was their final consultation. St. Arnaud had fixed and strong ideas on the situation; he was voluble in expressing them, and, though zealous and brave, he was somewhat shallow and self-opinionated. Lord Raglan's first care was to insure a good understanding with his impetuous colleague. He was hampered by the alliance; and there was no supreme Commander to give a decision at this moment when unity of action was indispensably necessary. The Chiefs parted, and came to no definite conclusion ; unless a hazy understanding can be called so, that the French were to try and turn the Russian left, but that the British could not do the same thing on the other flank "with such a body of cavalry as the enemy had in the plain." *

* Kinglake, ii. 239, etc., 250.

CHAPTER VI.

BATTLE OF THE ALMA.

Commencement of the battle—Advance of the Light and Second Divisions—Deployment of the First Division—Advance of the Guards and Highland Brigades—Defeat and flight of the Russians—No pursuit—Losses—Bravery and steadiness of the British troops—The Allies lose valuable time after the battle—Arriving at last before their objective, Sevastopol, they refuse to attack it—General description of Sevastopol.

AT one o'clock, Bosquet's division advanced to the attack. One brigade with the artillery, pushed through Almatamak and up the road there; the remainder, and the Turks, some 10,000 men, crossed the Alma near its mouth, and, ascending the pathway that leads thence to the cliff, found themselves far from the battle-field, and never fired a shot during the action. Canrobert took his division along the road at the farm, and debouched on the plateau a mile to the west of Telegraph Hill; but his own artillery followed that of Bosquet, and were with the latter's left brigade, a mile still further to the west. Prince Napoleon's division was on Canrobert's left, and made for Telegraph Hill; while Forey was in second line, in reserve. As the Turks were 7000 strong and the French 28,000, Marshal St. Arnaud had only 25,000 men and 68 guns in action.

The original formation of the British army had not been altered: the Second Division was on the right, the Light on the left, both in the first line, followed by the Third and First in the second line, the Fourth Division in reserve; four regiments of the cavalry covered the left, one followed in rear. The whole, 23,000 infantry, 1000 cavalry, and 60 guns—for part of the Fourth Division were still on the road from Old Fort—covered by the Rifles, now moved forward straight for the enemy's strong position on Kurgané, the right being directed upon Burliuk. The Russian skirmishers retired, setting fire to that village as the first line approached; while the latter, coming nearly within range of the hostile artillery, deployed. But too little ground had been taken up, and, in spite of every effort to rectify the mistake, the battalions overlapped, and were dangerously crowded. Lord Raglan, in pursuance of the arrangement already made with St. Arnaud, now delayed the attack until the French had time to complete the movement they had begun. But the Marshal was impatient, and before his troops could produce any impression on the enemy's left, he urged his colleague to wait no longer. In response to this strong request, Lord Raglan ordered his first line to advance.

The Second Division (Sir De L. Evans) was delayed by the conflagration raging in Burliuk; but the Light Division (Sir G. Brown), breaking through the vines and fording the river, gained a footing on the south bank, disordered by the obstacles they met, by the want of space, and by the hot fire poured upon them. General Codrington, heading his brigade and two battalions that joined him—one of Buller's and one of the Second Division—led them boldly up the slope under the fire of the battery behind the epaulment; while the rest of Buller's brigade covered his left flank from a threatening movement observed in that direction. On his right were three of Evans's battalions; the other two, under Adams, having crossed the Alma, below the burning village, pushed into the space to the west of the post-road.

The Russians, seriously alarmed at Codrington's impetuous onslaught, withdrew their heavy guns from the epaulment, except two, which they could not get away, and which were captured. Cheered by this retreat, the British gained the breastwork, and took possession of it; but they now found themselves face to face with large masses of the enemy's infantry and cavalry, supported by field-guns. The gallant rush in the face of a tremendous fire had come to an end; it was the moment for supports to arrive; but as they were not close enough to be available at this critical moment, the attacking brigade was soon afterwards forced back to the foot of the slope.

Meanwhile, the First Division (Duke of Cambridge) deployed and halted just beyond effective range, watching with enthusiastic animation and breathless interest, the movements of their comrades in front of them. There was more room for them, as they were not overcrowded by the Third Division (Sir R. England), which took up a position somewhat in rear. On the right stood the Guards Brigade in their usual order—Grenadiers on the right, Coldstream on the left, and Scots Fusiliers in the centre ; the Highlanders were formed on the left of the division. While they waited, spent round shot came bounding through the ranks like cricket balls. The men, longing to take part in the fray, were in exuberant spirits ; the least trifle amused them, and a little Maltese terrier called "Toby," belonging to the Coldstream drummers, drew loud laughter from the light-hearted soldiery as it gave chase to the Russian round shot which rolled slowly along the smooth ground.

At length Lieut.-Colonel Steele brought the order to advance, and never was it obeyed with greater alacrity and spirit, the whole division moving forward with admirable precision. Approaching the vineyards, the enemy directed his artillery upon our men ; but they quickly pushed their way through the tangled shrubs, and over a low wall obstructing their path up to the Alma, which they immediately crossed, and here they found shelter from the fire of the Russians.

As it had been impossible to reconnoitre the ground, each regiment had to take its chance of finding a favourable spot, or the reverse, for its passage; and it happened that the Coldstream reached the river, where it makes a large S-shaped bend, so that the greater part of the Battalion had to go through the water three times. Owing to the many obstructions in their way, all three Battalions were in considerable confusion when they arrived at the foot of the southern bank, and they at once began to reform their ranks under the partial cover it afforded. Colonel Upton, having halted the Coldstream, called out the markers to the front, quickly assembled the companies upon them, and then wheeled the Battalion into line, before making any further advance, in a manner that would have satisfied the most exacting drill-sergeant on parade in Hyde Park.*

Meanwhile Codrington's brigade were still in front, clinging to the epaulment they had captured, and engaged in a very unequal struggle with the enemy. Their distress was apparent from the river, and General Bentinck immediately ordered the

* See *The Crimea in* 1854 *and* 1894 (by General Sir Evelyn Wood, V.C., G.C.B.), p. 55 (London, 1895).

BATTLE OF THE ALMA. 81

Scots Fusilier Guards to hurry to their relief before there had been sufficient time to reform the line, and while the ranks were still disordered and the companies mixed up. As the Battalion moved forward, they met General Codrington's Aide-de-camp, who was sent to beg them to hasten to the front as quickly as possible, and they eagerly complied. Just at this moment a series of untoward circumstances occurred. The backward rush of some of the Light Division struck them with tremendous force; an order intended for the 23rd Fusiliers, "Retire, Fusiliers!" was heard in the field, and was believed by many of the Fusilier Guards to apply to them; the enemy was close, and in hot pursuit, and his artillery was firing furiously upon them. It was a critical moment, and one that would have been fatal to any but the best troops; but in spite of the gallantry of the Officers, who, running forward, endeavoured to rally the men, two or three companies were swept back by the retreating brigade, and were carried away with them towards the river, while the remainder halted, opened fire, and held their ground.*

* The following extract of a letter written by General Codrington, on September 27th, will be read with interest: "We were borne back, and when I saw we could not long bear up in these groups (from which I could not get them), I sent young Campbell [now Lt.-Col. Hon. H. Campbell, late Coldstream Guards] to the rear to the Battalion of Guards which I saw, to beg them to hurry their advance, otherwise we must lose all we had gained. . . . I saw the line of Guards coming up, though they were further off

G

As this was going on, the other two Guards Battalions, now completely reformed and in proper order, advanced steadily forward up the hill. Coming into alignment with the Scots Fusilier Guards, and perceiving the hot engagement that was still raging, the left company of the Grenadiers was wheeled back, and fired across the front, while the Coldstream, without changing position, opened upon the Russians as soon as they got the opportunity, and the latter retired. Though there was a gap in the Brigade which could not be immediately closed, the Guards—

"continued to advance in lines absolutely unbroken, except where struck by the enemy's shot; such French Officers on the hills on the right as, in an interval of inaction, were free to observe what our troops were doing, spoke of this advance of the Guards as something new to their minds, and very admirable." *

Soon they reached the epaulment, firing as they advanced, the enemy giving way before them, and

than I wished, and than they ought to have been in such a crisis; it was the Fusiliers in my rear to whom I sent, and I tried hard to keep our position, though in our irregular order, till they came; but I could not, the fire was heavy, the men collected in instinctive heaps and were borne back on the advance of the left wing of the Fusiliers, carrying, in fact, three or four companies back with them down the slope to the rocky shelter. . . . When the two or three companies of the Fusiliers were borne back with us, the right wing went on gallantly." The losses of this Battalion were very heavy, and amounted to 11 Officers and 170 men during the day. Among the many acts of bravery performed by Officers and men during the crisis, Lieutenant R. Lindsay (now Lord Wantage) gained the Victoria Cross for his intrepid conduct.

* Hamley, *War in the Crimea*, p. 59.

BATTLE OF THE ALMA.

as they came up to the crest of the hill the three companies, previously mentioned, rejoined their Battalion, and the whole Brigade was again complete.* To our left, protecting the left flank of the British army, were the Highlanders in echelon of battalions from the right; and this magnificent corps, handled with great ability, fired into the hostile columns that passed them on their way to the epaulment (round which the fight centred in this quarter of the field), and contributed in no small degree, to lighten the task of the Guards.†

* A point connected with this phase of the battle may be noted. The British soldier had never been trained to advance firing, and at first there was some difficulty in preventing him from halting to load, especially as the repeated cheering of the men drowned to a considerable extent the orders of the Officers. Many of the latter, however, springing to the front, showed by their example that the advance was on no account to be checked, and the line thereafter did not halt. Sir Colin Campbell drilled the Highland Brigade to advance firing, the morning after landing at Old Fort, and instructed them to open out, so that they should not crowd upon each other or interfere with each other's movements when loading and firing.

† Of the Coldstream, it is written that the Battalion was "drawn up in line with beautiful precision; because of the position of the ground on which it advanced, it had been much less exposed to fire and mishaps than either of the other Battalions of the Brigade, and it had not been pressed forward, as each of the other two Battalions had been, to meet any special emergency occurring on its front. Therefore it was that it fell to the lot of the Coldstream to become an almost prim sample of what our Guards can be in the moment which precedes a close fight. What the best of battalions is, when, in some Royal Park at home, it manœuvres before a great princess, that the Coldstream was now on the banks of the Alma, when it came to show its graces to the enemy. And it was no ignoble pride which caused the Battalion to maintain all this ceremonious

Nor had the British artillery been inactive. Pressing forward, they took up positions wherever they were to be found, whence they fired either upon the enemy's guns or into the solid masses of his infantry. At the moment when the Duke's division appeared upon the slope, three of Evans's battalions were engaged near the post-road; two more, under Adams, were further to the right, moving up the hill; England's Division was crossing the river, and the Fourth Division (Sir G. Cathcart) was still in rear, as a reserve. The first onslaught of the Light Division had shaken the enemy; and now, when opposed to the steady advance of the Guards and Highlanders, he did not long maintain the contest. The Russians were unable to fight in line. They remained throughout the whole day in dense columns.* This faulty formation, adopted to suit the quality of their troops, gave them greater weight had they been able to come to close quarters with their antagonist; but it prevented them from using their muskets, and offered a large target to our fire.

On the other hand, the fire of the two British

exactness; for though it be true that the precision of a line in peace time is only a success in mechanics, the precision of a line on a hill-side with the enemy close in front, is the result and the proof of warlike composure" (Kinglake, ii. 426).

* "They had a curious formation of close column, with swarms of skirmishers on each side; they seemed to run out of the ranks to fire, and then take refuge in their columns again; they would have been much safer outside altogether" (Tower, *Diary*).

brigades was fully developed. Moving as if on parade, the Guards in line kept up a continuous and well-aimed stream of lead, at short ranges, into the masses in front of them, while the Highlanders in echelon succeeded in striking the right flank of the enemy.* Unable to bear down on the thin lines that opposed them, the Russians wavered, and, with a ringing cheer, our men charged home, and drove them from the field. The English army had cleared the formidable position held by the enemy on Kurgané, as well as from that hill to the eastern slopes of the Telegraph, where the French had now arrived. Menshikoff's troops fled from the field, and their retreat was so precipitate that it was not even covered by cavalry or artillery. For a short time our batteries played upon their ranks; but Lord Raglan's request that Marshal St. Arnaud might complete the rout by sending forward his comparatively fresh troops, was met by a frivolous excuse, and there was no pursuit.

The British losses amounted to 106 Officers,

* "Scarcely a man had seen a shotted musket fired before, except at a target, and yet they looked as cool and self-possessed as if 'marking time' in an English barrack square" (*Our Veterans, etc.*, 133). "We soon drove the enemy before us up the hill and through the epaulment, but the guns had been taken out [except the two previously captured], and a regiment was retreating out of the rear of the work in very tolerably good order, firing at us, and in no confusion or disorderly haste. We gave them two or three steady volleys before they were out of shot; our men fired wonderfully steadily all the time. We fired sixteen rounds going up the hill" (Tower, *Diary*).

121 sergeants, and 1775 rank and file, total 2002, of whom were killed 25, 19, and 318 respectively. The French, who played a minor part in the action, exaggerated their casualties, which really numbered only 60 killed (including three Officers), and 500 wounded. The Russians put their losses at nearly 6000, but this was probably less than the truth. The Coldstream and the Highlanders had been protected to a great extent by the folds of the ground, and they were fortunately not under the direct fire of the Russian guns, as the other two Battalions of the Division had been. The casualties of the Scots Fusiliers have been already given; those of the Grenadier Guards amounted to 4 Officers and 137 men; the Highland Brigade (three battalions) lost 90 of all ranks. In the Coldstream there were two Officers and 27 men wounded,—of the former, Captain Cust, Aide-de-camp to Major-General Bentinck, died of his wounds immediately after the action; the other, Captain C. Baring, had his arm amputated.

Military critics are disappointed with this battle, and condemn both sides for displaying little tactical knowledge or talent. Menshikoff left almost everything undone, to enable him to make a stand on the ground he had himself selected for barring the march of the Allies. The influence of St. Arnaud, who at this time was in bad health, seemed to damp the usual ardour of the French; and on

BATTLE OF THE ALMA. 87

this occasion they hardly maintained the high standard of their brilliant military reputation.

We have seen that Lord Raglan and the Marshal had formed no definite plan of action before the fight began. If they intended to turn the enemy's left, and drive him off the road to Sevastopol into the interior, the English attack was too soon delivered; and if they hoped to push him towards the sea, they took no measures to effect that object. They pursued neither of these courses, and a mere frontal attack was undertaken, which resulted in dislodging the Russians, but which, in the absence of a vigorous pursuit, involved them in no serious disaster. Lord Raglan, moreover, having ordered the first line to advance, took up a position well in front of his own army, within the ground occupied at that time by the enemy. In this exposed place he watched the course of the battle, but he ceased to be able to control it. Hence the co-operation between his divisional commanders, necessary to the attack, was wanting, and we missed the opportunity of inflicting a greater defeat upon the enemy than we succeeded in doing. Of the bravery of both the Officers and men, of the steadiness and discipline under fire of the rank and file, who for the first time were in action, but one opinion has ever been expressed.

"All, therefore, that we had to be proud of was the dash and valour of the regiments engaged. These were very conspicuous, and worthy of the traditions of the Peninsular days. A French Officer, who was viewing the field, where our men lay, as they had fallen, in ranks, with one of our naval Captains, observed to him, 'Well, you took the bull by the horns—our men could not have done it.'" *

As has been said, there was no pursuit after the battle, and the enemy was allowed to leave the field unmolested. This was the more unfortunate, since the retreat of the Russians degenerated into a rout. But worse followed, for the morning of the 23rd dawned before we stirred from the scene of our success, and two of the most valuable days of the campaign were irretrievably lost to the Allies. The fault was St. Arnaud's, whom nothing could shake in his determination to remain where he was. Happily the strain of the alliance touched not the troops of either nation, and among them existed warm feelings of an honest *camaraderie*. Just as the First Division was about to fall in, a French brigade passed by on its southward march, and friendly expressions of mutual recognition and of good will were heard; from us, by lusty cheers and waving of bearskins and bonnets, and from them by hearty cries of "Vivent les Anglais! Vivent les Montagnards!"

Leaving the Alma, the approach to Sevastopol was made by easy stages. On the 23rd a halt was called at noon on the Katcha, where we had

* Hamley, *War in the Crimea*, p. 65.

BATTLE OF THE ALMA. 89

the mortification of learning that the heavy fieldpieces, which had done us so much damage on the Kurgané heights, had left but four short hours before our arrival. Next day, we reached the Belbek, thirteen miles from the late field of battle, and within striking distance of Sevastopol, the goal of our ambition. And now a strange thing happened. Far from attacking the very position we had come to assail, we even refused to make a reconnaissance to ascertain the nature of its defences, and the force and quality of the enemy holding it.

The expedition, we have seen, was expressly designed to be a speedy operation, and every step taken with respect to it was governed by that one idea; otherwise, it would never have been undertaken in the autumn of 1854. Hence, a coast destitute of secure harbours wherein to form a base of operations, was not considered unsuitable as a landing-place; communications between the Crimea and the rest of the Russian Empire were not intercepted; a line of advance exposed to attack by a relieving army was not rejected; a late season of the year did not put an end to the enterprise; and hence, also, there was no provision made for the winter.

These conditions were none of them in accordance with sound military science or practice; but they were accepted, and they led the army to the north side of Sevastopol—to the objective which the

Allies designed to reach when they landed at Old Fort. Arriving there, the Anglo-French armies came face to face with an obstacle; some works loomed in the haze before them, and they began to deliberate. Counsellors, not consulted when the expedition was planned, were now admitted as advisers, and they naturally viewed the problem without reference to the past. We had lost touch with the defeated Menshikoff, and it was thought that he probably had his army safe behind the entrenchments in front; the attack might not succeed, a delay might occur, and at any rate it was dangerous to wait when we had no secure base in our rear.

In short, the hazardous nature of the expedition which had been forced upon the Allied Commanders from home, suddenly burst upon them with a vivid light never experienced before, and they had to recognize, although unfortunately they did not yet acknowledge, that the surprise had failed, that a lengthened siege was inevitable, and that the descent on the fortress, as originally conceived, was a snare and a delusion.

And yet, had the position been reconnoitred, some interesting facts would have been revealed. We should have found the defences weak, imperfectly armed, and garrisoned only by 11,000 men, whose weapons for the most part were antiquated flint-locks, while others were only provided with

BATTLE OF THE ALMA. 91

pikes or cutlasses.* The field-force that fought on the 20th was not there at all. It had hastily retired to the south side to re-organize itself after the disaster it had suffered.

The possession of the north side of Sevastopol offered the Allies considerable advantages.† The town, barracks, dockyards, and arsenal are built on the south side of an extensive creek, deep enough to float the largest ships of war, which runs from the sea in an easterly direction four miles inland, 1000 to 1200 yards in breadth. This inlet, forming the roadstead or harbour of Sevastopol, is defended at its mouth by several strong forts, some of those on the north side being perched on cliffs 100 feet high. The northern bank entirely commands the south side, and rises from the water's edge more abruptly than the latter. These things were known to the Allies before they landed in the Crimea. It is obvious that, if the invaders could have established themselves on this northern bank, they would have taken the town and some of the forts in reverse; and that, if they could have brought up sufficient guns of the requisite calibre, the fortress itself would have been untenable, and the destruction of the ships in the harbour ensured by the force of plunging fire directed upon them.

While we lingered on the Alma, General

* Kinglake, iii. 43. † See Map No. 4, p. 102.

Menshikoff had not been idle, and he determined to secure all the advantages which the Russian fleet of the Black Sea might be able to confer. It was hopeless to suppose that this fleet could cope with our own magnificent ships which lay outside the harbour; and indeed, ever since the battle of Sinope, it had been carefully kept out of harm's way. The only use to which it could be put, was to convert it into an addition to the land defences of Sevastopol. But even then, it would be exposed to danger; for the enemy had a wholesome dread of what the historic daring of British seamen is capable of achieving when directed by an enterprising commander. On the night of the 22nd, therefore, he effectually barred the entrance of the roadstead by sinking seven vessels, and by constructing a boom across it, and thus he secured his shipping from any direct attack which our navy might have contemplated.

Thus the Russian war-ships became stationary floating batteries, and their function was to play their guns upon the ground that bordered the roadstead. For this device, also, the Allies must have been prepared, and might have taken it into consideration before even they started on the expedition. Now, the plateau on the top of the heights overlooking the town from the north, was much less (if at all) exposed to the enemy's naval artillery than the ground over which the invaders must advance, if they meant to deliver their attack from the south; and the fire directed upon this plateau would be uncertain and inefficient, since considerable portions of it were out of sight of the ships below.

The British Admiral, Sir Edmond Lyons, at that time second in command, never lost sight of the original plan of invasion: he advocated strongly an attack upon the north side, and was prepared to take a prominent part in the action he expected to follow. If successful, the closing of the harbour was of trifling moment. This powerful co-operation was impossible on the south side. Lord Raglan agreed with the Admiral, and was also in favour of striking a blow from the north, as had always been intended. But he was in a position of great difficulty. Some of his own advisers were against the proposal, and the French Marshal, always unfavourable to activity in this quarter, was sinking under a disease that carried him off before the end of the month.

The question whether this attack from the Belbek river would have brought about the immediate fall of Sevastopol, need not be further discussed; no attempt was made to ascertain whether it was practicable. Suffice it to say that General Todleben, who defended Sevastopol, afterwards expressed his deliberate opinion, and elaborately argued it out, that the northern plateau was untenable by the Russians, and that operations conducted against it would have led the Allies to a speedy success. Nevertheless, it is important to notice that the original design of taking Sevastopol by a *coup de main* under the effects of a surprise, was given up before even a reconnaissance was made to ascertain the strength of the objective, to which the Allies were committed by that very design. We shall now see that, refusing to pursue their plan, on account of the serious military errors it disclosed, the Allies were forced to adopt another plan, which equally, if not in a greater degree, violated the canons of the science of war.*

* The late Sir E. Hamley holds that General Todleben was wrong, and writes: " But he [Todleben] says the enemies' [allied] ships, approaching the shore, could batter the fort almost with impunity, [*i.e.* the Star-Fort, or the principal work on the north side of Sevastopol, which the Allies would have had to attack]. The impossibility of this is best shown by the fact that, in the subsequent engagement between the fleets and forts, one of the batteries on the cliffs (100 feet high) of the north side disabled several of our ships without receiving a shot in return, although they made it the object of their fire, and that the Star-Fort is distant inland from this battery 1000 yards. Thus, according to Todleben, the ships, while themselves under the fire of the coast batteries, which they could not injure in return, were to bombard a fort 1000 yards beyond these batteries, and which would be invisible from the sea" (Hamley, *War in the Crimea*, p. 71).

The bombardment spoken of, in which the English ships were injured, was only directed against the forts situated at the entrance of the harbour. From that point, no doubt, the Star-Fort could not be seen. But still Todleben made no puerile suggestion with respect to the geography of a place every inch of which he had good reason to know intimately. The Russian entrenchments on the north plateau could be reached by the guns of our fleet, from another spot off the coast, just round the promontory on which the coast batteries were built, and where our ships would be to a great extent (if not entirely) sheltered from the fire of the latter.

PART III.

BEFORE SEVASTOPOL.

CHAPTER VII.

FLANK MARCH ROUND SEVASTOPOL.

Predicament of the Allies—Determination to attack the south side—Flank march—Strange meeting with the rear of Menshikoff's army—Occupation of Balaklava by the British and of Kamiesh Bay by the French—The Allies refuse to assault Sevastopol; they prefer to bombard it—Depression of the Russian garrison, who fear a prompt assault—Their strength and the state of their defences—Successful efforts to strengthen the latter.

THE Allies, at this juncture, found themselves placed in a strange predicament. Their plans had hitherto been successful, and nothing remained to be done except to justify their first resolutions by standing firm to their original purpose. The critical moment at length arrived, and then, in the very presence of the enemy, they changed their minds. They would not operate against the north of Sevastopol; they would attack it from the south, and form a secure base in the harbours of Balaklava and Kamiesh, that indent the coast of the upland plain, called by the ancients the Chersonese.

In order to accomplish this new design, they had

to march the united armies from the Belbek to the south-west corner of the peninsula, quite close to the fortress they intended to capture. Added to this, the ground over which they had to pass was unknown. They left behind them the broad, open, and treeless plains, where they could march in battle array, ready for emergencies; they now approached a woody, difficult, and intersected country, and had to adopt long columns of route in moving across it. According to the information in their possession, moreover, a hostile army was sheltered somewhere within the lines of Sevastopol; it was believed to be securely posted behind the entrenchments on the northern plateau. They did not wish to meet it there, and, to avoid doing so, they were obliged to have recourse to the only alternative, and to commit a bad military error. They exposed the right of their long columns and their rear to imminent danger, and, courting disaster, invited the Russians to fall upon them, in a position where partial defeat must prove fatal to their existence.

On the 25th the main body, preceded by a regiment of cavalry, a troop of horse artillery, and a battalion of Rifles, left the Belbek, and the perilous flank march commenced. It was carried out in a manner which would have given the fullest advantages to the enemy had he availed himself of them. The general direction was kept, often by consulting the compass; but the difficulties of the country, the thick woods, and the haste which urged us forward, disarranged the order of the troops. At one moment, indeed, the head-quarters, leading the whole advance, were followed by a long procession of thirty guns without supports, and offered a tempting and easy reward to Russian enterprise. But, slow though we may be to recognize it, a miracle does sometimes take place, and in this case it showed itself in the fact, that the extraordinary march proceeded onwards without the slightest mishap. Not only this, but the British even captured some twenty carts from the enemy, though they failed to get hold of the horses, which were cut away directly we came into sight.

This meeting came about in a curious way. It happened, as we have seen, that Prince Menshikoff, far from taking post on the north plateau, was refitting his defeated army in the town of Sevastopol, south of the roadstead. He came to the conclusion that he ought to preserve his communications with the interior of the Crimea, and support the advance of the reinforcements he expected to come from Bessarabia. At dawn on the 25th, therefore, he, too, emerged from his retreat, crossed the Tchernaya at Traktir Bridge, and, advancing to Mackenzie Farm, marched towards Bakshiserai. Thus it came about that the two contending armies, moving on the same day, and for some time advancing towards one another by the same road, crossed each other's path, and that neither had the least conception of what the other was doing.

It was fortunate that, in this curious game of blind man's buff, Menshikoff did not strike our columns of route full in the flank; as it was, we just happened to drive our ram into the tip of his tail. For, as the head-quarter Staff, stumbling suddenly on the last portion of the enemy's baggage train as it passed unconsciously by, stood wondering at the sight, a few of our guns hurried up to the rescue, unlimbered, and secured some of his unhorsed carts. Among the booty was a carriage belonging to one of the Russian Commanders, in which were stars, crosses, medals, uniform, French novels, and a portfolio "of coloured prints, the morality of which will not bear discussion."

The experiences of the First Division on this march should not be omitted. After waiting ready equipped for two hours, the men at length moved off, at 8.30 in the morning, and plunged almost immediately into the forest.

"Everybody who has seen beaters pushing their way through a thick cover, may form a faint idea of the difficulties which beset, and the obstacles which retarded our progress. The heat was overpowering, not a breath of air percolated the dense vegetation. You scrambled on with arms uplifted to protect the face against the swinging back-handers dealt by the boughs; now your

THE FLANK MARCH.

shakoe was dashed off, now the briars laid tenacious hold on your haversack, or on the tails of your coatee. It was as much as you could do to see the soldiers immediately on your right and left. For the time, military order was an impossibility, brigades and regiments got intermixed. Guardsmen, Rifles, and Highlanders straggled forward blindly, all in a ruck. There was much suffering, and some stout soldiers dropped involuntarily to the rear, to be heard of no more." *

After four hours or more, the troops emerged on a lane blocked by the cavalry and baggage, and squeezed through. A little later they heard an explosion, and, pushing forward, they came upon the scene of the singular meeting that took place between the head-quarter Staff and the rear of the enemy's army. Continuing along a tolerably good road, they approached the valley of the Tchernaya after dark, and, crossing it at Traktir Bridge, they finally bivouacked near the village of Tchorgun, at ten o'clock at night, "completely exhausted, parched with thirst, and their clothes much torn by struggling through the wood." Indeed, they were fortunate, for it was one in the morning before the last British division reached its halting ground. The French, who followed their English allies, remained for the night midway on the wooded heights near Mackenzie Farm, where they suffered much from want of water.

Next day the movement continued; and the

* *Our Veterans, etc.*, p. 163.

cholera, that accompanied our troops without intermission, burst out with renewed malignity, and struck its victims down on the roadside along our line of march. After three hours, the division reached Kadikeui, about half a mile from Balaklava; while our ships, approaching, threw a few shells into an old Genoese fort, which commanded the harbour, and which was held by a handful of Greek troops in the Russian service; after a mere show of resistance, they surrendered without difficulty. The French also moved forward on the 26th, and established themselves on the Fediukhine heights near the Tchernaya. The Fourth Division, under Sir G. Cathcart, had been left behind on the Belbek, to embark the sick that remained there. On the same day (26th) he, too, started from his bivouac on the north of Sevastopol, and, following the track of the Allied armies, arrived on the Tchernaya without misadventure.

Thus the flank march was completed, and during the whole of the difficult and dangerous operation, lasting two days, the Russians stood by absolutely passive, and the Allies were entirely unmolested. Not a company was cut off, nor was a gun taken. This was the more remarkable since, perceiving the movement from a high tower in Sevastopol, they were accurately informed of our plan at midday of the 25th. General Menshikoff must also have known it, from the meeting that took place between the hostile armies near Mackenzie Farm. It was, indeed, fortunate that we had so forbearing an enemy.

Communications having now been fortunately re-established with the fleet, the British occupied the Bay of Balaklava, the French that of Kamiesh, where their respective bases of operations were formed. Thus we were placed on the right of the new line fronting northwards, and we were again posted upon the exposed flank.

About this time, an event of importance occurred to the French. Marshal St. Arnaud got so ill, that he was obliged to give up his command, and to leave the seat of war. He was to be taken to Scutari, but he died on the passage. General Canrobert succeeded him—a valiant, honourable, and straightforward soldier, but one little fitted to take upon himself the onerous responsibilities of his new position.

The Allies now found themselves occupying a fertile country, almost entirely denuded of inhabitants, who fled at their approach, covered with highly cultivated gardens, orchards, and vineyards, which teemed with vegetables and fruit in great abundance. Never were troops so amply supplied as during the first few days of their stay in this land of plenty; but the good things did not last, they were soon exhausted, and could not be replaced. The men were not easily restrained from enjoying to the full the luxurious feast which lay before them, after the fatigues of the forced flank march; though it is to be feared they suffered from its effects, and from the fact that they were still without tents. Cholera continued, and diarrhœa (its pilot-fish) increased considerably.*

The idea seems to have been pretty general among the troops that the flank march was intended to shift the position of the united armies from a strong front of Sevastopol to a weaker side, and that the attack was only delayed until we got close to the southern defences of the town. It was confidently expected that the assault would be soon delivered, and the landing of the siege-train did not put an end to that hope. As days went by, however, it began to be realized that operations of a slower nature were to be begun, and that a siege, not an assault, was to be undertaken. This surmise was entirely correct; though the Chiefs of the armies still held to the belief that, when a bombardment by siege guns had taken place, the defences would be destroyed, and the town would then fall before the winter set in.

Lord Raglan personally seems to have been disposed to make an immediate attempt against the enemy's lines, without incurring this further

* Of 76 cases of sickness that occurred in the Battalion in the month of September, 30 were fever, 24 diarrhœa, and 7 cholera (Wyatt, p. 24).

delay; and this view was certainly shared and supported by Sir George Cathcart, and was also advocated by Sir Edmond Lyons. It was urged that the Russian fortifications were slight and weak at the end of September, when the Allies got within striking distance, and, though we should be stronger against them as soon as the siege batteries were constructed and armed, yet the time required to do so could be utilized by the defenders in so strengthening their works, that the advantages of a delay would accrue to them, and to our detriment. General Canrobert, however, was cautious, and was disinclined to run any risks just as the supreme command was vested in him by the French Emperor. Others, among the British advisers at head-quarters, held the opinion that it was dangerous to deliver an attack unless prepared by artillery fire. They feared that the attempt might cost us 500 men, which loss they hoped would not occur if a siege were opened in the regular manner. Lord Raglan was forced to concur.

During this time the Russian commanders, left in Sevastopol after General Menshikoff's departure, were in a state of great depression, and believed that the town could not hold out against a vigorous assault. The entire garrison amounted to 35,850 men, made up of heterogeneous elements — one single battalion of regulars (750 men), militia, gunners, marines, seamen, and workmen. Of the latter, there were 5000—a useful body to create a fortress, if time were granted, but useless to repel an immediate attack. Of the sailors set free from the imprisoned fleet, there were 18,500, of whom a fourth part only were well trained or even decently armed.*

The south side, moreover, does not lend itself easily to a good defence.† A creek, hardly half a mile broad, called the inner harbour, runs inland for nearly two miles from the main roadstead, terminating in three ravines which ascend the upland of the Chersonese. This inlet divides the town from a suburb, called the Karabelnaya; and as both had to be held against the Allies, there was a formidable obstacle obstructing communications between them. The French, based on Kamiesh Bay, were opposite the western portion of Sevastopol, that is the town itself, from the sea to the head of the inner harbour. The British army on the right, faced Karabelnaya, and were responsible for the ground from the inner harbour to Careenage Bay,—another inlet, half a mile long, which also terminates in a ravine indenting the upland,—where the enemy's defences ended. The

* These numbers are taken from Hamley's *War in the Crimea*, p. 86. Todleben says there were but 16,000 "combatants" (excluding artillery) available for the defence of the south side (Kinglake, iii. 195).

† See Map No. 5, p. 124.

line held by the Russian garrison was about four miles in length: two miles from the sea to the head of the inner harbour, and the same distance onwards to Careenage Bay.

On the 25th of September, this long line was imperfectly defended. On the French section, the gorges of the Quarantine and Artillery Forts had been closed, and three bastions or redoubts had been constructed between them and the head of the inner harbour, where the Flagstaff bastion stood, connected, with but little interruption, by a naked loopholed wall. On the British section, there were four works, which were unconnected by wall or entrenchment, known as the Redan, the Malakoff Tower, the Little Redan, and No. 1 Battery, near Careenage Bay. Of these the Malakoff was "a mere naked tower, without a glacis, exposed from head to foot, unsupported by the powerful batteries which were destined to flank it, and uncovered as yet by the works which afterwards closed up round its base." The whole of the south side of Sevastopol, moreover, was armed with 172 guns, of which by far the greater number faced the French, and only a few the British position.*

* Kinglake, iii. 123, etc., 194, 347. Sir Edmond Lyons urged the immediate assault of the Malakoff hill, "then unoccupied, and advised the immediate construction of a battery there, which would make it necessary for the fleet to take care of themselves" (*Ibid.*, iii., Appendix, p. 491). The capture of the Malakoff in September, 1855, caused the immediate fall of Sevastopol.

The serious and very reasonable apprehension entertained by the Russian chiefs did not, however, prevent them from taking every measure to fortify their position, directly they understood that the Allies were approaching the south side in force. The greatest activity prevailed day and night in the garrison and among the inhabitants, the women and children taking their share of the labour, and thus the works designed by the Russian Engineer Officer, Todleben, were rapidly thrown up. The Anglo-French Commanders never interrupted these operations, nor did they make any demonstrations to try the quality of the defences. They contented themselves with distant reconnaissances, so that in a short time the entrenchments were greatly strengthened, especially the Malakoff, and began to look more formidable than had been the case before; the armament also was being changed, the lighter guns giving place to heavier ordnance drawn from the ships and arsenal.

CHAPTER VIII.

A REGULAR SIEGE UNCONSCIOUSLY BEGUN.

Description of the upland of the Chersonese occupied by the Allies—Position of Menshikoff's army—Of the French—Of the British—Weakness of the right flank of the allied line—Nothing done to defend it—Supply of tents to the troops—Preparation for the projected bombardment—Official confidence in an immediate success—Severe duties—How the enemy utilized the unexpected respite accorded to him.

THE upland of the Chersonese,* on which the Allies had established themselves, is a sloping plain, trending from a line of hills, called the Sapuné Ridge, 500 to 700 feet high, that bounds it on the east, from the head of the roadstead of Sevastopol to a point on the coast some four miles west of Balaklava. The upland is scored by numerous ravines, running from the ridge in a general north-westerly direction to the town and coast; but on the eastern side of the ridge the ground falls abruptly and almost in a cliff-like manner into the valley of the Tchernaya river, which discharges itself into the roadstead.

* See Map No. 4, p. 102.

The distance from Sevastopol to Balaklava is nearly eight miles. Of the two roads connecting them, one, the Woronzoff road, was metalled, and, proceeding along the Causeway Heights, formed the main communication with the south of the Crimean peninsula. The other was a mere cart-track or pathway, more to the south, which leaving Balaklava, ascended the ridge over the "Col de Balaklava," three miles from that place, and joined the Woronzoff road two miles further on, on the upland.

This extended position had to be defended from attacks that were to be feared from Menshikoff's army. The latter, having left Sevastopol, was in easy communication with the town, and was securely posted on very defensible ground, from whence it could advance upon the right of the Allies or upon our base at Balaklava. Moreover, the Russians would, before long, be strongly reinforced by troops which, as we have seen, were hurrying without opposition from Bessarabia into the Crimea; but when this event would take place was still uncertain. The Allies had lost all touch with the enemy's army they had defeated at the Alma, and their hesitation to assault the weak defences that covered Sevastopol directly after the flank march, was in a measure due to their ignorance of what their opponent was doing. In reality he was then many miles away, and had no intention of resuming hostilities without further assistance. He was re-organizing his men, and waiting for the fresh forces he expected from the north.* Only for the moment, therefore, was the right flank of the invaders free from danger, and under no circumstances could it have been left unguarded.

The French divided their army into two Corps. The 3rd and 4th Divisions, under General Forey, formed the besieging force, and took post before Sevastopol, their right on the great ravine which runs into the inner harbour, their left on Streleska Bay. The 1st and 2nd Divisions, together with the Turkish contingent, constituted a Corps of observation, under General Bosquet, and were entrenched on the Sapuné Ridge, facing the east, between the Woronzoff road and the Col previously mentioned.

The whole of the British army was engaged in the siege, before the suburb of Karabelnaya, the left on the ravine, in communication with the French, the right upon ground not far from the Sapuné heights. The defence of Balaklava was provided by the 93rd Regiment (withdrawn for the purpose from the Highland Brigade), 1,000 Marines, a battery of Artillery, and a body of Turks (3,500 of whom had been recently despatched to the Crimea, the remainder, two battalions, being

* Kinglake, iii. 215.

lent by the French). These troops, which included a provisional battalion formed of 25 to 30 weakly men drawn from every regiment, were placed under the command of Sir Colin Campbell, who was detached from his brigade. In front of them, in the valley, was Lord Lucan's cavalry division.

These measures did not, however, secure the right flank of the British siege-works. At this point, the cliff-like appearance of the heights overlooking the Tchernaya partially disappears, and the upland falls towards the roadstead and the river, in numerous spurs, intersected by ravines. This broken country was known to the Allies by the name of Inkerman, and along its foot there ran a road from Balaklava, which, skirting the Tchernaya to the roadstead, proceeded to Sevastopol along the southern shore of the latter. The river, moreover, was crossed at its mouth by a bridge and a causeway, over which another road led to Bakshiserai.

This was a vulnerable point in the line adopted by the Allies, who far from being able to invest the place they intended to besiege, were too weak even to establish themselves upon the head of the roadstead, and prevent an irruption from the town, or an attack from the direction of Bakshiserai upon the right of their position. To guard this vital point, only a strong piquet was employed, and a battery of two guns of position, called the

A SIEGE UNCONSCIOUSLY BEGUN.

"Sandbag battery," constructed to strengthen it, had soon to be disarmed, as it was found impracticable to support the guns by infantry. The flank, in short, was left undefended, because the whole of the British army was required to undertake the siege, and because Bosquet's corps had entrenched themselves on an inaccessible position on the ridge, where no enemy could attack them, and where they could neither give efficient support to the defences of Balaklava, nor be of any immediate use should an onslaught be made on the unguarded spurs of Inkerman. In other words, we suffered from the effects of a divided command.*

We left the Guards Brigade, on the 26th of September, near Balaklava, at the end of the flank march. For the first few days there was little done. "Troops passive and grape-gorging, with the exception of strong fatigue parties engaged in the slow and laborious office of landing the siege guns from the transports, which now cram the harbour of Balaklava."† On the 2nd of October, the First Division marched to the front, and about this time the British army was thus bivouacked before Sevastopol. The Second Division on the right, with the First in support, nearly a mile in rear; next came the Light Division, separated from them by the Careenage Ravine. These three divisions

* Kinglake, iii. 291 ; Hamley, *War in the Crimea*, 124.
† September 29th (*Our Veterans*, etc., p. 177).

manned the British Right Attack. The Fourth and Third Divisions were posted south-west of Cathcart's Hill, and continued the line to the west, in rear of the Left Attack, to the ravine, on the other side of which lay the French siege corps, near Mount Rodolph. The work of bringing up the battering train continued without interruption, and some heavy guns from the ships were drawn to the batteries by sailors, who, forming a brigade under command of Captains Lushington and Peel, took part in the operations which were soon to commence.

It was fortunate that tents were at last issued, on the 5th of October; for the men, having been constantly bivouacked since the disembarkation at Old Fort, nearly three weeks before, were again attacked by sickness. Cholera reappeared on the day after the troops stood on the upland plain before Sevastopol, and an Officer of the Coldstream, Captain Jolliffe, died of it on the 4th. It seems that the delay in providing shelter, even of an indifferent nature, was due to the want of transport, which still failed us. Nothing apparently could induce our Government to give the army this indispensable requirement. The boon of again having a tent to cover them in the chilly autumn nights of the Crimea, was keenly appreciated by Officers and men. But comfort is a relative term, and, judged from the ordinary standpoint, the slight

A SIEGE UNCONSCIOUSLY BEGUN.

shelter which was supplied, was inadequate and insufficient.

The constant labour which the Russians devoted to the improvement of their fortifications became apparent to regimental Officers, as they anxiously scanned the enemy's works during their leisure time.

"Within the last few days," writes Colonel Wilson, on the 7th, "an amazing change has taken place in the aspect of the town. The base of the Great Tower (the Malakoff) is now 'shored up' with earthworks; and defences of similar construction—some far advanced towards completion—are being thrown up along the entire line commencing at Careenage Bay on the east, and terminating near the cemetery on the west [near the Flagstaff bastion]. Hence, in the course of a week, if not sooner, Sevastopol will have assumed the likeness of a vast entrenched camp."

On the same day, it seemed to leak out, that "the place looked so much stronger than had been anticipated, that perhaps we might not take it this winter;" and it was devoutly hoped that precautionary measures would be taken in time, against "the onslaughts of Generals Rain, Frost, and Snow, no matter how great soever may be head-quarter confidence in the overwhelming efficacy of our opening fire." *

It was, however, still officially considered that the projected bombardment would shatter the Russian defences, and that the speedy capture of

* *Our Veterans, etc.*, p. 191, etc.

Sevastopol would be the result. This opinion was also shared by many of the Officers of the British army, and every nerve was strained to make the operation a success. On the 10th we broke ground, and began the construction of three batteries.* Two, known as Chapman's and Gordon's, called after the Engineer Officers in charge, were some 1400 yards from the Redan, and the trench connecting them became eventually the first parallel.

Chapman's battery, 41 guns, was placed on Green Hill, between two ravines that descend into the inner harbour, viz. the valley of the Shadow of Death and the Woronzoff ravine. Gordon's battery, 26 guns, stood on Mount Woronzoff (also called Frenchman's Hill), between the Woronzoff and the Docks ravines. On the next hill, between the Docks and the Careenage ravines, the Victoria or Right Lancaster battery was built, armed with 6 guns (5 of the Lancaster pattern), more than 2000 yards from the enemy's lines. The French began their siege-works on the 9th, on Mount Rodolph, and placed 53 guns in battery, 1000 yards from the enemy's fortifications. Thus the Allies had 126 guns in position, not counting the field artillery. The enemy had 118,—64 facing the French, and 54 the British,—besides 223 of lesser calibre.

The Battalion, in common with the other troops stationed before Sevastopol, took their full share in

* See Map No. 5, p. 124.

the construction of these batteries, by supplying working parties and covering guards to resist *sorties*. The operation was new to all ranks, who had received little training in these special duties, the greater part of which had to be performed at night. But any confusion incidental to the circumstances of the case speedily passed away, and from start to finish the men stuck to their work, and did it thoroughly, under a heavy and unreturned fire, that constantly poured upon them from dawn to dark from the Russian lines.

"On the 14th October," Colonel Wilson writes, "the duties grew very hard. For myself I have been at work four nights out of five, and so have many others. . . . But in this respect, of course, the rank and file are the principal sufferers. To what insignificance do our hardships sink when compared with theirs! In the case of the private, downright manual labour—picking, shovelling, dragging, lifting—is superadded to watching. In his instance, no little dainties . . . vary the nauseous salt junk, and the wish-wash of green coffee. In his instance, the tatters—which were a uniform once—only cover the wearer's nakedness imperfectly: that ragged patchwork has long ceased to combat with the wind and rain. . . . Oh! what painful illustrations of the cheap and nasty principle, are those filthy dangling shreds and bursted seams! How one's heart yearns toward the unflinching British 'common soldier' so sternly superior to privation, so proudly reckless of his life! Brave heart! unconquerable soul! Crimean hero, whom we cannot glorify too much!"*

* *Our Veterans, etc.*, p. 211.

The excellence of the work performed by the Brigade is thus described in a recent publication, already alluded to:—

"The spade work of the soldiers varied considerably, but from the Royal Engineers' journal of work done in Bulgaria, and from what I saw early in the siege, that of the Guards Brigade was undoubtedly amongst the best. This may have arisen from the memory of instruction at Chobham camp in 1853, or from regimental pride, or from both causes. . . . By the end of August the infantry had made six thousand gabions and seven hundred fascines; for every one of these passed as serviceable, the soldiers received 14d. and 7d. respectively, which included the labour of cutting and carrying the brushwood which was close at hand. In the Guards Brigade each section of three men produced three gabions daily; in the Line the average did not exceed one gabion daily per section. Throughout the long ensuing siege, the working parties in the trenches did well or badly in proportion to the efficiency of the Officers. When they sat and smoked, paying no attention to the men, the sergeants followed suit, and but little progress was made. On the other hand, when the Officers, keen and sympathetic, knew how to get cheerful work out of their men, the spirits of the directing Engineer Officer rose considerably." *

* Wood, *Crimea in 1854 and 1894*, p. 87. As the training at Chobham camp lasted but a short time, and amounted in reality to very little, and as the work performed in Bulgaria and before Sevastopol afforded more practical instruction than could possibly have been given at Chobham, does it not seem probable that the excellence, attributed to the Brigade, arose much more from what is called regimental pride, from the character of their system, and from the efficiency of their Officers, than from any other cause?

A SIEGE UNCONSCIOUSLY BEGUN. 119

The following extracts from Colonel Tower's diary give, moreover, an idea of the nature of some of the duties discharged by the men, and the conditions under which they were performed:—

"*Oct.* 14*th.* Paraded at 3 a.m. for a covering party in rear of Chapman's battery. The enemy annoyed us very much all day, throwing shot and shell, but, by dint of creeping about and keeping well under the parapet, we all got safe back to camp at 6 a.m., after twenty-seven hours in the trenches.

"*Oct.* 16*th.* On covering party in rear of the sailors' battery. There was a large heap of stones, two to three feet high, behind which we laid down as flat as we could; about 10 a.m. a red flag was hoisted on the Redan, and immediately every gun they had mounted commenced pitching into our battery, . . . for about half an hour, evidently to try their range. Every sort of missile they could cram into their guns came whistling over us and knocking our heap of stones about. We lay as still as mice, and the shot rattled about like hail, and went bounding away over the hill in our rear towards the camp; Goodlake and self, Francis Baring and Bob Lindsay were our party. In the middle of the *jeu d'enfer*, old Gordon the Engineer appeared walking over the open towards the battery, the shot striking the ground all round him; he never quickened his pace, and seemed perfectly unconscious of his imminent danger: but fortune favours the brave, and although he ought to have been struck fifty times, he coolly walked up the hill with the utmost indifference."

In preparation for the bombardment, fixed to commence at 6.30 a.m. on the 17th of October, the troops were held in readiness in their camps to fall in at a moment's notice; arrangements were made in case the army was ordered to move forward to assault the Russian position, scaling ladders, tools, etc., were collected, and a body of sharpshooters was specially organized. In the First Division, the latter were placed under Captain Goodlake of the Coldstream, whose gallant services soon earned for him the Victoria Cross.*

But the first onslaught on Sevastopol failed to produce the results that were expected from it.

---

* By *First Divisional Order*, Oct. 16th, ten men and a Non-commissioned officer from each battalion, good shots, volunteers preferred, were selected to act as sharpshooters, under a Captain and a Lieutenant of the Brigade of Guards, and a Lieutenant of the Highlanders. "The sharpshooters will have to approach within 400 or 500 yards of the enemy's works, there to establish themselves in extended order (by single men) under cover of anything which may present itself to afford protection. They will endeavour to improve their cover behind any obstacle by scraping out a hollow for themselves in the ground, and they will carry with them provisions so that they will be enabled to remain, being once under cover, for many hours (even twenty-four) without relief. Whilst so established, they will endeavour to pick off the enemy's artillerymen in the embrasures. The approach of the sharpshooters to the spot they must occupy, must be rapid, in a scattered order ; each man acting for himself, and exercising his intelligence to the utmost of his ability. Each man will select the spot which suits him best, and be guided only in that choice by the cover he may find and the command it may give him of an effectual fire into the embrasures." It is to be noted that the Officers ordered to perform this important duty were in no way "selected" for it, but were taken by "roster." In Crimean days, as well as during the Peninsular war, it was considered that all Officers were fitted to discharge the ordinary duties which their profession required of them.

A SIEGE UNCONSCIOUSLY BEGUN.

The Allies found the enemy placed in far other circumstances than had been the case when they first presented themselves before the south side on the 26th of September.

At that date the advantages gained by the battle of the Alma had not been entirely dissipated. The Crimean field army, under Menshikoff, was beaten, and was far away from the scene of hostilities, refitting and awaiting reinforcements; the garrison of Sevastopol—composed of a mere medley of details, imperfectly armed, and many of whom could scarcely be called "combatants"— was physically and morally weak; the entrenchments were slight and incomplete; the guns to oppose an attack were light. On the 17th of October a great change had been effected. The forces from Bessarabia were arriving; the Russians had been able to reconnoitre the valley of the Tchernaya, and to threaten our exposed right flank and our base of operations; they spared as many as 25,000 of the regular army to strengthen the garrison of the town; the *morale* of the latter had been raised; the defences were much improved— they assumed the appearance of genuine fortifications; the armament was greatly increased, and had been rendered formidable.

CHAPTER IX.

THE FIRST BOMBARDMENT.

Importance and magnitude of the operation—Results of the first day's fire—No attack—Continuation of the bombardment—No better result—The insecurity of the British right flank—Augmentation of the Coldstream for the purposes of the war—Russian reinforcements begin to arrive—Battle of Balaklava—Cavalry charges—Consequences of the battle—*Sortie* against our right flank—Its failure—Its object—Another bombardment projected early in November.

NEVERTHELESS, the first bombardment of Sevastopol was an operation of great importance and magnitude. The Allied fleets took part in it in full force, though it was not possible for them to produce any real effect; for the land defences were out of their reach, and the sea forts were extremely strong. Still all the artillery the invaders could muster, discharged their thunders upon the fortifications which covered the south side of the town and the entrance of the roadstead.

The French, subjected to a hotter and closer fire than we, suffered severely, and between ten and eleven in the morning, two explosions having

THE FIRST BOMBARDMENT. 123

occurred in their batteries, their guns were silenced. The British, on the other hand, were very successful. Directing their fire upon three of the enemy's works, they inflicted considerable damage on the Flagstaff battery, silenced the Malakoff, and almost demolished the Redan, the salient of which was blown to pieces by the explosion of a powder magazine. The defences of the Karabelnaya were completely paralysed, an immediate assault was expected, and the troops to oppose it being demoralized, fell back in confusion.*

But no attack took place. The French were unable to advance against the lines which had silenced their siege guns. It was too much to ask them to allow us to go on, under cover of their friendly co-operation and support. The enemy, in a word, gained by the Anglo-French alliance, and the common interests were obscured under the pressure of international courtesy. Thus a severe strain was still to weigh down the resources of the two Great Powers of Europe ; an insignificant fortress was to baffle their united efforts ; their armies were to be destroyed on the upland of the Chersonese by cold and famine ; and, while our British Engineers alone could survey with complacency the results of their skill, evidenced by the speedy destruction of the defences around Karabelnaya, the Allies were not one whit nearer the accomplishment

* Hamley, *War in the Crimea*, p. 105.

of their object than they had been before the bombardment began.

Still the Chiefs of the invading forces were sanguine that their fire at last would tell, and would allow them to storm the place together, at points where each had breached the defences opposed to them. But in this expectation they were, as they deserved to be, disappointed.

The bombardment was continued on the 18th, and the British batteries alone took part in it—for the French were not ready, and were improving their earthworks after the disaster of the day before,—not, however, against the wreck which we had created by the evening of the 17th, but on renewed and freshly armed defences that were repaired in the night by the ceaseless energy of the garrison, whose labours were undisturbed by any countermove on our part.

Again, on the 19th, the united artillery fired on the hostile batteries with complete success on our side, but once more the French guns were silenced. The bootless bombardment continued till the 25th, ever with the same result: the lines covering the Karabelnaya were open to attack, but the forts opposite Mount Rodolph were unsubdued. Thus no advantage was gained, or indeed could be gained, under the rule which the Allies had imposed upon themselves to the benefit of the enemy, who, not slow to perceive the situation, took every

THE FIRST BOMBARDMENT. 125

advantage therefrom. A great display, therefore, was all that took place, which cost the Russians nearly 4000 men, while the Allies lost less than a fourth part of that number.

As the fire proceeded from day to day, the attention of the First and Second Divisions was directed to their right flank.

"Started an hour before daybreak on outlying piquet on the heights to our rear, and was kept the whole day in a state of excitement by a large force of Russians, cavalry and artillery, in the plain below; some took up a position on the hills in front of Balaklava, and some remained near where we bivouacked at the Tchernaya bridge, evidently threatening Balaklava. Some of them advanced towards us, and brought some artillery and opened fire. Presently a battery of ours unlimbered in the bushes by my piquet, and got ready for action; the 2me Zouaves were also sent, and there was a report that the enemy was advancing up the Inkerman gorges; in short, we thought we were in for a scrimmage. But after a short time the Zouaves and artillery were sent back to their quarters, and I was left face to face with the Ruskis. After dark their fires blazed all over the plain, but nothing occurred. I was with my sentries all night. They evidently intend making an attack on Balaklava when we assault the town, which doubtless must take place soon." *

The enemy, seen upon this occasion, was again observed by a piquet of the Coldstream on the 20th, among the Inkerman ruins (beyond the Tchernaya),

* Tower, *Diary*, Oct. 18th.

mounting guns. Towards evening he opened fire, and directed his aim upon the camp of the Second Division, until the Sandbag battery, previously mentioned, was constructed, and armed with two 18-pounders. The British fire soon drove away the guns from the ruins, but the 18-pounders had to be removed to a less exposed position.

Nine Coldstream Officers reached the Crimea and joined the Battalion on the 17th, the first day of the bombardment; but they were not accompanied by any men, and the strength of the rank and file was not therefore increased.

It should be stated here, that, on account of the war, the Regiment received an augmentation, first on the 13th of February, and again a little later. The establishments were as follows :—

	Colonel.	Lt.-Colonel.	Majors.	Captains.	Lieutenants.	Ensigns.	Adjutants.	Qr.-Masters.	Surgn.-Major.	Surgeon.	Assist.-Surgns.	Solicitor.	Sergeants.	Drummers.	Rank and File.	Battalions.	Companies.
Feb. 1st, 1854	1	1	2	16	20	12	2	2	1	1	2	1	72	37	1280	2	16
Mar. 1st, 1854	1	1	2	16	20	12	2	2	1	1	3	1	88	37	1600	2	16
Aug. 1st, 1854	1	1	2	20	24	16	2	2	1	1	4	1	118	46	2200	2	20

Of the twenty companies, twelve were at home and eight at the seat of war, but the latter were strong companies on paper, and the former weak. It was further ordered that the service Battalion

THE FIRST BOMBARDMENT. 127

was not to bear upon its strength less Officers than were required for 10 companies, the Adjutant not included.* Hence the two mounted Officers who, before the receipt of this order, were posted to companies in the field, were placed upon the 1st Battalion establishment, and nominally belonged to companies at home.

During the first few days of the operations against Sevastopol there were several casualties among the Officers of the Grenadier Guards. On the 16th, Captain Rowley was killed, and, two days later, the same fate overtook Colonel Hood, the gallant Commanding Officer who had greatly distinguished himself by his coolness and intrepidity at the Alma. The losses of the Coldstream at this moment were happily less. It was not till the 20th, that the first man was wounded in the trenches; but next day, Lord Dunkellin was unfortunately captured. Commanding a working party without arms—for at that time the men told off to dig were sent to the front unarmed,—he lost his way in the darkness, and, stumbling upon a piquet which he thought was English, he went forward by himself to ask where he was. As it happened, he found himself within the enemy's lines, and was taken; his men, however, luckily escaped under cover of the night.†

---

* *Brigade Order*, London, Sept. 5, 1854.
† This incident does not appear to have modified the rule by

Prince Menshikoff so far recovered from his defeat on the 20th of September, that he occupied the hills in the neighbourhood of Mackenzie Farm, and took possession of the roads leading therefrom into the valley of the Tchernaya on the 7th of October. He had good reason to be proud of the achievements of the garrison of Sevastopol, and to rejoice at his own singular good fortune. The town was fast growing into a powerful fortress, sufficiently strong to resist any sudden assault, and likely for months to occupy the energies of a far more numerous force than stood before it at that time. He himself was placed in an unassailable position. Secure as regards his communications with the interior of Russia and with Sevastopol, he not only received without difficulty the fresh forces that were hurrying to his assistance; but he also hemmed the invaders into a small corner of an exceedingly inhospitable country, restricted their enterprise, and threatened them with destruction in case a reverse were to happen to them. History, indeed, fails to record any great genius in this Russian General, nor were his troops of that high

which working parties were sent to the trenches at night, across an unknown and intersected country, without arms or an escort, if we may judge from the following General After Order of the 22nd: "The Commander of the Forces directs that all parties, whether armed or on fatigue, which may be ordered to the front, may be accompanied by a Staff Officer competent to guide them." On the 11th of November, however, it was ordered that all working parties were to take their arms with them (*First Divisional Pass Order*).

order to account for the immense advantages he gained at this moment. He was simply fortunate in the Governments and in the leaders of his antagonists, who, unable to combine to carry out any single plan, continually changed their intentions, until a surprise on the north side was converted into a lengthy siege (without investment) of the south side.

The Bessarabian reinforcements began to reach Simferopol early in October, and on the 15th, General Liprandi arrived there. A few days later it was determined to make an attack on our base at Balaklava, with some 25,000 troops (22,000 infantry, 3400 cavalry, and 78 guns) commanded by that Officer. The attack took place on the 25th, a day immortalized in our military history by the bravery of the British cavalry, particularly by the charge of the Light brigade, "one of the most brilliant ever remembered in the annals of war," though it resulted in the destruction of that corps.*

Balaklava was covered by two defensive lines, the outer and the inner. The outer line, more than two miles in length, running along the Causeway Heights and near the Woronzoff road, had the support of a few small earthworks, "mere

---

* General G. Klapka, *The War in the East, from the year* 1853 *till July*, 1855 (translated by Lieut.-Colonel A. Mednyansky), p. 96 (London, 1855).

scratches with the spade, a donkey might have been ridden into some of them," * armed with only nine 12-pounder guns in all, and occupied by about two battalions of Turks. The inner line, near Kadikeui, was 3000 yards in rear, and was held by the 93rd Regiment, the Marines, a few invalids, and the rest of the Turks. The Russians, advancing in force at dawn on the 25th, brought 30 guns (some of them of heavy calibre) against the earthworks on the Causeway Heights, —which were isolated, entirely unsupported, and commanded by neighbouring ground,—and captured two of them on the right of the line, after a stubborn resistance; a third soon after fell into their hands.

They then pushed forward their cavalry, of which four squadrons reconnoitred towards Kadikeui. The latter came within range of the 93rd, drawn up in line, who received them with a volley, and with such determination that they quickly wheeled about and fled to the rear. The rest, a solid column, nearly 3000 strong, supported by 32 guns, moving in somewhat the same direction, came suddenly close to the British Heavy cavalry brigade, who, without the slightest hesitation, charged, and in a few moments routed them, and sent them back in confusion, past the front of the Light brigade. Unfortunately Lord Cardigan

* Hamley, *War in Crimea*, p.110.

THE FIRST BOMBARDMENT. 131

did not fall upon the flying mass and complete their discomfiture. So they got away down the valley that lay between the Fediukhine and Causeway heights, both of which were held by the enemy's infantry and artillery, and took up a position about a mile and a quarter away, behind some Russian guns.

And now "some one blundered," and the Light brigade made their famous charge, over this dangerous ground, flanked on each side by well-posted artillery, straight into the guns and the cavalry at the end of the valley. The story of this gallant deed is well known. The Russian gunners and cavalry were swept away, and forced to retreat before the impetuous onslaught of our weak squadrons, but the brigade was broken, and indeed destroyed. It numbered 670 sabres at the commencement of the action, and at the conclusion its mounted strength was only 195. The enemy was quite unable to cut off the retreat of the remnants of our light horse, as they rode back after their desperate expedition, very few prisoners were taken, and the French, making a spirited and successful charge upon the Fediukhine Heights, prevented the Russians from harassing our men from that quarter, as they emerged from the deadly and unequal conflict.

Heavy firing had been heard in the British camps before Sevastopol at dawn, and, when the serious nature of the attack was perceived, orders were sent to the First and Fourth Divisions to march down to meet the danger. Two of Bosquet's infantry brigades, as well as the French cavalry, which had by this time reached the seat of war, were also brought to the field of battle. When our troops got to the Sapuné Ridge, and looked on the plain beneath, they saw with breathless interest the first encounter between the contending horsemen.

"The Heavy cavalry charge," says Colonel Tower, "was just going on as we came in sight of the Turkish redoubts; we could indistinctly see the grey horses and bearskin caps [the Scots Greys] swallowed up in a dense mass of grey-coated Russians, their sabres flashing in the sun." *

The subsequent charge of the Light brigade was not so apparent to our infantry:—

"The threatened attack of Balaklava," continues Colonel Tower, "turned out to be nothing; and when it appeared to be all over, the Light cavalry started on their suicidal expedition. We could see them over the line of hills of the Turkish redoubts, and then they vanished to be seen no more. When the remnants returned, I got leave to fall out, and walked up to the Turkish redoubts, and almost the first thing I saw was poor Nolan's body,

---

* *Diary*, Oct. 25th. Readers of the late Sir Edward Hamley's *War in the Crimea*, p. 113, will remember the vivid description which he has given of this brilliant cavalry charge, as it appeared to him and to the troops (among them the Coldstream) standing on the heights above.

THE FIRST BOMBARDMENT. 133

his chest knocked to pieces by a round shot; the whole plain was dotted about with men and horses, some struggling on the ground, some loose horses galloping about without riders; a great many Russian cavalry were lying about where the Heavy cavalry had driven them back,—our men had used their sabres with good effect."

Despite the glorious conduct of our troops upon this occasion, we lost a good deal and gained very little. The eastern portion of an unsupported advanced line of redoubts on the Causeway Heights was captured by the weight of numbers, and the outer defences of Balaklava were occupied by the enemy. But his further movements towards Kadikeui were crushed by a handful of our Heavy cavalry, and our Light brigade proved their superiority over him by a useless feat of daring which is unparalleled in warfare.

Thus, though Balaklava was still safe, we were deprived of the use of the Woronzoff road as a means of communication between our base of operations and the upland, and we had only the unmetalled path which led over the Col to rely on. We shall see that this result of the battle of the 25th was a serious one for the British army besieging Sevastopol. There was, indeed, some idea of turning Liprandi out of the Causeway Heights; but had it been definitely formed, the infantry would have descended from the ridge on which they stood by the Woronzoff road, whence the object would have been more easily accomplished. Instead of this, however, they were moved onwards to the Col, and remained during the day covering Balaklava. No forward operation was undertaken, and it was probably considered that we had not sufficient troops to hold the outer line efficiently. So the main road was placidly given up to the enemy, and at nightfall the Guards Brigade and the Fourth Division returned to camp, while the remaining two Highland regiments were left at Balaklava to strengthen the garrison at that important place.*

The vulnerable point on the right flank of the British position has already been adverted to, also the position taken up by the French Corps of observation under General Bosquet. We have seen that this force could not help the Allies to retain possession of the Woronzoff road, nor could it, as we shall see, secure the right of their siege-works from serious attack.

* The battle which deprived us of our principal road, cost the Allies—

English,	40 Officers ;	386 sergeants, rank and file ;		426	total
French,	2 ,,	50 ,,	,,	52	,,
Turks,	9 ,,	250 ,,	,,	259	,,

Total, 737 men, and 409 horses. The Russians lost some 600 men, of whom the greater number fell before the British Heavy cavalry. The latter suffered but little in that superb charge, though they had many casualties when shielding the recoil of the Light brigade (*Our Veterans, etc.*, p. 255).

The first attempt to disturb this flank was made at noon on the 26th, when a force emerged from Sevastopol, of which 700 men advanced up the Careenage Ravine, while the remainder, 4300 men and four guns, crossed that obstacle, and directed themselves upon Shell Hill, in front of the camp of the Second Division. The former column was met by the sharpshooters of the Guards, under Captain Goodlake, who, drawing up his insignificant detachment behind a ditch that ran across the ravine, held the hostile column in check, and barred its further advance,—even capturing several prisoners,—until, a little later, some men of the Rifles appearing upon the scene, the enemy was driven back.*

The main column, endeavouring to reach Shell Hill, met the outposts of the Second Division, some 250 strong, who, instead of retiring before so superior a force, stubbornly resisted it, and held it at bay, until, outflanked and pressed back by numbers, they retreated slowly and in good order. But the Russians gained nothing, for the divisional artillery, reinforced by a battery of the First Division, had time to come into action, and when the enemy appeared upon the crest of the hill, he was met by the fire of our

* This was one of the acts of gallantry performed by Captain Goodlake during the war, for which he was awarded the Victoria Cross.

guns, which speedily repulsed him, and made him retire precipitately to the fortress, pursued by the piquets, and under fire of the Lancaster battery. In this combat, where the Russians acknowledge the loss of 270 men and 80 prisoners, as against 12 killed and 77 wounded on our side, Lieutenant Conolly, of the 49th Regiment, greatly distinguished himself. He was promoted Brevet Major, obtained the Victoria Cross, and a commission in the Coldstream. The Brigade was not employed in this action; they stood in reserve out of musketry fire, and watched the fight, ready for emergencies, but their services were not required.*

This *sortie* was intended, according to Todleben, to distract our attention from Balaklava; and it may well be that Liprandi, knowing its importance, was under grave apprehension lest the Woronzoff road might be wrested from him. It has also been thought that the Russians were endeavouring to effect a lodgment on Shell Hill, preparatory to the attack they meant soon to deliver on our right flank at Inkerman, and this is very likely. But, if so, they had an inadequate force to accomplish such a purpose, and by this time they had ample experience of the fighting qualities of the British troops, who, man for man, were immensely superior to their own.

* The Russians appear, upon this occasion, to have understated both their strength and their losses.

Indeed we had every need of the sterling bravery of our gallant soldiers, for a great crisis was at hand. The strength of our Crimean army was becoming alarmingly weakened, not only by the wear and tear of active service and losses incurred on the field, but through the unusual amount of sickness that prevailed, and the arduous nature of the campaign in which we had become engaged. In the Coldstream there were 190 more admissions into hospital in October than there had been in September.* On the other hand, the actions of the 25th and 26th increased the confidence of our men when opposed to the enemy. They felt themselves more than a match for him if they could only get leave to be at him; but they little knew how severe the trial would be that awaited them in a very few days.†

On the night of the 28th, many of our camps were alarmed, and believed they were about to be

---

* Wyatt, p. 28.
† Colonel Wilson, describing the excellent tone that prevailed among our men at this time, notes the behaviour of the wounded on the 26th, as they limped or were carried on stretchers past the Brigade. He says it was "wonderful, the very reverse of what might have been looked for. Far from drooping in spirits, most of them were in buoyant spirits. Sometimes a fine youth with a badly fractured arm, hurraed lustily as he passed; another, whose thigh a round shot had smashed, would—faint as he was—raise himself up a little on his litter, and brandish his rifle triumphantly. I observed that nearly every man, whether slightly or sorely hurt, still clutched his musket. . . . A bullet through the heart alone conquers such soldiers" (*Our Veterans, etc.*, p. 266).

attacked. The outposts watching the plain of Balaklava heard cavalry approaching, and a great deal of firing in the dark took place—the sentries blazing away whenever they saw, or fancied they saw, the phantom horsemen, "who seemed perpetually galloping, but never coming any nearer. Staff Officers kept arriving to know what the commotion was about. Of course I could give them no information." A regiment of Zouaves and the guns in a French redoubt poured volleys into imaginary columns coming to storm our position. "The Russian drums all along the Fediukhine Heights beat to arms; and I sat down quietly on a stone in advance of my sentries, and could hear nothing more, but made up my mind Liprandi intended to give us a benefit in the morning." When the morning broke the mystery was cleared. It was found that a number of Russian horses had stampeded from their lines, and that no enemy was near. A hundred or more were caught, and served to mount a few of our cavalry, while the remainder scampered back across the plain to their legitimate owners.*

The weary monotony of the siege continued after the *sortie* of the 26th, the troops being largely employed in the trenches, constructing approaches or batteries, or acting as covering guards, generally under a heavy fire from the fortress in front of them.

* Tower, *Diary*, Oct. 28th.

"The enemy is barricading the streets, and we shall have to fight every inch of ground. I fear we have a great many of our sorrows to come, more especially wintering here; too horrible to contemplate! An army of 30,000 men in our rear with a large force of cavalry, and Sevastopol, which seems to be getting stronger every day, in our front. Any number of general actions is better than a siege. In the trenches for twenty-six hours at a time (we used to mount now at 2 a.m., with nothing but biscuit and salt pork to eat), shells constantly troubling one's life, and showers of dirt covering you every time a shot strikes the parapet."*

The French were sapping up towards the Flagstaff Battery with the greatest energy. They were becoming strong enough to withstand the guns of the garrison, and to retrieve their failure of October 17th–25th. Another bombardment, to be followed by an assault, was contemplated, and the Allied Commanders had full confidence that this time, at least, the effect would be decisive. They even agreed to meet on the 5th of November to arrange the details of their projected operation. But neglected opportunities too often rise in judgment against a General in the field. The 5th was the day of Inkerman, and all our plans were completely frustrated.

* Tower, *Diary*, Oct. 27th.

PART IV.
BATTLE OF INKERMAN.

CHAPTER X.

CONDITIONS UNDER WHICH THE BATTLE TOOK PLACE.

Large Russian reinforcements reach the Crimea—Menshikoff determines to drive the invaders into the sea—Position and strength of the enemy—Numerical strength of the Allies—Length of the line to be defended by them—Plan of attack—Prospects of the Russians—Their confidence of victory—Description of the field of Inkerman—Position of the Allies opposing the attack—Hearing the sound of fire, the Guards move quickly to the front.

THE Russian reinforcements which, as we have seen, began to arrive in the month of October, continued their advance upon the Crimea, so that early in November the hostile forces at the seat of war amounted, all told, to more than 120,000 men capable of taking part in the operations of the campaign.* The moment had now come when the enemy determined to deliver his well-prepared attack upon the invaders, and hoped to rid the Crimea for ever of their presence.

* Sir E. Hamley, in his *War in the Crimea*, p. 129, estimates these forces at 110,000 to 115,000, including the enemy's sailors. He has, however, apparently omitted to include men whom he previously counted as part of the garrison at the end of September (see *ante*, pp. 105 and 106).

It must be confessed that he had a good opportunity of accomplishing his object, and that every advantage was on his side. He could choose his own time and place of attack; his forces were far more powerful than those of the invaders, both in numbers and in position; and, by the reconnaissance or *sortie* of October 26th, he found out (if he did not already know it) that our vulnerable right flank was unsecured by any fieldworks to make up for our other deficiencies. The onslaught, then, that was to drive us away from Sevastopol, and to sweep us into the sea, was to be directed upon this flank, upon ground which our soldiers called Mount Inkerman, and Sunday, the 5th of November, was chosen as the day upon which to put the design into execution.*

On the evening of the 4th, Prince Menshikoff established his head-quarters near the mouth of the Tchernaya, and his troops were posted as follows:

The garrison was not increased beyond the numbers it contained towards the end of October.

General Dannenberg, head-quarters on the Old City Heights, midway between Mackenzie Farm and the head of the roadstead, commanded a corps of 50 battalions, 1 squadron, and 134 guns (of which 54 were guns of position). This corps was divided into two columns, namely, General Soimonoff,

* See Map, No. 6, p. 166. Properly speaking, Inkerman was on the other side of the Tchernaya, called by us Old City Heights.

19,000 infantry and 38 guns (22 of position), whose troops were temporarily sheltered in the lines of the fortress in the Karabelnaya; and General Pavloff, 16,500 infantry and 96 guns (32 of position), concentrated on the Old City Heights.

To the left of Pavloff, there was another force of 16 battalions, 62 squadrons, and 88 guns (15,000 infantry), composed mostly of Liprandi's column, but now under Prince Michael Gortchakoff, whose head-quarters were at Tchorgun.

Lastly, there was a body of 4000 infantry and 36 guns guarding the road to Bakshiserai, somewhere near Mackenzie Farm.

Thus, besides the garrison which amounted to nearly 60,000 men, placed in what was now a secure stronghold, amply covered and well armed, there was a force of 54,500 infantry, a powerful body of cavalry, and 258 guns available to operate against the undefended flank of the Allies.

The latter, on the other hand, had received a few reinforcements, but not sufficient to compensate for the immense losses to which they had been subjected. On the evening of the 4th, they numbered but 58,000 infantry,—16,000 British, 31,000 French, and 11,000 Turks; and this small force was further weakened by the fact that the Allied Commanders, totally unacquainted with the war-like qualities of their Ottoman auxiliaries, would not allow them to develop their value, and

L

left them no chance to assist in the approaching battle. So far did Lord Raglan's prejudice go, that the 6000 attached to the British army, were not suffered to take part as combatants, and when Omar Pasha proposed to send him a further contingent he refused the offer.* Hence there were practically only 47,000 British and French infantry left to meet the grave crisis which now confronted us.

These troops were disposed on an irregular curve which stretched from Streleska Bay (north of Kamiesh Bay) along the front of the enemy's lines of Sevastopol to the heights of Inkerman, thence southwards on the Sapuné Ridge to the Col, where it ran more to the east, near Kadikeui, and covered Balaklava. This line measured twenty miles in length, it was unsupported by any central reserve, and was everywhere in contact with powerful masses of the enemy.

Menshikoff's onslaught was to be delivered as the first gleam of light appeared at dawn on the 5th, when his forces were to be before our outposts, ready to press the advance home. The principal attack was confided to Dannenberg's corps, whose two columns were to converge upon the British

* Hamley, *War in the Crimea*, 128; Kinglake, v. 33, 34 note, 41 note. Sir Evelyn Wood says, in his recent publication, that he has "never understood why these Moslems, who came out so grandly at Silistria, were considered unfit to fight alongside the English and French troops" (Wood, *Crimea in 1854 and 1894*, p. 199).

unguarded position at Inkerman,—that of Soimonoff, issuing from the Karabelnaya by the road that skirts the south bank of the roadstead, that of Pavloff marching down to the Tchernaya and crossing the river by the causeway and bridge near its mouth. Gortchakoff was to support this operation, and endeavour "to seize one of the ascents to the Sapuné Ridge;" and the garrison was to "cover by its fire the right flank of the assaulting columns, and, should there be confusion in the enemy's batteries, to storm those batteries."

The Russians were elated by the bright prospects before them. " Future times, I am confident," wrote their Chief, "will preserve the remembrance of the exemplary chastisement inflicted upon the presumption of the Allies. . . . Heaven visibly protects Holy Russia. Have the kindness to bring this to the knowledge of our august Sovereign for the great satisfaction of his magnanimous heart." Two of the Grand-Dukes, sons of the Tsar, arrived in the Crimea, to encourage the Muscovite troops, and to bear witness to the "exemplary chastisement" about to be inflicted. But the " magnanimous heart " was not to be satisfied, for Menshikoff forgot to take into account, what a handful of British soldiers are capable of doing when sorely pressed, and when protecting the honour of their Queen and country, even against overwhelming odds.

A general description of the ground known as

Inkerman (or Mount Inkerman) has already been given. The Lancaster battery, now nearly dismantled, and holding but one gun, had been planted on the Victoria Ridge between the Docks and Careenage ravines, and more than a mile in rear stood the camp of General Codrington's brigade of the Light Division.

To the east, another main spur, jutting out from the upland, fills up the space between Careenage Ravine and the Tchernaya, broken by water-courses which descend into the ravine, the roadstead, and the river. Into the ravine, there is one water-course, the Wellway, which joins it 400 yards in rear of the Lancaster battery; and into the Tchernaya there is another, the Quarry Ravine, through which a post-road runs connecting the upland with the head of the roadstead. Between the Wellway and the Quarry Ravine, the main spur is some 1300 yards broad, and supports a rise, called Home Ridge, that bends to the north under the name of Fore Ridge, and thence slopes away towards the Tchernaya, in two spurs, which overlook the valley, and which are divided by St. Clement's Gorge, viz. Inkerman Tusk and the Kitspur. On the Kitspur the Sandbag battery had been erected on commanding ground : it was a mere short wall of earth, only eighteen paces in length, too high to shoot over except where cut by two embrasures; it was unprovided with a banquette, and at this moment it was vacant and unarmed.

Astride the post-road the Second Division was encamped, immediately behind Home Ridge, in front of which the main spur is contracted to 250 yards in breadth. But at a distance of 1400 yards from the ridge, the main spur again widens out considerably, and here there is another rise, called Shell Hill, flanked on each side by buttresses, West and East Jut, which the enemy had vainly tried to capture on October 26th. About a mile in rear of the Second Division, and always on the same main spur, near a ruined windmill, stood the camp of the Guards Brigade, the Coldstream being somewhat in rear, and separated from the rest by a narrow ravine.

Thus, in the first instance, available to resist an attack on Inkerman, there was one division, viz. the Second, of 3000 men and 12 guns; supported in rear by the Household Brigade, 1300 men, and 12 guns of the First Division, and, on the left, though with a great obstacle intervening—the Careenage Ravine—Codrington's brigade, 1200 men. To the rear, some two miles from the Guards, lay the northern portion of Bosquet's Corps of observation, which at this time was in closer communication with the Highlanders and Marines, at Balaklava, than had been the case before October 25th. To the left, were Buller's brigade of the Light, and the Fourth and the Third Divisions, distant respectively from Home Ridge, 1½, 2½, and 3 miles. These latter troops were covered by the defences which the trenches and batteries afforded, as was also Forey's French siege corps, which, as already mentioned, took up the line from the British Left Attack to Streleska Bay. But no such protection was available for the division and the two brigades more immediately threatened in the vicinity of Inkerman.

Though both Commanders of the Allied armies felt anxiety on account of this exposed flank, nothing was done to make it secure. General Canrobert paid us the compliment of placing extraordinary reliance on our troops,—especially the *bonnets de poil*, as he called the Guards; on the other hand, Lord Raglan, weak in numbers, thought he could not spare any of his men from the trenches. Still, the omission to safeguard this vital position with earthworks has never been explained; for as Turks could have been obtained for this purpose, and as Engineer Officers were available, the excuse given, like many others put forward to cover our deficiencies in this extraordinary war, can hardly be deemed satisfactory. Of the value of works of defence to be occupied in case of attack, it is sufficient to point out that, if we were victorious without them, we should have been far stronger with them, and the battle (if it had taken place at all under these circumstances) could not have failed to result in greater disaster to the enemy, and in much less loss to ourselves.

The Guards furnished piquets to watch the flank

HOW IT BEGAN.

and rear of the British army. On the 1st of November a stronger force was considered necessary to accomplish this object, and the Brigade supplied eight piquets daily. Six (numbered 1 to 6) mounted an hour before daybreak for twenty-four hours, under the Field-Officer of the day, while the other two (Nos. 7 and 8) were posted as a reserve from sunset until an hour after sunrise, the whole during the night being placed under the command of a "full Colonel of the Brigade." *

Besides finding three working parties in the trenches, each 40 to 50 men strong under an Officer, the Coldstream furnished, on the 4th, piquets Nos. 5 and 8, and again on the 5th, Nos. 3, 5, and 6. Thus before dawn on the morning of the battle, the Battalion had two piquets (Nos. 4 and 5 companies) coming off, and three piquets (Nos. 6 and 7 companies) going on duty; so that four companies were absorbed, and when the first alarm was given, only half the Battalion (Nos. 1, 2, 3 and 8 companies) were in camp. The Colonel on duty, during the night 4th–5th, should have been Lord F. Paulet, but as he was incapacitated by illness, Colonel Upton took his place; moreover, Lieut.-Colonel Newton, detailed Field Officer of the day for the 5th, had left long before daylight began to appear. The next senior Officer was Lieut.-Colonel Dawson, and, when the first alarm was given, he quickly formed up what remained of

* *Brigade Order*, Nov. 1, 1854.

the Battalion, and immediately marched them to the front where the battle was heard, to the support of the Second Division, who were then seriously engaged with the enemy.

"MacKinnon, Ramsden, and I," writes Colonel Tower, "were all three living in one tent, and were awakened at daybreak, or soon after, by firing in the direction of Inkerman; we thought little of it, as we were accustomed to alarms, and the piquets constantly fired; but presently a big gun or two told us it was more than piquets. The bugles sounded in the camp, and 'fall in directly' was echoed by the sergeants along the line of tents. We hurried on our arms, as we always slept in our clothes, and found the Battalion falling in. Vesey Dawson was in command, on a chestnut horse; Granville Eliot, Adjutant, on his old grey arab, Bashi-Bazouk. It rained a great deal during the night, and that memorable Sunday morning dawned a nasty damp foggy day; the mist was rising from the ground and the brushwood was quite wet; we could only see a few yards before us, but we could hear the pattering of musketry, and the firing had been going on fully half an hour before we came on the scene of action. We left camp in column of fours, but before we got to the Second Division tents one or two round shot came right through our ranks, and we began to have an idea how close the enemy was, and of the serious nature of the business. We formed line, and advanced through the Second Division tents, many of which were knocked down and shot through. . . . We were the battalion on the extreme right of the army, and my company (No. 1) was on the extreme right of the Battalion." *

* Tower, *Diary*, Nov. 5th.

CHAPTER XI.

EARLY STAGES OF THE FIGHT.

Events of the morning—Unexpected approach of the enemy—Confusion in the Russian arrangements for the attack—First struggle with the British outposts—The Second Division soon involved—Arrival of General Buller's Brigade—Inequality of the numbers engaged—Arrival of the Guards' Brigade; their strength and composition—Situation on the field at that moment—The Guards move to the Kitspur, and join the rest already engaged there.

MEANWHILE, what had happened was this. Although we knew that an attack was imminent, we were unable to tell the precise day on which it was to take place. The night 4th–5th passed quietly, there was no firing, no alarm, no spies came to warn us. The sentries on outpost, and the piquets, heard a rumbling noise in the valley, but the sounds were deadened by the heavy rain that fell during the 4th and throughout the night, and they were not sufficiently distinct to induce us to concert any definite arrangements to meet the emergency.

In so far the enemy acted with caution and

ability; the attack came upon us as a surprise, even though we expected it. He failed, however, to marshal his immense masses to the best advantage. The orders given to Dannenberg's forces were vague, and there was a confusion as to whether both Soimonoff and Pavloff were to operate on the eastern side of the Careenage Ravine, or whether the former was to advance along the Victoria Ridge and the latter against Inkerman.

Obviously, had this plan been adopted, Codrington's brigade and Evans' division would both have been in imminent danger; and had either been driven in, the results must have been disastrous. Fortunately, the two unwieldy Russian columns jammed themselves together on the broken ground east of the ravine, and interfered by their numbers and proximity with each other's movements.

Soimonoff, arriving on the ground a little before his colleague, commenced the attack with his powerful column. Advancing cautiously and silently in three lines covered by skirmishers, he had 6000 men in the first line, followed by 3300 and his heavy guns, and 9000 with the light artillery in reserve. The latter was the first hostile body perceived by the British advanced piquets; who, though they could then see nothing, heard their approach. On discovering them, they opened fire, and these volleys were heard by General Codrington, who, according to his usual practice, was near the Lancaster battery reconnoitring to the front with his relieved piquets, before the day broke. He at once got his brigade under arms, moved them to the edge of the ravine near the battery, and lost no time in conveying the alarm to headquarters and to the left. Buller then moved out towards the threatened point, and the Fourth and Third Divisions were in readiness to march.

The enemy soon pressed back the outposts of the Second Division, and the camp being aroused, the troops formed on Home Ridge; while the 22 heavy Russian pieces establishing themselves on Shell Hill, opened on the ridge and on the ground in rear of it. By this means the Russians hoped to crush the British supports that were supposed to be in their ordinary place. But, as a matter of fact, we had none there, a single thin line held the crest, and the fire beyond it succeeded only in destroying the camp and the horses left behind.

While this was going on, the twelve field guns of the division were neither silent nor inefficient, and General Pennefather (in command, Sir De Lacy Evans being at Balaklava, on the sick list *) now pushed forward bodies of 200 to 500 men to reinforce the piquets, who were slowly retiring before the advance of the masses opposed to them. One of these detachments, 500 strong, under General

* He came up later in the day, but refused to take the command out of Pennefather's hands.

Adams, moved to the right, towards the Sandbag battery; and another, hurrying to the left, soon came in contact with a huge hostile column which bore down on them in the mist. The Officer in command had just time to sing out, "Fire and charge!" and the men obeying with loud cheers, the enemy was driven back, right through the line of his guns on Shell Hill, before the impetuous onset could be arrested.

The result of this hand-to-hand encounter between a thin line of red-coats and a strong column of the Russians, was often repeated during the day. The battle, in short, resolved itself into a series of personal combats between small British detachments and dense masses of the enemy; the former, under the nearest Officers, dashing boldly, without supports, against the latter wherever opportunity offered or danger pressed. There was no central control, nor were manœuvres attempted; both were impossible. But the activity, intelligence, and courage of the few—to be counted by hundreds against thousands—never flagged for an instant, and the unwieldy forces opposed to us, though so much more powerful in point of numbers, were shattered and driven back in confusion.

"No doubt the mist was favourable to the fewer numbers, hiding from the Russians the fact that there was nothing behind the English lines, which came on as boldly as if strong supports were close at hand. It needs some plausible supposition of this kind to account (however imperfectly) for the extraordinary combats which ensued, where the extravagant achievements of the romances of chivalry were almost outdone by the reality." *

Soimonoff, leaving 10,000 men in rear of his guns on Shell Hill, made his first real assault with 9000 infantry, who, to avoid our artillery fire, moved along the eastern slope of the Careenage Ravine. Part of Pavloff's corps, 6000 men, had by this time arrived on the scene, and they got into the Quarry Ravine, and, bearing across Inkerman Tusk, made for the Sandbag battery. Thus the narrow flat of the main spur, connecting Home Ridge with Shell Hill, was swept with fire from the enemy's guns, and on one side of it (our left) were 9000 Russians advancing, while 6000 more were threatening our right front at the head of the Quarry Ravine and on the spurs in the vicinity overlooking the Tchernaya. General Buller reached the field at this juncture, with 600 men and a battery from the Fourth Division. To meet the onslaught of 15,000 men suitably supported by artillery, against both our flanks, Pennefather, therefore, had just 3600 men and 18 guns.

Soimonoff's advanced troops on our left met with a transient gleam of success. They captured three guns, which were hurrying into action, and

* Hamley, *War in the Crimea*, p. 141.

they managed to push into the Wellway. Had they been able to emerge on the plateau near Home Ridge, they would have taken the British position in reverse.* But this column was quickly discomfited by a gallant charge of a few men of the 77th Regiment, and by a piquet of the Grenadier Guards under Lieut.-Colonel Prince Edward of Saxe-Weimar, posted close by. Nor did the remainder of Soimonoff's corps hold their ground, for they also gave way when met by the steady line of British infantry, and the whole attack upon our left was soon repulsed; indeed, one of our groups, having driven in immensely superior forces, pursued them, and halted not until Shell Hill was reached. The three English guns taken by the enemy were speedily recaptured, and were found to be uninjured. The Russian General, Soimonoff, moreover, was killed at this period.

Nor did Pavloff's 6000 men fare any better, though they were confronted by only 700 to 800 Englishmen. At the head of the Quarry Ravine, the leading hostile battalions were charged by 200 men of the 30th Regiment, and were routed; while the rest, attacked by General Adams and the 41st Regiment near the Sandbag battery, were also driven back in confusion.

* Apparently this advanced column was composed of sailors or marines, not reckoned in Soimonoff's corps; they were, therefore, additional to it (Kinglake, v. 117).

It was now nearly 7.30 in the morning, and everywhere the struggle had resulted in our favour. But the battle was only in its infancy. Soimonoff's reserve, 10,000 strong, was intact, and the remainder of Pavloff's corps, 10,000 men, had arrived, together with his long train of artillery, which, placed on commanding ground, prolonged the line of guns from Shell Hill to the end of East Jut. Dannenberg now assumed command of these 20,000 infantry, and of the columns whose first attack had failed. He determined to employ his masses against our right, and so co-operate more closely with Gortchakoff, who, as we have seen, was manœuvring in the valley, with orders to seize the Sapuné Ridge.

This latter corps had very early assumed a threatening attitude as far north as the heights for which the Guards Brigade were responsible, and this fact somewhat delayed their advance to the front.* But it was soon perceived that the enemy in this quarter was making a mere empty demonstration, that the real crisis was round Home Ridge, and that the piquets were sufficient in the present emergency to guard the hills overlooking the Tchernaya. The Grenadier and Scots Fusilier Guards, encamped closer to the scene of action, were therefore moved forward to take their share in it, followed soon after by the Coldstream (four

* See Kinglake, v. 70.

companies strong, under Lieut.-Colonel Dawson, as we have seen), and the whole came into action about 7.30, when the introductory phase of the fight was over, and just as the new attack was developing itself.

Shortly after the departure of the Regiment, the two relieved Coldstream piquets (Nos. 4 and 5 companies), having been kept out somewhat longer than usual, on account of Gortchakoff's movements, came into camp, and, finding it empty, advanced to the front, as did also Colonel Upton. The strength of the Brigade was as follows:—

	Officers.	Sergts.	Drmrs.	Rank & File.	Total.
Grenadier Guards ..	22	24	17	438	501
Coldstream (6 cos.)	17	34	14	373	438
Scots Fusilier Guards	20	23	17	332	392
Brigade Staff ..	3	—	—	—	3
Total	62	81	48	1143	1334

Dannenberg's advance was directed against the Sandbag battery, a work, although quite unfit for defence, and worthless when gained, yet served as a rallying-point, which the enemy endeavoured to capture, and which we determined to defend. Round it and near it, therefore, there surged the bloody and lengthened contest in which the Brigade was about to take a leading and conspicuous part. The attack was of a far more fierce and formidable nature than those which preceded it, and which were almost as child's play compared with what

EARLY STAGES OF THE FIGHT. 161

followed. Instead of yielding to an impulse to fly when the heads of their columns recoiled before our impetuous charges, as had invariably been the case in the early morning, the Russians, still assailed by the same dauntless and romantic British courage, now fought with greater determination. They worked round our flanks and rear, and refused to be carried back by the retreating bodies which our men repulsed. The advance, in short, was better regulated, better fed, and better covered by artillery.

Adams was still holding the Sandbag battery, and had received reinforcements after his first success; our troops were also at the head of the Quarry Ravine, where a short wall of loose stones, called "the Barrier," blocked the post-road. Little breathing-time was allowed them after the repulse they had just inflicted on the enemy, and a desperate struggle recommenced at these points. The small British detachments, overpowered by numbers and threatened in flank, were forced back; they retired fighting, and in good order, losing many men, among them General Adams. Three guns, under Captain Hamley (the late Sir Edward Hamley, whose book has been so frequently referred to), effectually checked any desire the Russians might have indulged in to harass our retreat. At this juncture the Guards Brigade arrived on Home Ridge; and it will be useful to take a rapid glance at the position as it was at that moment.

M

On the left, General Codrington was chained to the slopes near the Lancaster battery, and could not move therefrom without endangering the whole line. He received, though unwillingly, slight reinforcements, and his force then amounted to 1400. Later, additional troops reached him from the Third Division, and some artillery; but the latter were overpowered by heavier fire, and the one gun in the Lancaster battery could not be used till near the conclusion of the battle. During the day he held the ridge, maintained a heavy fire upon the enemy in Careenage Ravine, and stood ready to oppose any hostile advance that might have been contemplated up its course. His casualties amounted to about 180 men.

Next, in and near the Wellway and in front of it, were the various groups who had repulsed Soimonoff's first attack, including the company of Grenadier Guards previously mentioned; in all, about 1000 men—that is, allowing for losses, less than a third of the whole force that held Inkerman during the preliminary stage of the battle. It was not known that the enemy meant to concentrate all his efforts on our right, and to leave the other flank practically unmolested, so these men were also chained to the places where they stood, expecting fresh adventure, and, when any of them had to be moved to meet an emergency elsewhere, others replaced them in the position they held.

Of the rest, a proportion were men exhausted or unrallied after their previous exertions, and it is calculated that some 1400 men only remained to defend Home Ridge and the Kitspur, 700 on each. As we have seen, those holding the latter were slowly retiring.

Of reinforcements arriving, the Guards, 1300, had just reached the ridge, as well as 12 guns of the First and 6 of the Light Divisions. The Fourth Division, 2000, under Sir G. Cathcart, was approaching, so that some 4700 men and 36 guns might be reckoned upon for immediate purposes, while 1600 French and other of Canrobert's troops were moving forward.

The enemy, on the other hand, was still very strong, though he had lost part of the 15,000 troops that first attacked, some of whom, indeed, were streaming away from the field panic-stricken, down the Careenage Ravine into Sevastopol, and over the Tchernaya bridge. But he had his powerful and numerous artillery securely posted on West Jut, Shell Hill, and East Jut, and, besides the greater portion of the 15,000 men, there were 20,000 fresh troops. Of these latter, 10,000 were in reserve, and the other 10,000 in the Quarry Ravine, in the neighbouring glens, on the post-road, and in the Sandbag battery which they had just captured.*

---

* According to the theory of Mr. Kinglake (whose excellent work on the Crimean War has been largely drawn upon, in

The enemy had secured a footing on the plateau of the Inkerman main spur, and the Guards Brigade, coming up at that instant, were launched

preparing this volume), the 15,000 men who attacked in the early morning in two columns, one 9000 strong on our left and the other 6000 on our right, were so completely shattered by their first encounter with the detachments of the Second Division, that they *all* fled away, and not a man of them took any further part in the battle. Also that, of the 20,000 infantry remaining to the Russians, practically only 10,000 were engaged, the reserve of 10,000 being most of it kept back. Thus, while 15,000 were dispersed into space with the utmost ease, in less than an hour, by very few opponents, almost as if by magic, the 10,000 made so good a resistance that they were with difficulty vanquished, in three hours and a half, by the 4700 Englishmen who were on the scene at this moment, aided by 1600 French, who appeared soon after, and by the Algerines, Zouaves, and other troops of the same nation, 4000 strong, who reached the ground between ten and eleven o'clock. Nor is it alleged that the early attacks of the enemy were delivered by worse troops than those who came into action at 7.30 a.m.

This theory was evidently not believed by some who fought at Inkerman, and Colonel Tower is of opinion that when the Guards first entered into the struggle, they met the Tarutin and Borodino regiments; that is, the eight Russian battalions which formed the main portion of the first attack made by the enemy with 6000 men on the Kitspur, and which, by Kinglake's account, were not only repulsed, but clean driven from the field never to appear there again, by the bold onset of 700 to 800 Englishmen.

The losses during the day of the two Russian columns, that took part in the first attack, before 7.30, amounted to some 5000 men; and this fact seems to show conclusively that the 15,000 men continued the fight, as stated in the text, long after the hour when Mr. Kinglake says they disappeared from the battle-field. The casualties of the 10,000 men under Pavloff, who came into action at 7.30, were somewhat greater, proportionately, than those of the first two columns. The losses of the reserve (10,000 men), which to a great extent was kept back out of the struggle, were proportionately much less. (P. Alabine, *Notes of the Expedition in* 1853-5, published in the Russian language, at Viatka, 1861, gives the losses by Russian regiments.)

EARLY STAGES OF THE FIGHT. 165

against him, the Grenadiers in front, then the Scots Fusiliers, the Coldstream following a short distance in rear. The leading Battalion charged, and drove the Russians back to the crest; the next formed on its left, and Dawson prolonged the line to the right.

" Thus the narrow strip of height on the beak of which arose the two-gun work [the Sandbag battery] was thinly edged by the *Tria juncta in uno*, ranged two deep: the Duke of Cambridge and General Bentinck in command." *

* *Our Veterans, etc.*, p. 287.

166   BATTLE OF INKERMAN.

CHAPTER XII.

STRUGGLE ON THE KITSPUR.

The Sandbag battery on the Kitspur, the central point of the main attack—A contest against very superior forces—A confused but exceedingly fierce struggle—Impossibility to describe accurately the exact details as they occurred—Arrival of the Fourth Division under General Cathcart—His manœuvre and its failure—Arrival of the French—Exhaustion of the Guards—They withdraw to Home Ridge.

MANY of the rifles at first missed fire, for the incessant rain had saturated everything; but by snapping off caps to dry the channel and by other means the arms were got to work.* The failure to use their weapons at this crisis caused great confusion, as may well be imagined, for there was a dense mass of Muscovite grey coats and flat caps in front, advancing against the Brigade.

" We were almost among them *at once*, we were certainly not twenty-five yards from them. . . . They yielded ground and we advanced a little, showing a most decided front, but they kept pouring a most deadly fire into our ranks, which began to tell fearfully. The

* Some of the nipples had even to be unscrewed (Tower, *Diary*).

enemy's artillery were posted on Cossack and Shell hills, and they had seventy or eighty guns at least, but the mist prevented their laying their guns properly for our lines, and they worked the Second Division heights [Home Ridge], whilst we were far in advance of that; the road was also a point on which they concentrated their fire. Big gaps began to be visible in our line, our dark great coats and bear-skin caps towering above the bushes made our men conspicuous in the grey mist. . . .

"Several times I saw heads of Russian columns coming swarming through the bushes, the Officers in front waving their swords and shouting to the men; but directly they saw us there was a hesitation, a huddling together, an indecision, and a decided tendency *not* to come on. They fired quickly and nervously, and generally over our heads; they were so close to us before they saw us, and they were on lower ground than we were; if they had advanced in anything like a decided manner, we *must* have been entirely swamped and annihilated. But our fellows stood their ground manfully, and the more the Ruskis came up, the quicker our fellows rammed down their cartridges and blazed into them. . . .

" Our men were getting very few and far between; our poor company, No. 1, suffered terribly, but we yelled and screamed and fired at the columns we saw in our front; they were immensely superior to us in numbers, ten to one at least, and seemed now to stand their ground very well; they pressed us *hard*. But determination and dogged courage kept them back, and not a yard would we yield. The numbers in front of us increased every second, and we were really hand to hand with them; the bushes were full of English and Russians mixed up together. The groans of the wounded, Officers yelling and screaming at their men, the soldiers shouting at one another, and (I have no doubt) using their favourite expressions, and the firing almost deafened one.

"The Brigade was getting very much mixed up now. . . . Several other regiments and men of the Second Division piquets furnished us with stragglers who were of the right sort. Our Brigade line, or remnant of our line, was the rallying-point of everybody who was animated with a right spirit. Oh, for breech-loaders at this moment, how we could have swept them off as they came up the hill! . . . I kept taking ammunition out of dead men's pouches to feed the pouches of the living, screaming if I saw any fanatic Ruski that required shooting. . . .

"Some one behind or in the ranks hallooed out, Charge! Granville Eliot galloped forward right at the mass in front of him, Cowell, Bob Lindsay (Fusilier), young Greville, and myself were all close together, and we ran forward with all the men that were near us. It really was a critical moment in the battle, at least in our *local* part of the battle. Eliot fell from his horse, shot through the head; Cowell staggered and fell by the same bush; young Greville was shot through the body. The enemy was frantic at this moment; the few men who charged with us were all shot, and I found myself entirely surrounded by flat caps. . . . I could see no one but Russians anywhere near; one fired at me, the powder almost singed my cap. I could see some bearskins on my right through the bushes, and accordingly made for them as hard as I could lay legs to the ground, and I suppose Bob Lindsay and the men who were with us did the same.

"There was a small two-gun sandbag battery on the crest of the hill, into which the remnants of the Brigade were retiring; the Grenadier Colours were already there.

The Russians had been driven out of it just before.* There were perhaps a hundred men of the three [Guards] Regiments in the little battery, and crowds of Russians hemmed us nearly all round; we extended men on the left and rear to prevent their cutting off our retreat and getting in behind us. Column after column kept pouring up the hill, and every moment our chances of retreat looked worse and worse. The parapet in front of us was too high to fire over, and the enemy kept climbing into the embrasures and up the exterior slope of the parapet; but one after another they fell, shot by our men as they showed. . . . We could see lines of bayonets outside the parapet, and could hear them howling and cheering one another on; it was now *fearfully* exciting. . . . We kept them at a respectable distance; our line extended some way in the rear and left: but they kept getting nearer, and our men fell very thick. . . . Vesey Dawson I saw shot by a Russian creeping into the embrasure; Sir R. Newman of the Grenadiers was also killed, and some other Grenadier Officer fell wounded.

"Our ammunition was beginning to fail, some of the men had not had a round of their own for a long time: the dead furnished the living; but now even that began to fail, and the men in their excitement threw stones, lumps of earth, anything they could see, over the parapet among the Russians, and they came back again amongst us with interest. One of the most remarkable things about Russian troops is the noise they make in action, and I think it is catching, as I never heard our men make such a yelling as they did all this day; I know I was as bad as the rest, because I could not speak for hoarseness that evening and the next day. How long

* For their gallantry upon this occasion, Colonels Lord Henry Percy and Sir Charles Russell, Grenadier Guards, got the Victoria Cross.

the game of throwing stones lasted I cannot say, but it seemed a long time. There was a visible diminution of bayonets outside the battery, and we had really driven the enemy back a great deal on our left; it was more that they ceased coming on than that we were driving them back. We were still surrounded by them, and they were firing into us as hard as they could.

"Of course we could do nothing but retire; this we accordingly did, the Grenadier Colours being our rallying point: but in our weak state, with only a handful of men, *very* few Officers, and very little ammunition, retiring in the face of a body of the enemy was no easy matter, although the enemy were not in the same strength they were, nor did they seem to be animated with the same spirit they had shown previously. They retired from outside the Sandbag battery certainly; because I remember going outside the battery with several men and pursuing, or rather firing into the enemy, as there were large bodies of them below the battery amongst the bushes; I very nearly got killed for my pains, as I got too far down the hill, and found the top above me lined with Ruskis, and had to run the gauntlet through the bushes along the side of the hill to rejoin the remnants of our Brigade with the Grenadier Colours. . . .

"At this moment the *Indigènes* [the Algerines] came into action; they were the first individuals that appeared on the stage, and well do I remember their black faces and blue uniform coming tearing through the bushes. . . . When we got to the Second Division heights [Home Ridge] we were given ammunition. . . . As to what occurred in the front after this I cannot pretend to say, I only know firing went on with considerable vigour for some time; but the battle *had* turned in our favour.

"The French troops advanced in masses down the road and over the Second Division heights [Home

Ridge], but the *real* fighting all along the line was over when we retired and when the *Indigènes* advanced. Some heavy guns on the Second Division hills had cut up their artillery on Cossack and Shell hills very much; the distant rumbling of musketry was going on and some heavy firing still, but it got further off. . . .

"I am *perfectly certain* the brunt of the battle was over when we were retiring out of Sandbag battery: the sun then came out, and it was perfectly clear; our heavy guns began to tell upon the enemy's artillery on Cossack Hill. The fog having lifted, I saw the whole battle for the first time when we retired out of the Sandbag battery; before then, we had been entirely enveloped in mist and fog. I put this period at about 8.30 or 9, perhaps a little later, but no Frenchman appeared on the right of the battle till after this time, 9.30. . . . I am perfectly confident the Russians were in retreat when Bosquet's *Indigènes* came into the action. . . . When the *Indigènes* came through the bushes, some of our men joined them to have a last shot at the Ruski, and they probably formed along the hill in our old position, and peppered into the retreating columns as they went down the hill."*

This account of the fierce struggle between the Brigade and overwhelming masses of the Russians, written in the private diary of an Officer of the Regiment, gives a few of the confused events that took place immediately near him. Colonel Tower belonged to No. 1 company, and as Colonel Wilson was with No. 8 company, a few words describing what occurred about him may be also reproduced.

* Tower, *Diary*, Nov. 5, 1854.

"Amid a dense fog raged wholesale murder; the mortal strife was hand to hand, foot to foot, muzzle to muzzle, butt-end to butt-end. It must not be supposed that we always stood rooted on our ground, that we never budged. No, the fight rested not steadfast for an instant. It was now backward, now forward, now sideways. Here, a Grenadier party, after a frantic tussle, would be forced by overwhelming swarms out of the battery; there, a knot of Coldstreamers would arrest the advance of an entire Russian battalion; in another place, a cluster of Fusiliers, rallying after a repulse, would fling themselves upon a column, and with the sheer might of strong hearts, arms, and steel, send it slap-dash over the height's crest. This ceaseless wrestling to and fro accounts for the Sandbag battery being occupied alternately by men of the different Guards Regiments (or, more properly speaking, by mixed parties of the three Regiments larded with brave Liners). Whenever Pavloff succeeded in ousting one band of defenders from the work, a comrade batch would rush in, and, by a combination of bullet, bayonet, and gun-stock, thrust forth the intruders. . . .

"Time marches so marvellously fast in battle, that it is utterly impossible for men, plunged in the *mêlée*, to form an idea of how they stand with the clock. I have therefore no notion at what period reinforcements reached us. All I know is, that towards the end of the fight I saw many Linesmen fighting intermixed with Guardsmen. . . . Despite melting ranks, despite fresh regiments which continued to stream up the hillside, despite the growing scarcity of ammunition, the English clung to their battery with the grip of despair. If, by chance, the bull-dog's hold was for an instant shaken off, the next moment his teeth closed tighter than ever on the sandbags. . .

"The Russian Officers behaved like true soldiers. They ever were in front of their less adventurous rank and file, urging them on with voice and uplifted sword; nay, they rushed freely on certain death, with the view of inflaming the sluggish spirit of their followers. . . .

"And now half the Brigade—a grandiose title for 1300 men—strewed the ground; some slain outright, others bleeding to death, others vainly imploring to be carried off the field. Oh! that I must write 'vainly,' but in the devilish turmoil not a man whom God had shielded could be spared to carry away the wounded. The honour of England, nay, the very safety of the army, demanded that all living should be breast to breast with the Russians. . . . Meanwhile the Guards seemed at their last gasp, every minute found them less able—not a jot less willing—to repel the enemy. Hardly a man tasted food that morning, hence individual strength began to flag; where companies contended now only subdivisions struggled, hence collective power was ebbing fast. Nor was this all, ammunition had become frightfully scarce; in many cases, indeed, the soldiers had none left, so they were reduced to rifling the pouches of their fallen messmates; and when that resource failed, to pounding away at the ugly Calmuck visages with stocks and stones." *

It is unnecessary to proceed further with this account, for the writer now gives his experiences, when his excited men, having forced a superior number of Russians into hurried flight down the hillside into the valley, rushed after them in pursuit, in spite of their Officers' efforts to call

* *Our Veterans, etc.*, p. 290, etc.

them back. It is sufficient to say that any description of the struggle between the Guards and the masses which Dannenberg brought against them is impossible. The combatants were in close proximity, the contest was fought out in a thick fog, and on broken ground covered with tough hornbeam bushes and oak scrub, so that our men were speedily dispersed into groups, and few could really say what their neighbours were doing.*

* The following extract, from an account furnished by a Coldstreamer present at the battle, will be read with interest : *Sergeant W. Wilden, No. 1 Company*, writes :—" Suddenly the alarm came, 'fall in,' every man rushed for his rifle and ammunition ; the order was so sudden many had not turned out, and several took their places in the ranks only partly dressed ; poor Captain Ramsden was killed in his brown shooting-suit. . . . During the early part of the day, I should think about 8 or 8.30, the atmosphere became so thick with fog, rain, or mist, and the smoke from firing on both sides, I was not able to see more than eight or ten of my comrades, and scarcely able to distinguish the enemy, although within a few yards of him. At this juncture an alarm ran through our shattered ranks that the enemy was surrounding us. This turned out to be true, for he was working round our right flank to obtain possession of the small Sandbag battery. . . A terrible struggle took place for possession of this battery ; the enemy pushed his columns to the front in great numbers, and at the same time his left flank was gradually working round and attacking our right. At this time I should think about two companies of our Battalion held the battery. Here our losses were very heavy. We held it apparently for some time, and kept the Russian massive columns in check, until an unfortunate crisis happened ; our ammunition was exhausted, and, as our ranks were so terribly shattered, we were compelled by superior numbers to retire from the battery, or, in other words, we were driven out, and left it in the hands of the enemy ; but only for a short time, for we rallied and charged the enemy at the point of the bayonet and recaptured the battery. Here a dreadful struggle

But the main features of the contest are fairly clear. The Russians, securely posted in the Quarry Ravine, St. Clement's Gorge, and on the eastern slopes of the Kitspur, made their main attack against the latter, and as their assaulting columns were driven from the crest, they rallied again in the hollows beneath, and kept surging upwards, and renewing the strife. For some time the Brigade drove back the successive waves of the advancing enemy unassisted, except by the broken fragments of Adams' men; but a little later, when Cathcart's division approached, some 500 of his troops were pushed forward, and joined in the fray, while another portion moved to the head of the Quarry Ravine, and regained the Barrier. The latter, reinforced from time to time, remained there during the rest of the battle, and though the enemy passed them by, now as he advanced and again as

ensued, a hand-to-hand fight took place, in which bayonets were freely used on both sides, and at one period stones were resorted to to beat the enemy back from the north-western embrasure. . . . Although several bayonet charges were made upon the enemy, we were unable any longer to hold our ground against overwhelming numbers, and greatly exhausted, we were compelled gradually to retire, at the same time disputing every inch of ground. Here the enemy gradually advanced, and many of our wounded comrades were bayoneted or killed by the enemy. At this moment, the welcome sound of the bugles of the gallant Bosquet's division of Zouaves reached our ears; their numbers enabled them to force the enemy back and regain the position we were gradually losing. We then retired . . . Two long 18-pounder guns were about this time drawn by hand to replace those dismantled, and were used until the close of the battle."

he retired, it seems he never closed in on their rear or reconquered the post.

Colonel Upton, reaching the ground some time about 8 a.m., with No. 5 company of the Coldstream, and a company of the Scots Fusilier Guards, also coming off piquet,* endeavoured to close an undefended gap which existed between the Sandbag battery and the Barrier, and he prevented the enemy from seizing its advantages at that moment. But his force was insufficient to hold it for more than a brief space, and his men were most of them drawn into the vortex of the principal fight. Hence, it was not difficult for the Russians, pressing through the gap, to work round the left flank of the Brigade, and to penetrate to their rear.

Most of the Fourth Division, having been split up into fractions, were sent wherever the pressure of the battle required their presence; but a residue of 400 men under General Torrens remained, and with this force Cathcart hoped to relieve the Brigade in their arduous struggle, and assail the enemy in flank by descending the slopes on our right. The attempt, though successful at first, was not fortunate, and it failed to accomplish the results that were expected from it. The men soon dispersed in groups, were almost surrounded, and had to fight their way upwards with the Russians above

---

* It appears that No. 4 company of the Coldstream moved forward separately, and joined the main body of the Battalion.

them. It was here, moreover, that the valuable life of Cathcart was lost, and that Torrens (some time in the Grenadier Guards) was severely wounded.

This manœuvre appears to have changed the principle on which the Brigade had been resisting the hostile columns, and many who hitherto never pursued the beaten bodies of the enemy beyond the crest, now rushed after them down the slopes into the hollows beneath. In this way the group near Captain Wilson got out of hand, and pursued far down into the valley of the Tchernaya, where they were met by shots from Gortchakoff's riflemen, "who sprang up among the bushes, and blazed full in our faces." Meeting some stray groups of Cathcart's submerged detachment, the whole party reascended the heights, and lost heavily as they climbed up. Here they found themselves between two fires, and ascertained that the enemy was really above them, for at first they thought they were mistaken for Russians, and were being shot at by English soldiers. Avoiding this danger, by taking an upwards direction to the left, they stumbled upon a dead ammunition mule, and eagerly replenished their pouches, as for some time they had not had a round among them. Having at last reached the top, they found that the fog had lifted, that the Brigade was not where they had left it, and that Zouaves and Algerines (the *Indigènes*) were approaching the ground, and were driving the

N

enemy back as Colonel Tower has already told us. Wilson and the last of his men joined this attack, and many fell; he finally attached himself to the French 50th of the Line as they advanced, and then finding he could do nothing more, he sought the Coldstream, eventually falling in with them near Home Ridge, which he reached before the shattered remains of the Battalion got there.

CHAPTER XIII.

REPULSE OF THE RUSSIANS.

Operations of the French—Successes of the British artillery—Repulse of the Russian attack—Retreat of the enemy—No pursuit—What the garrison of Sevastopol did during the day—Operations of the Russian forces in the valley of the Tchernaya—Their unaccountable inactivity—Great losses incurred on both sides—Those among the Coldstream Officers abnormally large—Reaction after the struggle—A scene of carnage—Extraordinary gallantry of the British troops.

FROM the moment our men began to descend the slopes their means of maintaining their post on the Kitspur seemed to diminish. Under any circumstances, the struggle of the few against the many was gradually exhausting the power of the former, and reinforcements were urgently required. It was fortunate, therefore, that our allies now appeared upon the scene.

Bosquet, who for some time in the early morning had been observing Gortchakoff, came speedily to the conclusion that that General meant to remain quiescent; he therefore sent forward some of his troops without delay, to Home Ridge, where the danger was most pressing. Two Battalions, 1600 strong, arrived first. One, the French 6th of the Line, pushing towards the Kitspur, struck in flank the Russians, who,—advancing through the gap (previously mentioned), which was ever getting wider,—were endeavouring to operate against our rear. This French battalion, however, soon got into difficulties, and the other, the 7me Léger, was sent to its support.

But before this was effected another crisis occurred; for the enemy, urging forward his numerous forces up the ravines which he occupied, brushed past the Anglo-French then on the Kitspur, and made a very determined onslaught on Home Ridge itself. This serious manœuvre was repulsed by the gallantry of a few British detachments present on the spot, and of the 7me Léger. The defeated column was driven back, so that the two French battalions were brought together.

It was now 10 a.m., and another French force, a brigade with some artillery, led by Bosquet in person, reached the battle in two columns: in the first, some rifles, a battalion of Algerines, and one of Zouaves (1900); in the other, more Zouaves, and the French 50th of the Line (2200). There was still a good deal of difficulty in forcing the enemy to recede; for as the first column pursued him, they advanced too far, and fresh hostile forces were able to move up the ravines leading to the main spur, thereby threatening our allies in rear. But on the arrival of the second column, the Russians, now thoroughly broken by their losses and by the stubborn resistance which held them in check, gave up the contest. They were finally driven off the Kitspur and out of the ravines which had been so useful to them during the struggle, by enabling them to re-organize after so many repulses inflicted by our slender forces. Kinglake thus speaks of a band of the Coldstream during this phase of the fight :—

"The Zouave battalion was advancing . . . when the bearskin all at once reappeared. It was from the wooded steeps of the hillsides that the spectre uprose. Since the time when last we observed it, the small band of Coldstream men collected by Wilson had remained in the brushwood below watching always for some such occasion as the one that now offered. Amid a roar of joy and welcome—for the Zouaves and the Guards were close friends—these Coldstream men joined the advance, aligning on the right of the French. . . . What followed was slaughter." *

Meanwhile we had already gained an immense superiority over the enemy's artillery. As early as about 9.30, two 18-pounder guns of position had been brought on Home Ridge, and after a short space of time the power of the hostile batteries began to wane. The French guns, coming up, posted themselves on our right, and the bombardment

* Kinglake, v. 402.

continued with increasing advantage on our side, though the number of our pieces was not half that of our opponents. Some of our men on the left and centre of our line also advanced, and added to the misfortune of the gunners on Shell Hill. The battle was really decided at eleven, though the artillery continued to fire till much later. As soon as the bulk of the Household Brigade returned to Home Ridge, and after ammunition had been served out, the men were reformed, and were moved up to protect the guns against any sudden assault. This duty was "worse than fighting the infantry, for we got no revenge for the men we lost," and we incurred casualties not a few.*

---

* Letter of Mr. Taylor, late Quartermaster Somersetshire Militia, then in the Coldstream. One shell killed and wounded eight men. Colonel Upton was wounded at this period. See, also, *Our Veterans, etc.*, p. 299.

The action of the Guards at Inkerman seems to be imperfectly described in Kinglake. According to that writer, the bulk of the Brigade came out of action at 8.30; though he notes that the force under Wilson joined the last attack undertaken by the French about 11 o'clock, and allows that the companies which followed Upton were in the field as late as 10. Giving Bosquet's impressions of the scene presented to his observation at that hour, he says, "High above on the right, where there sauntered a red-coated Officer with the *bonnet de poil* and a singularly unconcerned air (Colonel Upton), some men of the Guards could be seen lying down among the brushwood" (Kinglake, v. 382). Yet Tower and Wilden, whose accounts have been given, state that they were relieved on the Kitspur by the Algerines and Zouaves—that is, after 10 o'clock; and Wilson, who, according to Mr. Kinglake, was on that portion of the battle-field later than any other Guardsman, tells us himself that he got back to Home Ridge *before* the bulk of the Brigade reached it. Some isolated groups, separated

The retreat of the Russians commenced about one o'clock, and was covered by a column of their reserve; which, attempting to advance, was quickly dispersed by a few rounds of the 18-pounders. There was no pursuit. The enemy slipped away, and "seemed to melt from the lost field; the English were too few and too exhausted, and the French too little confident in the advantage gained, to convert the repulse into a rout." Our allies, deducting losses, numbered at the end of the engagement some 7000 infantry, for, besides the troops already mentioned, three battalions (2400) arrived on the ground at eleven; they also had 700 cavalry and 24 guns present. Lord Raglan was anxious to complete the victory by falling on the rear of the flying Russians, but his cautious colleague would not consent; for he still feared an attack from Gortchakoff's untouched forces, and was unwilling to expose his men to the fire of the ships that were moored in the roadstead.*

While the battle was going on, the garrison of Sevastopol kept up so poor a demonstration, that we were able to denude our camps of men, and push them to Inkerman. Besides the men on duty in the trenches, the greater part of the Third

during the fierce struggle in the fog and brushwood from the main body, possibly found themselves on Home Ridge before; Taylor says he helped to pull up the two 18-pounders, which, as we know, took place about 9.30.

* Hamley, *War in the Crimea*, p. 157.

Division watched the fortress, and they were subjected to no further inconvenience than that which the fire from the place, intensified on this day, entailed. About 9.30, however, the enemy made a *sortie* against Forey's siege corps, under General Timofeyeff, with 5000 men and 12 guns. The blow, though it met with some success at first, failed, and the Russians were pursued by our gallant allies back under the shelter of the fortress. Thus little was done by the garrison to assist Dannenberg, and that little was of trifling value.

Gortchakoff's operations during the day were still less effective. He made a few feints, fired upon the Sapuné Ridge, and, it is said, did lose 15 men. He thereby gave the companies on piquet (among them, Nos. 6 and 7 companies of the Coldstream) the opportunity of engaging him with distant volleys, without apparently causing much, if any, loss to our side. In short, he did nothing, when by attacking Bosquet, he would have prevented that General from advancing to our assistance at Inkerman. His orders were "to support the general attack, to draw the Allied forces upon himself, and to try and seize one of the ascents to the Sapuné Ridge." Mr. Kinglake, however, tells us that these written orders were explained away by "oral communications" into something different,[*] and makes us believe that there is a mystery which

---

[*] Kinglake, v. 59 (note), 69.

has never been explained, hanging over the operations of this Russian Commander, who, on that day, held so much power in his hands. What we do know is that Dannenberg, in spite of his overwhelming numbers, was unable to secure a footing on the Kitspur, that this was due to the manner in which it was defended by our scanty forces, and that in this defence the Household Brigade played a glorious part, and suffered much in consequence.

The losses were very great on both sides: those of the enemy, who moved in heavy columns, being more than those of the Allies, though relatively, in proportion to numbers at the seat of war, he suffered less than we did. The Russians had 10,729 killed, wounded, and prisoners, including 256 Officers. The English 2357 of all ranks, of whom 130 were Officers (or 39 Officers, and 558 men killed, and 91 Officers and 1669 men wounded). The French 929, among them 49 Officers (or 13 Officers and 130 men killed, and 36 Officers and 750 men wounded).* The Brigade lost nearly half its effective strength, viz., out of a total of 1334:—

	Officers.	Sergts.	Drumrs.	Rank & File.	Total.
Killed	12	9	1	177	199
Wounded	20 †	20	4	357	401
Missing	—	—	—	4	4
Total	32	29	5	538	604

* The above were the losses on the field of Inkerman. The total casualties on the 5th of November amounted to: Russians, 11,959; English, 2573; and French 1800 of all ranks (Kinglake, v. 443, 457).

† Including Major-General Bentinck, who was severely wounded,

The Coldstream suffered in like proportion, but the casualties among the Officers far exceeded those that occurred in the other Regiments. In fact, almost all the Officers were swept away. Out of seventeen present,* four only escaped uninjured, viz. Captains Strong, Wilson, Crawley, and Tower. Of the rest, eight were killed or died soon after of their wounds, viz. Lieut.-Colonels Dawson and Cowell, Captains MacKinnon, Bouverie, Eliot, and Ramsden, and Lieutenants Greville and Disbrowe. The remainder were wounded; viz. Colonel Upton (slightly), Lieut.-Colonels Halkett and Lord C. FitzRoy, Captain P. Fielding, and Lieutenant Amherst (all severely). The losses of the Battalion amounted to—

	Officers.	Sergts.	Rank & File.	Total.
Killed	8	3	73	84
Wounded	5	11	107	123
Total	13	14	180	207

The principal casualties were in the flank companies. No. 1 entered the action with 50 to 60 men, and No. 8 was slightly stronger. The former lost one sergeant and 43 rank and file, and the latter two sergeants and 41 men. No. 2 came next, losing 37 men.

Where a Battalion has so freely shed its lifeblood in the stubborn defence of the position

* Of the Coldstream Officers on the Staff (not counted among the seventeen mentioned) none were wounded, though actively engaged on that day.

assigned to it, it may seem strange that no official notice should be taken of the death of the Officer who led it into action, and who directed its movements until he fell, and more especially when in the Brigade to which the Battalion belonged, no other Commanding Officer lost his life. Yet this is what occurred with respect to the memory of the gallant Colonel Dawson, and the feelings of his brothers in arms were not inadequately expressed in the following lines, written by Colonel Wilson :—

"The despatch which informed England of this dearly bought victory, commended the services of many of the living and blazoned the merits of many of the dead; but from that encomiastic scroll there was at least one remarkable omission. To the memory of Colonel Vesey Dawson, shot through the heart while in command of the Coldstream Guards, was conceded not a passing word of eulogy or of regret. It is melancholy to reflect that on this humble page should stand the only record of how as brave a soldier as ever drew a sword, as noble a gentleman as ever earned the respect of his fellow-men, fought and died." *

We are told that this great victory caused no outward elation among our troops. A reaction succeeded the excitement of the struggle; the danger now past began to be realized for the first time ; and the men, though hardened to the miserable scenes which war creates, were almost awed

* *Our Veterans, etc.*, p. 306.

by the terrible carnage and devastation that met their eyes on the hard-fought field. The Second Division camp was laid flat, the tents uprooted and scattered, canvas saturated with blood carpeted the ground. Our own camp swarmed with the wounded and the dying, and the sight sent a chill of depression through the few survivors as they returned to their bivouacs. Everywhere on the narrow space of the battle-ground the victims lay thick, some killed, others groaning in agony, and nowhere thicker than in and around the Sandbag battery, where the contest raged the fiercest. Here the dead were literally piled up on one another as they fell.

"The whole battle-field, which could all be seen at a glance, except where concealed by brushwood, looked perfectly *covered* with bodies; between the Second Division hills and the crest of the Inkerman hill is a very short distance, and the entire action having been fought on that limited space, there was an awful scene of carnage upon it. . . . Before evening we got all our wounded off the field; the dead, of course, remained there, and the poor wounded Ruskis who were a great deal too numerous to take off. . . . From the heights I could see the Russian army winding up the road; the whole country was covered with troops straggling over the causeway over the Tchernaya marsh; they were a long time crossing. Arabas full of wounded, guns, etc., lumbering up the way, but they had quite enough of it. . . . Our hospital was a most piteous sight. . . . Our poor fellows were all dying or dead. . . . The camp was miserable, and I could only thank God I was not lying in the hospital tent with half my limbs smashed to pieces, or lying on a stretcher ready to be buried."*

Saddest of all, was the cruel thought surging in every mind that many of our brave wounded had been basely bayoneted as they lay helpless on the ground, by an uncivilized enemy, who, unable to drive off the few that held the plateau against him, wreaked his vengeance on the defenceless, as soon as they fell into his hands. We had ample evidence of this savagery—established, moreover, by a special inquiry—that cast so black a stain on the Russian army, for, when our men hurled the foe from a corner from which he had driven us, we found our wounded stabbed to death.

Thus was the battle of Inkerman fought and won by small bodies of the British and French armies, over an overpowering hostile force of more than 35,000 infantry, amply supported by artillery ; who, having stolen in during the night up to our outposts, endeavoured to break through the Allied line round Sevastopol, at a point where we were weakest, and where we had absolutely no defences.†

* Tower, *Diary*.
† It cannot be insisted too often that the Sandbag battery was a battery only in name ; and that its importance consisted in the fact that it served as a rallying-point, on account of its being a conspicuous object, round which the main struggle on the Kitspur raged. Russian exaggerations have given it a wholly fictitious value ; even Todleben, describing the fight a little after eight o'clock, says that the Okhotsk regiment (3000 strong) attacked the Sandbag

The result proved the immense superiority of our arms over those of Russia; so also does it give us some indication of what would have happened if we had boldly attacked Sevastopol at the end of September, before, or immediately after, the flank march, or even during the bombardment in October.

The British fought with a valour and constancy that surpassed even the glorious traditions of the past. Led by Officers who hurled themselves like the old Knights Errant into the thick of every danger, they nobly followed on with that unflinching steadiness produced by constitutional bravery, by devotion to their leaders, and by the splendid discipline that was the predominant characteristic of our Crimean troops. Their bold extension and their courage in maintaining it, even without supports and when opposed to heavy columns, made the Russians think that the line of red-coats was but a fringe of our strength, and they hesitated when they ought to have acted boldly. We were, moreover, provided with a superior rifle, and so when the enemy, emerging from the ravines, found himself met by a heavy and shattering fire, his columns were brought to a standstill, and he lost the advantage which his solid formation might have given him. He was far from being imbued

battery, held by their "worthy rivals—the intrepid Coldstream," that they expelled the latter, and that nine guns were the reward of this brilliant feat of arms! (see Hamley, *War in the Crimea*, p. 160).

with the spirit that animated our men, and he lacked the determination to close with them.

"Had he, at the commencement of the battle, pushed these columns resolutely forward, it follows nearly as a matter of course that, by sheer momentum of his heavy masses, the British lines would have been broken through and trampled down utterly. It would have been a question of weight alone. As it was, no devotion, no exertions on the part of the Russian Officers, could at the outset spur their battalions to one grand combined rush. Time was frittered away in a series of persevering but desultory attacks, which were invariably repulsed, thanks to English valour and English firearms." *

* *Our Veterans, etc.*, p. 309. It is proper to add that the Russian Rifle corps, 1800 strong, were armed with as good a weapon as our Minié, also that some of the British battalions (the 20th Regiment, for instance, who distinguished themselves greatly in the battle) carried the old smooth-bore musket, known as "Brown Bess" (see Kinglake, v. 475).

PART V.

THE WINTER OF 1854-55 *IN THE CRIMEA.*

CHAPTER XIV.

DISTRESS OF THE ARMY.

Prostration of both sides after the battle of Inkerman—Sevastopol not to be taken in 1854—Tardy arrangements made for the winter—Depletion of the ranks—The right flank is at last secured—Violent hurricane of the 14th of November; stores scattered and destroyed—The winter begins in earnest—Causes of the sufferings that overwhelmed the army—How Government attended to its wants—No road between the base and front—Miserable plight to which the army was reduced.

THE battle of Inkerman exhausted the energies of the combatants and for a few days they recoiled from each other, stunned by its effects. The Allies had gained a Pyrrhic victory ; another such victory, and their forces must be annihilated. The enemy also had received a crushing defeat, which shattered his military prestige and ruined the *morale* of his army. Neither side was in a condition to operate against the other, and each faced his opponent listlessly, almost helplessly. But Menshikoff, though disgraced in the field, deserved the gratitude of his Imperial Master, and had every reason to be content with what he had achieved ; for he had gained an advantage of supreme importance. He had put it out of the power of the Anglo-French invaders to finish the war during the year 1854, and thus, while chaining them fast to the bleak and narrow upland of the Chersonese, he had the satisfaction of knowing that they would be exposed to the rigours of the approaching winter.

This result was all the more disastrous to us, since, not having foreseen it, we were in no position to meet it, and were unprovided with the means of maintaining our troops in the inhospitable region to which we had become committed. In short, the Allies were about to be handed over to foes far more destructive and terrible than those they had hitherto met. Instead of contending against Russian weapons, they were now also to struggle with the forces of nature and the fury of the elements.

On the 6th of November it was finally determined to put off the projected bombardment, and to winter in the Crimea. The Commissariat Department, informed of this decision, was then, and then only, ordered to make such preparations as would enable the army to remain on the upland. But the tardy order came too late, for in less than ten days the winter began in earnest, and nothing could then be got ready to save the troops from the cruel trials that awaited them.

DISTRESS OF THE ARMY. 197

On the day after the battle, the Allies were engaged in burying the dead, in removing the Russian wounded who still lay on the ground, and in clearing the field of the traces of the struggle. An invitation addressed to General Menshikoff to agree to a truce, and to send out his men to bury their own dead, was refused, for that prudent commander was naturally disinclined to give his troops so sombre and depressing an object-lesson of their utter inefficiency in the field. His army, however, met this invitation in another fashion, and, whether in error or by design, they answered it by firing upon our burying parties.

As another attack was feared, the front was cleared of incumbrances as soon as possible, and the wounded were promptly taken to Balaklava. Their sufferings were considerable; there was a scarcity of hospital comforts and appliances at the seat of war, and the ambulances in use were unfitted for the purpose of conveying injured men.

Much affected by the heavy losses sustained by his " First Brigade," the Duke of Cambridge came early into the Guards' camp, where the few men present turned out to cheer him.

"Accompanied by his Aide-de-camp, the brave and popular Macdonald, the Royal General was assiduous in his attentions to the wounded Guardsmen, sympathizing in cheering tones with the livid wretches that still breathed, and shedding tears of manly sorrow upon the mangled clay of those who had completed their last tour of earthly duty." *

The funeral of the numerous Coldstream Officers formed a most sad procession. Seven—Dawson, Cowell, MacKinnon, Eliot, Ramsden, Disbrowe, and Greville—were laid to rest in one grave, in a small rocky ravine near the Windmill. Bouverie's body was only recovered late on the 6th, and he was buried by the side of Lieut.-Colonel Hunter-Blair of the Scots Fusilier Guards, who survived the action twenty-four hours.

"It was really enough to unman anybody; poor fellows! far away from all their friends and relations; poor Greville, whose death killed his mother, everybody loved him; we laid them side by side, and I remember the earth pattering on their poor bodies with dull hollow sound." †

Colonel Upton, though badly hurt, was able to remain at his post till the middle of November, and he assumed the command of the Brigade, *vice* General Bentinck, wounded, and of the First Division from the 7th, when the Duke of Cambridge was sent to Balaklava, on the sick list. The command of the Battalion thus devolved upon Colonel Lord F. Paulet. The Coldstream was, in

---

* *Our Veterans, etc.*, p. 314.

† Tower, *Diary*. All the Guards Officers were buried in this spot. During the winter of 1855, more than a year later, their bodies were exhumed, and were properly interred on Cathcart's Hill, where they now lie.

truth, a mere skeleton of the fine body which embarked at Portsmouth in the spring of 1854. It only mustered now 11 Officers and 307 men, while no draft,—except a small one of 58 men, which, having left London on the 26th of October, reached the Crimea on the 22nd of November,— was on the road to compensate for this serious deficiency of strength in the field.

When news of the battle arrived in England, strenuous efforts were made to fill up the attenuated ranks of the army, by sending out fresh battalions and reinforcements to those already at the seat of hostilities. But the campaign, ever since July, when we were first encamped near the pestilential lake of Devna, had sadly drained our resources—far more rapidly, indeed, than the home authorities had anticipated,—and though recruiting had been actively going on, the large demands which this war created could not be satisfied. In this way, the next (the third) draft sent to the Coldstream only amounted to 153 men, and could do little to restore our depleted ranks to an efficient state. This draft started on the 24th of November, and arrived in the Crimea on the 18th of December.*

In France, however, there was not such a dearth

* The average age of the small draft of 58 men reaching the seat of war in November, was twenty-one, and their service nearly two years. The averages of the next draft arriving in December, were twenty-one and a half years and eight months, respectively.

of fighting men as seems to have been the case in England, and considerable reinforcements were despatched to the east, so that somewhat later (in February) our allies were able to extend the siege-works that surrounded the south side of Sevastopol.

We have seen that the omission to strengthen the unguarded flank at Inkerman by earthworks had led to serious consequences. The critical nature of the battle made this so clear, that, when the fight was over, though we had fewer men to spare than were available before, this vital position was at once placed in a state of defence. English, French, and even Turks—held hitherto to be an incumbrance—were set to perform this duty, and Fore Ridge and Shell Hill were soon crowned with works, commanding the approaches to the scene of the recent struggle, and securing it at last, as far as possible, from further molestation.*

The ordinary routine of siege life had hardly recommenced after the rude shock which interrupted it on the 5th, when the winter burst upon the Crimean peninsula with a suddenness and

---

* Recent events having opened the eyes of authority, the shoulder was put vigorously to the wheel. Hence the fortification of an all-important point which, previous to the battle, had either been considered unnecessary, or had been pronounced impossible of achievement with the means at disposal, was actually executed with sorely straitened means after the battle. In a word, few hands contrived to do what comparatively many hands had been judged incapable of doing. "Where there's a will there's a way" (*Our Veterans, etc.*, p. 325).

violence that marked a distinct feature in the story of the war, and brought innumerable troubles upon the Allies engaged in it. The weather lately had been cold and stormy, varied upon occasions by short gleams of sunshine and partial warmth. At daybreak on the 14th, however, a violent hurricane, accompanied by a deluge of rain, unexpectedly arose, and swept with terrific force over the country, and not only blew away every tent standing on the upland, scattered the stores upon which the army depended, and stopped all communications, but also dashed to pieces or disabled much of the shipping laden with supplies that were then very urgently needed.* The ground was speedily converted into a deep and impassable sea of sticky mud, which flew about in large quantities; the temperature fell, and snow came down.

The men of the various regiments huddled together like sheep, behind bushes or rocks, or wherever they could find some protection against the violence of the elements. The condition of the houseless troops was miserable in the extreme, both during the day and long afterwards, for they had nothing wherewith to repair their losses. But

* It is said that only three tents remained upright in the English camps (Nolan, i. p. 650). But a fourth, belonging to Lieut.-Colonel Carleton, also survived, and it was the only one that did so in the Guards camp. The Turkish tents, placed in a sheltered position, made a better resistance than ours, and comparatively few were swept away.

it was worse with the sick and wounded, who were exposed to the full force of the cyclone, and to the cold and the rain.

A considerable amount of shipping had been left outside the harbour of Balaklava, instead of being safely berthed inside the landlocked bay. Of the vessels anchored in this dangerous position, many went to pieces on the rocks forming the iron-bound coast; altogether twenty-one were sunk, and their valuable cargoes were all lost. H.M.S. *Retribution*, with the Duke of Cambridge on board, narrowly escaped destruction. On that fatal first day of a severe Crimean winter, the troops were deprived of vast quantities of ammunition, food, clothing, and forage, and there was no reserve at hand from whence they could be replaced.

The difficulties and sufferings that now overwhelmed the army began with this storm, but they are clearly to be traced to the aimless manner in which the campaign had been conducted. The original intention had been to surprise Sevastopol; but it soon disappeared out of sight, and no step was taken to capture the town in accordance with the conditions under which the expedition landed on Russian soil. On the contrary, a regular siege was gradually commenced, and a completely new plan was thereby adopted. But the change was never recognized, its bearing upon the fortunes of the war was not appreciated, and no stores were accumulated at the base of operations to meet the requirements of the lengthy proceedings into which the invaders had drifted.

This was the more unfortunate, since, when the Allied Commanders undertook the flank march, and shifted their ground from the north to the south side of Sevastopol, they found themselves obliged to operate upon a barren upland which afforded no supplies, and very soon they even lost the advantage of drawing forage from the valley of the Tchernaya. Thus, after the 25th of October, if not before, nothing whatsoever was to be obtained from the land in which the army was established, and every single article had to be transported by sea from a distance. The battle of Inkerman at last revealed the true position in which we stood ; but it was then too late, and when the storm destroyed the vessels lying outside the harbour, which contained considerable addition to our scanty stores, it must be acknowledged that this position was indeed deplorable.

Nor should it be forgotten that requisitions put forward were imperfectly attended to by the authorities in England, and that there was often confusion at the base (Scutari and Balaklava), which appears to have been incompletely organ- ized. Owing to these circumstances, many mis- fortunes overtook the British army, some of which may be cited. Though a request was made early in September for 2000 tons of hay, only 228 tons were received in the Crimea by the 1st of February, 1855.* In November an application was forwarded for 3000 tents, and for a steam mill and bakery; but more than six months elapsed before they arrived at the seat of war.†

Again, we have seen that a substantial portion of the kits were left behind in the squad bags, at Scutari, at the end of May; also that, on landing at Old Fort, the packs were taken away from the men. The former seem to have been allowed to remain where they were stored. But an effort was made in the middle of October, just a month after they had been left on board ship, to recover the knapsacks; though apparently with very indifferent success. And thus, the troops remained, exposed to the severe inclemency of the weather, without any change of clothing, in the worn-out and tattered garments that had uninterruptedly done duty, day and night, from the beginning of June, when they landed at Varna.

Lastly, biscuit and salt pork formed the usual, indeed the never-varying ration served out to the British soldier. This diet was his only food, and it produced scurvy, as was only to be expected. To counteract this plague, limejuice and vegetables were thus urgently required, but neither was available. It is true that small quantities of

* Kinglake, vi. 128, note.   † *Ibid.*, pp. 98, 138.

vegetables were sometimes to be had, but then they were sold to the starving men at famine prices.* A tardy requisition was made in October for limejuice, and half the quantity demanded (20,000 lbs.) reached Balaklava on the 19th of December; but there it remained almost unnoticed, and this antidote against the scourge of scurvy was only unearthed on the 29th of January following. Nor was it apparently ordered to be issued to the troops as a ration, until the middle of February.†

Arising directly out of the incomprehensible

* *General Order, Memo.*, Nov. 1st: "Commanders of divisions will send to-morrow at 9 a.m. to the Quartermaster-General's office, on the wharf at Balaklava, for potatoes. . . . They must be paid for at the spot at the price of £1 1s. per cwt." *Ibid.*, Nov. 6th: "Those corps or divisions which desire potatoes should send to Balaklava for them; the price is £1 1s. per cwt. . . . The money required to pay for them must be sent at the same time." It appears that later, after December 10th, whenever vegetables were available they were supplied to the men gratis; but as they had to fetch them from Balaklava under circumstances of extreme difficulty (as will presently appear), it is scarcely to be wondered that the wearied troops did not always avail themselves of the boon (see Kinglake, vi. 138, note).

It should further be stated here, that Lord Raglan, "in consideration of the length of the siege operations, the constant labour the men have been called upon to perform, the inclemency of the weather, and the cheerfulness and good will they have manifested in the discharge of their duty," granted the unusual issue of working pay to the troops employed in digging, etc., in the trenches, at the rate of, for Non-commissioned officers as overseers, one for every twenty men, 1s. by day, 1s. by night; for rank and file, 8d. by day, 10d. by night (*General Order*, Nov. 14, 1854).

† Wyatt, pp. 41, 55. Limejuice, after February 16th, was issued three times during the month.

manner in which this extraordinary war was conceived and carried on, another circumstance, more powerful for evil than the apathy with which the necessities of the army were regarded by the Government, caused famine and distress to oppress our troops. We had no road between Balaklava and the front; and hence, when supplies reached the former place, we were without means of conveying them to the spot where they were to be consumed. And yet the distance to be traversed was under eight miles.

It has been shown that, of the two roads connecting the English before Sevastopol and the base, one, the Woronzoff road, was metalled; the other, over the Col, was but a mere pathway or cart-track: also that on the 25th of October, we lost the use of the former, and were restricted to the latter. During the autumn this pathway was serviceable; indeed, so firm and open was the country, that waggons and guns could easily move across it anywhere. But when the torrents of rain flooded the ground on the 14th of November, the whole aspect of the upland became altered, and the track as well as the plain were converted into a deep morass, over which communications were rendered almost impossible.

The French, with proper forethought, constructed a good road between Kamiesh Bay and their camps, directly they occupied the Chersonese; but as all the British troops were required to push forward vigorously the siege-works, and as we indulged in the misplaced confidence that Sevastopol would fall immediately after the bombardment of the 17th of October, we never even thought of securing our communications, until after the 5th of November, when it was decided to winter in the Crimea.

The rejected Turks, offered by Omar Pasha, might certainly have performed this important service while the weather was clear and dry; but the prejudice against them has already been mentioned, and their assistance was refused. After the battle of Inkerman we took measures to construct the road, and we acted as we did with respect to the defences near Home Ridge; tools were hastily procured from Constantinople, and Turks were at last employed. But it was then too late. The unfortunate men were unprovided with food and shelter, and the weather was severe; they died so rapidly that the living were all required to bury the dead, and in a short time this ill-fated contingent disappeared altogether.

The scarcity of forage and the want of a road acted and reacted on each other, and formed the principal causes of the winter troubles. The horses and mules died of starvation, and it was useless to replace them, as there was not wherewithal to feed them. The transport, miserably insufficient as it always had been, dwindled into nothing, and all but disappeared; troop horses of the cavalry were impressed into this service, but they too perished. Carriage traffic soon ceased, and an attempt was then made to convey supplies on the backs of the wretched beasts that survived. This expedient also failed; the quagmire of tenacious clay intervening between the port and the front, the famine, and the exposure to cold and wet, all operated together, and the animals could work no more. Thenceforward there was nothing for it but to make the men themselves wade through the deep mud, and fetch up such things from the base as they required, to keep body and soul together.

The duty was no inconsiderable addition to their ordinary toil, for while they were decreasing fast in numbers, the labour in the trenches did not abate. The journey also sometimes took twelve hours to accomplish, and during the time it lasted they were without food, shelter, or rest.* This miserable makeshift was, of course, entirely inadequate to supply the troops, and the more bulky or heavy articles, however necessary to the wellbeing of the army, could not be brought to camp at all.

The serious error by which magazines had not been established in time at the seat of war, was repaired quickly by the great energy displayed at head-quarters, and in December considerable

* Hamley, *War in the Crimea*, p. 170.

DISTRESS OF THE ARMY. 209

quantities of every kind of stores were available at Balaklava, but there most of them remained unused, because, as Government would not supply forage (and it seems it was not easily procured out of England), there was no transport, and as there was no road to span the morass, means did not exist of crossing it and of reaching the front.

The winter all through Europe was a peculiarly severe one, and there was no exception to its inclemency in the Crimea, where the season was specially cold. All the combatants suffered from its effects. Even the Russians felt it acutely, though housed and provided with a tolerably fair transport service from their well-stored magazines on the Sea of Azof. Our French allies also underwent many privations, due to the general difficulties that affected the invaders established on the barren upland and exposed to the wind, the snow, and the rain; but more especially on account of the small *tente d'abri* which sheltered them at night, and which was not so useful as our bell tent.

But the British army suffered most. Like the French, our men were sent to trenches filled with water, where they remained wet to their knees for many hours during the day and night; but, unlike them, these hardships were of constant recurrence. Reinforcements were rapidly sent to General Canrobert, and his force was strong enough to enable him to give his soldiers rest when their tour of

P

service in the siege-works was finished. But the British had no such exemption ; their numbers were insufficient for the purposes of the campaign ; and they practically were always at work. Lord Raglan computed that they were "on duty five nights out of six, a large proportion of them constantly under fire."* If we add, that they were seldom dry ; that they had little or no fuel except brushwood and roots ; that they could not cook their food ; that the coffee served out was in the form of the green unroasted berry ;† that the ration of rice failed from the 15th of November to the end of December ; that the boots were defective and bad ; and that there was no warm clothing available until the beginning of the latter month ;—it will be readily seen that the hardships undergone were of no trivial character.‡

* Letter to the Duke of Newcastle, Dec. 26th.
† Many of the men now existed almost entirely upon the biscuit and ration of spirit ; the camp was often strewed with portions of uncooked salt meat, and partially roasted or green coffee (Wyatt, p. 40). The green coffee ceased on February 22nd, and compressed vegetables were supplied for the first time on the 26th (*ibid.*, p. 56).
‡ In the Coldstream some warm clothing and blankets were issued to the men early in December, more were obtained later, and in January a further supply was procured. Lord Raglan directed (January 6th) that each soldier should receive a pair of boots gratuitously (*General Order*). The following is the clothing served out to the Battalion (including the Regimental hospital) between the 6th of December and the 28th of February: Great coats, 392 ; trousers, 100 pairs ; sheepskin coats, 459 ; tweed coats, 29 ; fur caps, 503 ; flannel shirts, 147 ; jersey frocks, 861 ; pairs of

Nor did the men's sufferings end here, for when exhausted by toil and privations there was no alleviation to those whose health and strength had given way. So badly organized were the hospital arrangements, that we are told the climax of misery was only reached in the places set apart for the sick. Circumstances necessarily made the field-hospitals in the front rude habitations for numerous patients seized and tormented by painful complaints.* The transport of invalids to Balaklava was, moreover, a difficult proceeding and an agonizing ordeal. But arrived at the port, their troubles should surely have come to an end.

It was not so, however, for such was the confusion prevalent at the time, so great the number of the sick, that they were subjected, if possible, to

socks, 1527; flannel drawers, 994; mitts, 993; boots, long and short, 532; comforters, 446; gregos, 55 (Wyatt, pp. 41, 45, 57). The long boots appear to have given little satisfaction. On account of the cold — the thermometer sometimes ranging from eleven to fifteen degrees Fahrenheit,—it was not easy to make the men take off their boots at night; their wet feet often being swollen, were pressed by the leather, and thus frost-bite was induced (*ibid.*, p. 42).

* The indefatigable Surgeon of the Coldstream in the Crimea, Dr. Wyatt, tells us that a marquee was applied for (November 17th) to replace the ill-ventilated bell tents used as a Regimental hospital. It arrived next day, but without ropes, and these, though repeatedly demanded, were only obtained a fortnight later, through Colonel Steele, Lord Raglan's Military Secretary, who at last procured them from a man-of-war. On the 18th of December another marquee was required (the sick were becoming very numerous), and it arrived on the 29th, also without ropes and deficient of five pieces of canvas; in this case the error was only rectified, after six weeks' delay, on the 30th of January.

worse treatment during the voyage across the Black Sea and in the great hospital established at Scutari. In short, this hospital was a loathsome lazarette, "crammed with misery, overflowing with despair," until Miss Nightingale and a number of Nuns and Sisters, having arrived on the scene early in November, acquired such influence and acted with such admirable prudence and energy, that gradually—the evil was too great to be arrested at once—order was restored, sanitary conditions were introduced, and the sick were well tended and cared for by the gentle and able nursing of kindly ladies.*

The British forces before Sevastopol were rapidly melting away in consequence of the combination of misfortunes that overwhelmed them. Diseases of a violent type broke out, and cholera, typhus, diarrhœa, dysentery, scurvy swept away the ranks; frost-bites were common, and even men reported fit for duty, were so weakened as to be scarcely able to continue their labours under the hard circumstances that surrounded them. The drain was excessive upon our strength in the field, and the small army was in truth threatened with extinction.

Between the 1st of November and the 28th of

* Hamley, *War in the Crimea*, pp. 172, 179, etc. After the battle of Inkerman, the depôt which had been established at Scutari early in June, was re-organized and placed under the able command of Colonel Lord William Paulet (November 23rd), through whose energy many improvements in the hospitals were effected (see Kinglake, vi. 437). An acting Sergeant-Major (Sergeant White of the Coldstream) was appointed there November 19th.

February we lost as many as 22,506 men, not including the killed in action; of whom 8898 had died in hospital, while the remainder, 13,608, were lying there sick on the latter date. In spite of fresh regiments and drafts which reached the Crimea after Inkerman, the total effectives all told at the seat of war, reckoning the troops at Balaklava, amounted then to only 17,311 men. In January there would have been about 3000 to 4000 men of the infantry available to repel another attack of the enemy, had he attempted to repeat the operation of the 5th of November.* The British would have had a smaller force at the end of February.

The Coldstream shared to the full the calamity which has just been so imperfectly described. Taking part in the constant duty which exhausted the army, exposed to the cruel suffering that the winter brought about, and conspicuously displaying the virtues of strict discipline and of uncomplaining fortitude which enabled our men to preserve a bold and defiant front against the Russians, the lot of the Battalion can scarcely be separated from that which afflicted and honoured its brethren in arms standing before Sevastopol. Its fate was the same as theirs, its sorrows were equally acute, its bearing likewise was proud and dauntless, its glory bright and lasting. But its losses were heavy, as the following table will show:—

* Kinglake, vi. 202, etc.

	Regimental Hospital.		Sick Transferred to Scutari.	Remarks.
	Admissions.	Deaths.		
Nov. (including wounded at Inkerman)	277	22	153	Eight died of cholera and eleven of wounds.
December	221	17	99	
January	186	37	91	The average daily sick was more than sixty-three per cent. of strength present.

On the 1st of November the effective strength of all ranks in the field was 600 Officers and men ; 1st of December, 451 ; 1st of January, 353 ; 1st of February, 173 ; and at the end of February there were fewer than 100.*

---

* Wyatt, p. 58. It should not be forgotten that the two drafts (*ante*, p. 199) which reached the Battalion on November 22nd and December 18th, numbered together 211 men. It appears that there was considerable sickness and mortality among the young and unseasoned soldiers who composed the drafts.

CHAPTER XV.

OPERATIONS DURING THE WINTER.

Indignation in England, and the measures taken to relieve the army—Admirable manner in which the misfortunes were borne by the British soldiers—Testimony of the commission of inquiry —The Russians quiescent during the winter—Operations of the Allies — The French extend their siege-works — The Turks brought to the Crimea and occupy Eupatoria—Their successes at the battle there—The Guards brigade are sent to Balaklava.

BUT there was an end at last to these mournful circumstances that oppressed our forces fighting in the Crimea ; and with the first peep of spring a new era of hope dawned upon the army. The news of the winter troubles roused a strong feeling in England, and the nation was stirred to its depths with sympathy for its brave and suffering soldiers, of whom no country had more reason to be proud, and with resentment against the supposed delinquents who were accused of bringing about the disaster. Greater activity and energy were displayed at home, and a railway was begun to connect Balaklava with the front, so that by the end of March it reached the Col on the edge of the upland, at a time when the road, constructed by ourselves and the French, was made to the same place. A Land transport service was also at length organized. Subscriptions were collected, and clothing, food, stores, and even luxuries poured into the Crimea, and into the hospitals established at and near Scutari.

The Government was overturned, and a Commission of inquiry was instituted, both in England and at the seat of hostilities, to report upon every circumstance connected with the war. The result of these investigations, as well as the conclusions arrived at by another that sat later (in 1856), need not be alluded to in this volume. But one point cannot be omitted which deals with the conduct of the troops, who, in the dark hour of trial, did honour to their Queen, to their country, and to their noble profession.

"Great Britain," says the report of the Commissioners sent to the Crimea, "has often had reasons to be proud of her army, but it is doubtful whether the whole range of military history furnishes an example of an army exhibiting, throughout a long campaign, qualities as high as have distinguished the forces under Lord Raglan's command. The strength of the men gave way under excessive labour, watching, exposure, and privation; but they never murmured, their spirit never failed, and the enemy, though far outnumbering them, never detected in those whom he encountered any signs of weakness. Their numbers were reduced by disease and by casualties to a handful of men, compared with the great extent of the lines which they constructed and defended, yet the army never abated its confidence in itself, and never descended from its acknowledged military pre-eminence. Both men and Officers, when so reduced that they were hardly fit for the lighter duties of the camp, scorned to be excused the severe and perilous work of the trenches, lest they should throw an undue amount of duty upon their comrades; yet they maintained every foot of ground against all the efforts of the enemy, and with numbers so small that, perhaps, no other troops would even have made the attempt. Suffering and privation have frequently led to crime in armies as in other communities, but offences of a serious character have been unknown in the British army in the Crimea . . . intemperance has been rare. Every one who knows anything of the constitution of an army must feel that, when troops so conduct themselves throughout a long campaign, the Officers must have done their duty and set the example." *

The Russians, on the other hand, except for the great labour and care expended on the fortress, remained almost quiescent during the winter months. Restricting their energies to the defences of Sevastopol and to the annoyance of the besiegers, they made the fortress exceedingly strong, and pushed advanced works in front of the line they had already occupied. The greater portion of their field army was brought into the town to reinforce the garrison, the remainder being quartered in the neighbouring villages, or in the Tchernaya Valley. But

* First Report, 1855, pp. 2, 3.

no offensive operations were undertaken, notwithstanding their immensely superior numbers; and this was the more fortunate, since in the midwinter our forces were so weakened that the English trenches were guarded by only 350 men. This extraordinary inactivity on the part of the enemy has excited astonishment, and it may well be asked—

" how it was that an enemy who possessed such enormously superior forces in men and material, and who could, at any time during a period of months, have directed on some selected point of the siege-works thousands of troops that would have found only hundreds to meet them, did not muster the courage for such an enterprise, when it promised deliverance to the fortress and ruin to their foes." *

* Hamley, *War in the Crimea*, p. 194. Whether the Russians were destitute of the necessary courage to take advantage of the obviously favourable chances that the winter offered them of sweeping away the feeble residue of frozen and plague-stricken Englishmen that still survived before Sevastopol, or whether their conduct was the result of a deliberate design, may perhaps be revealed at some future time, when eventual consequences of the Crimean war have been fully developed. It may easily be imagined that the Government of St. Petersburg shrank from converting the existing war of cabinets, hitherto purely local, into a general struggle of nations and principles (Klapka, *War in the East*, p. 101). For had Great Britain been driven from the Crimea, she would surely have taken her revenge, and have removed the contest from a barren and useless fortress, where unhappily she became involved, to a vital point in the armour of her foe. If there were to be a war at all, it is obvious that the struggle for Sevastopol was the least expensive and the most advantageous form of hostilities that the Tsar could engage in. He lost comparatively little if the contest should prove adverse to his arms, more especially if he could prolong his

On the part of the Allies, the approaches to the fortress were pushed forward with considerable activity, both by ourselves and by the French, but there was little actual fighting except what was brought about by the siege operations. In the beginning of February, the French, who, thanks to the liberal supply of men sent to the seat of war, were growing in numbers, undertook to extend the siege-works on our right ;* thus continuing the line of trenches towards the roadstead of Sevastopol. Bosquet's Corps was employed for this purpose.

Another element of strength was brought into the field during the winter, to which brief allusion must be made. It was at last determined that Omar Pasha's army should be removed to the Crimea from Bulgaria, where it was unable to influence the course of hostilities. The concentration was effected at Eupatoria, and, on the 17th of February, before the movement was complete, the Turkish force there amounted to 23,000 men. The Russians, having reinforced the troops they had in this part of the peninsula to 20,000 men,

resistance against the united efforts of the two great Powers of Europe. The more he succeeded in doing this, the more he gained a fictitious prestige, the more he exhausted our resources, by the dissolving process which the winter must surely effect, and the more he made the Western nations beware for the future how they again attempt to thwart his plans.

* Our allies had 56,000 men in the Crimea in November, 65,000 in December, and 78,000 in January (Hamley, *War in the Crimea*, p. 176).

attacked the place on that date, and were repulsed with a loss of some 800 men.

This success seems to have been decisive, in so far that the Allies now held firmly a point within striking distance of the enemy's communications through the isthmus of Perekop ; but its value was considerably lessened by the following fact. In the autumn of 1854, General Menshikoff was dependent upon this line to draw reinforcements from Bessarabia, and, as he found it open, he advanced freely along it, and reached Sevastopol before the 5th of November, as has been already related. This advantage gained, the road through Perekop became of comparatively minor importance, and the enemy thenceforward relied upon the line from the Sea of Azof. His communications in this quarter could, of course, only be threatened by a force based somewhere in the neighbourhood of Kertch ; but that place was avoided, and Eupatoria was selected. Hence the achievement of the 17th of February, while it might have been followed by satisfactory results had it taken place early in October, was, to a certain extent, a barren victory, and served only to show that our Turkish auxiliaries were capable of performing some service in the war.*

The Guards Brigade, having suffered so severely

* Colonel (now Field-Marshal Sir Lintorn) Simmons was present with Omar Pasha as British Commissioner with the Turkish army. He served in that capacity from the summer of 1853, until the end of the war.

at Inkerman, and being the only infantry force in the front composing the First Division (the Highlanders occupied Balaklava since the 25th of October), it was necessary to reinforce that division by adding thereto the 97th Regiment (November 23rd). This regiment was armed with the old smooth-bore musket, but as sickness diminished the ranks, the Minié rifles of non-effective Guardsmen were handed over to the survivors of the 97th and of other corps similarly situated.

On the 22nd of November the position of the camps of the Grenadiers and Scots Fusiliers were moved to the spot where the Coldstream was established. Two days later, a new disposition of the piquets was ordered; of the eight furnished by the division, six were found by the Brigade and two by the 97th. The strength of these piquets, 50 men each, allowed a double sentry every fifty paces of the entire front; three piquets were placed in reserve, and all were "to be encouraged in making fires, as it is desirable that our full strength should be estimated." * On the 25th of December the piquets were reduced to 30 rank and file each.

During Colonel Upton's absence at Balaklava on sick-leave, Colonel Lockyer commanded the Division until the 15th of January, when the former returned to the front; the senior Guards Officer

* *Divisional Memo.*, Nov. 24, 1854.

present commanded the Brigade during this interval. Colonel Lord Frederick Paulet was also away on the sick-list until the 16th of January, and the Battalion during this time was under Lieut.-Colonel Newton. On the 17th of January the Brigade lost the services of their Paymaster, Captain South (late 20th Regiment), who, having been present with them ever since they left England, was obliged to leave the Crimea through ill-health. His duties were undertaken by a committee, composed of Colonel Hamilton (Grenadiers), president, and Lieut.-Colonel Stephenson (Scots Fusilier Guards), and Captain Sir J. Dunlop (Coldstream), members.

On the 26th of November the Household Brigade furnished a detachment of 200 men, under a Captain and Lieutenant-Colonel, to the neighbourhood of the monastery of St. George, on the coast west of Balaklava, for the purpose of making gabions, which were required for the siege-works. Of these, the Coldstream provided 70 men, with Officers and Non-commissioned officers in proportion. The detachment was relieved by a similar party on the 21st of December, and again on the 20th of January by 150 men, each Battalion finding a Subaltern Officer and 50 men, with the usual number of Non-commissioned officers.

Major-General Lord Rokeby arrived in the Crimea on the 2nd of February, and assumed the command of the First Division and of the Brigade. Thereupon, Colonel Upton reverted to the Battalion; but not for long, for, owing to the promotion of the Lieut.-Colonel of the Regiment, he was gazetted to that command (February 20th), and left soon after to take up his duties in London.* By this change Lord Frederick Paulet became Major of the 2nd Battalion at home, and Colonel Gordon Drummond obtained the command of the 1st, at the seat of war.

When the sick of the army left the front for Scutari, no regular information regarding them was obtained by the Regimental authorities, and to correct this serious inconvenience, a Captain and Lieutenant-Colonel from each Battalion of the Brigade was sent to inspect the hospitals where Guardsmen were treated, and to arrange a more proper system for future adoption (February 16th). Lieut.-Colonel Dudley Carleton, who represented the Coldstream, reported that the admission of men into hospital, as well as the patients' death or discharge, were imperfectly registered:

* In parting from the Battalion when it was still before the enemy, and after having held the command during a very eventful period, Colonel Upton issued an order of which the following is an extract: "He has known their gallantry and firmness before the enemy, their endurance, and their discipline under every trial and pressure. . . . To the young soldiers one word at parting: let them ever hold in view the conduct and bearing which have characterized their older comrades, that they in their turn may pass them on to others, and so uphold and carry forward the name of the distinguished Regiment of which they now form a part."

"their kits were either stored or condemned without regular authority, or were left in the hold of transports, carried up and down during many voyages, and not unfrequently plundered. When a man died, no regular record was kept or transmitted to his regiment, although professedly done. No returns whatever had been sent to the Battalion of men dead, invalided home, or otherwise employed." *

Colonel Carleton remained absent six weeks, and during this time he established a system of fortnightly returns, which thenceforward were regularly despatched to the Crimea, and he placed a sergeant of the Coldstream on the staff of the hospital at Scutari to carry it out.

It has already been mentioned that the winter troubles added to the losses incurred at Inkerman, and, in the absence of sufficient reinforcements from home, had destroyed the efficiency of the Brigade at the seat of war. At the end of January the three Battalions could hardly muster a tenth of their proper strength, and numbered only some 312 men able to do duty.† Lord Rokeby seems to have been so struck with their exhausted appearance, that he endeavoured to obtain for them an exemption from trench duty for a time; but as the Order book shows them to be still continually at

* Wyatt, 53. The three Officers were, Lieut.-Colonels Hon. C. Lindsay, D. Carleton (now Lord Dorchester), and Hon. S. Jocelyn (late Earl of Roden).

† Kinglake, vi. 204, quoting from the *Report of the Sevastopol Commission.*

work, it is evident that it was not possible to comply with the proposal. Towards the end of February, however, it was found absolutely necessary to make a complete change, and to move them to Balaklava, there to rest and to recruit their strength after the very arduous labours in which for so long they had been engaged. Accordingly, on the 22nd, the Grenadiers marched there, followed by the Coldstream on the 24th, and by the Scots Fusilier Guards about the same time. In the Regiment there were less than 100 men of all ranks on parade. For some time previously it had become manifest that, if the men continued to live under existing conditions, it was but a question of time how long the Battalion could survive except on paper. Of the sick left behind, 41 followed on the 27th, and 75 were conveyed next day by French mule transport (the usual conveyance lent us by our allies, and indeed the only transport procurable, since our own arrangements had broken down) ; but the last detachment was not removed to Balaklava until the 28th of March.* The Guards remained at the base till June, 1855 ; but though absent more than three months from the front, they missed little chance of performing any useful military service.

* Wyatt, pp. 54, 65.

PART VI.

THE FALL OF SEVASTOPOL.

CHAPTER XVI.

EVENTS OF THE SPRING OF 1855.

Stay of the Brigade at Balaklava—Improvement in the condition of the men—Return of the Guards to the front, June 16th—Changed aspect of affairs before Sevastopol—Review of events during the time spent at Balaklava—Interference by Napoleon III. in the course of the war—Second bombardment—Operations paralysed—General Canrobert resigns, and is succeeded by General Pélissier—Energy displayed by the latter—Third bombardment.

THERE are not many incidents of interest to record during the stay at Balaklava. The men were lodged in huts, but as these were situated near a burial ground and close to the stables of the Land Transport Corps, the advantages gained by a change from the fatigues and hardships of the siege to the base of operations were sadly diminished, and several cases of maculated fever for the first time appeared. In March, another site having been selected on the west side of the harbour, in a more favourable and sanitary position, and huts having been constructed, the Battalion moved there towards the end of the month. The better food, the shelter, the increased comfort, and the rest now enjoyed by the men, produced a satisfactory effect upon their health, to which the improvement in the weather also contributed ; for, the short, though terribly severe winter had passed away, and with the spring the temperature became warm and pleasant. During March, 101 men were admitted into hospital, of whom 24 were suffering from typhus, and the mortality amounted to 10 ; while next month, 53 men only were admitted, and but 5 deaths occurred.*

The Battalion were employed principally in the ordinary duties performed at the base of operations, guarding the stores and buildings or other places set apart for the use of the army, and unloading the ships that arrived in Balaklava. Drills were carried out, and the troops practised, in occupying the trenches at night, to meet any sudden attack which the enemy might contemplate.

The danger of such an attack was lessened by the fact that the enemy had relaxed his hold, as far back as the end of December, upon the heights on the left bank of the Tchernaya, captured by him on the 25th of October, though he continued to occupy the line of the river. It was still necessary to restrain his activity in this quarter, and several reconnaissances took place to prevent his advance. As was only natural, the Officers at

* Wyatt, p. 65.

Balaklava, when off duty, rode frequently to points where operations of interest were being undertaken, but the Brigade itself was not engaged at this period.

The gabion-making detachment was continued near Balaklava to supply the siege-works before Sevastopol.

Early in March, convalescents from Scutari, wounded at the Alma and at Inkerman, returned to the Battalion ; but the next (the fourth) draft did not arrive until the 1st of May, when 7 Officers and 307 men, whose average age and service were $22 \frac{1}{12}$ years and 7 months respectively, landed at Balaklava. Thereupon Colonel Lord F. Paulet (having previously been promoted to the command of the 2nd Battalion) was ordered to proceed to England, while Colonel Gordon Drummond assumed the command of the 1st Battalion in the Crimea.

As the summer approached, the weather became extremely hot, and towards the middle of May, 90 degrees were registered in the shade. Cholera again broke out among the troops, but, warned by the visitation of this plague in the previous year, every precaution then known to medical science was taken to avert it. The number of sick increased during May and June, the admissions into hospital being in the first month 134, and the deaths 5, and in the second month 267 and 36 respectively ; of the latter, 24 men died of cholera.

On the 16th of June, the Brigade returned to the front to join in the operations which were intended to be undertaken by the Allies on the 18th, the anniversary of the battle of Waterloo.* The Battalion was 488 strong (excluding Officers). Three Officers and 61 men were left behind sick, as well as 15 convalescents; altogether 111 men were abstracted from the effective strength.

On reaching the upland the old positions were scarcely to be recognized by the rank and file who had remained more than three months at Balaklava. The French having already extended the British Right Attack, occupied the ground in front of the Karabelnaya from the Dockyard Ravine, past the Careenage Ravine, and along Mount Inkerman to the heights overlooking the roadstead. Innumerable siege-works cut up the plateau, the lines were

* The Highland Brigade marched up with the Guards, and thus the First Division, under Lieut.-General Sir Colin Campbell, was once more complete before Sevastopol. Shortly afterwards the following changes were made in the British army. The Highlanders were separated from the Guards, and having several battalions added to them, formed the "Highland Division," commanded by Sir Colin Campbell. Lord Rokeby, promoted locally Lieut.-General, commanded the First Division, formed of the Guards Brigade, under Brigadier-General Craufurd; and of the 2nd Brigade, viz. a battalion of the 9th, 13th, 31st Regiments, and of the Rifle Brigade, under Colonel Ridley. About the same time, the Second, Third, Fourth, and Light Divisions were commanded by Major-Generals Markham, Eyre, H. Bentinck, and Lieut.-General Sir W. Codrington respectively. The Cavalry, under Lieut.-General Sir J. Scarlett, was divided into three brigades: the Heavy, Light, and Hussar brigades.

pushed further forward, a large force was concentrated on the spot, and the face of the country —so bleak and barren in February—was now covered with the green carpet of a luxuriant vegetation.

We must now take a hasty glance at the state of affairs prevailing before Sevastopol and elsewhere, which controlled the war, while the Guards were at Balaklava. In spite of the united efforts of the British and French occupying the ground before the Malakoff, the enemy succeeded in extending his works to his front, and in materially strengthening the lines that covered the Karabelnaya. The fact was becoming more apparent that General Canrobert, gallant soldier though he was, was not disposed to risk the chances of making a bold move against the Russians ; and that the latter, under the distinguished leadership of Colonel Todleben, were enabled thereby to prolong the struggle.

But Canrobert was not entirely his own master in this matter, for towards the beginning of the year 1855, the Emperor Napoleon interfered with the conduct of the operations in the Crimea, in a manner to impede seriously the progress of hostilities. Declaring himself to be dissatisfied with the course pursued, the Emperor conceived the idea of delaying the siege until he could isolate Sevastopol from the rest of the peninsula ;

and he even proposed to go himself to the Crimea to carry out his design. He was happily dissuaded from undertaking this latter part of the project—dangerous both on account of his inexperience in war, and because of the instability of his authority in Paris,—and it was finally abandoned, after he had been received as a guest at Windsor (April 25th). But he still adhered to his determination to enforce some hazy plan which his vanity had formed, and thereby he increased considerably the difficulties of the Allies.

Added to this, there was a renewal of negotiations at Vienna. The Tsar Nicholas died early in March, and though his successor, Alexander II., was clearly in the hands of the war faction, some feeble attempt was made to patch up a peace. The negotiations failed; but the events alluded to could not but exercise some influence over the fortunes of the war, by fettering the action of the French army engaged in it.

This appears to be shown by the results that followed the second bombardment of Sevastopol, which commenced on the 8th of April. Immense preparations had been made to ensure its success, and it was confidently expected by the Allied hosts that this bombardment would at last lead to an immediate and triumphal assault of the fortress.

"Ten days did the terrific storm of iron hail endure; ten days did the Russian reliefs, holding themselves ready to repel attack, meet wounds and death with a constancy which was of necessity altogether passive. On the 19th they saw the fire of the Allies decline, and settle into its more ordinary rate ; they saw, too, that the sappers were again at work with their approaches, and reading in this the signs of a resumption of the siege, and the abandonment of the policy of assault, they once more withdrew their sorely harassed infantry to places of shelter and repose. Then they began to reckon their losses, which amounted for the ten days, in killed and wounded, to more than 6,000 men. The French lost in killed and disabled, 1,585 men; the English, 265.*

All this expenditure of lives and of war *matériel* effected just nothing, nor was anything even attempted against the enemy ; for the French, though having an opportunity to assault, not possessed at that time by their British allies, were "kept waiting for Louis Napoleon, and were restrained from engaging in any determined attack." †

In order to accomplish the views of the Emperor Napoleon, a French army of reserve was being collected near Constantinople, and as it was expected soon to reach the Crimea—to undertake the plans which had been sketched out in Paris,—two important operations against the enemy were delayed. First, a further bombardment, arranged to take place at the end of April, and to be followed by an assault, was put off ; and secondly, an expedition,

* Hamley, *War in the Crimea*, p. 212.
† Kinglake, vii. 195 ; compare Hamley, *War in the Crimea*, p. 225.

at last agreed to, against the Russian communications in the Sea of Azof, and which had actually started to Kertch (May 3rd), was recalled.* Both these events caused much embarrassment to Lord Raglan, who, understanding imperfectly even then the Emperor's proposals, found his own plans thwarted by the supine and unintelligible conduct of his colleague.

The confidence reposed in the latter was naturally shaken ; and when, a few days later, Napoleon's scheme was fully revealed to the Allied Commanders, was discussed, and was found to be impossible of execution, General Canrobert felt his position to be intolerable, and he resigned the chief command of the French army. It is right to add that, though Canrobert's character unfitted him to direct the difficult operations which lay before him, he was well suited to assume the lower functions of a commander of a division or army-corps. Being of a loyal and soldierlike disposition, and unwilling to leave the seat of war, he begged that he might revert to the position he originally occupied in the French army when the war broke out, and recommended that General Pélissier (who had reached the Crimea in January) should be appointed the

* "I merely record that both armies were certainly, if not discontented, amazed, when an expedition which started on the 3rd of May to Kertch, to destroy Russian magazines and stores, was recalled three days later, on the receipt of a telegram from Paris" (Wood, *Crimea in* 1854 *and* 1894, p. 264).

new Commander-in-chief. These proposals were sanctioned in Paris by telegram, and were immediately carried into execution (May 19th).

The change in the French command completely altered the state of affairs in the Crimea. The vacillating weakness of Canrobert and his subserviency to the foibles of his Imperial Master, were at last replaced by the hardy daring of Pélissier and by his manly disregard of an ill-timed interference in the conduct of the war, which could only end in disaster. The forces fighting against Russia, moreover, were increasing ; while the strength of that Empire was ebbing fast. In April nearly half of Omar Pasha's Turks, about 45,000 strong, were taken from Eupatoria to the Chersonese, and next month a compact division of 15,000 Sardinians—who had joined the confederacy against Russia—landed in the Crimea, under the command of General La Marmora. The enemy about this time, by reason of his immense losses, had little more than 100,000 men in the peninsula ; the Allies were more numerous, and could dispose of about 180,000 men.* Thus, it was becoming apparent, that by vigorously pushing on the siege, Sevastopol must fall, and that the resources of Russia—so fatally allowed to accumulate in the early stages of the war—were beginning to fail.

* English, 28,000 ; French, 100,000 ; Turks, 45,000 ; Sardinians, 15,000 (Kinglake, viii. 7).

Immediate arrangements were made to storm the advanced works which Todleben had constructed, to occupy the Tchernaya and the plain of Baidar that lay beyond it, and to attack Kertch and the Russian base of supplies formed on the coast of the Sea of Azof. On the 23rd of May, after severe fighting, the French gained an important advantage over the enemy near Quarantine Bay; and, two days later, he was also attacked on the Tchernaya and driven out of Tchorgun. About the same time, the expedition to Kertch, composed of 15,000 English, French, and Turks, started for its destination. Operations in this quarter were entirely successful, and by the middle of June the Allies, having struck deep into the resources of the Russians, cut their chief line of supply, and in no small degree carried out practically the policy of investment which the Emperor professed to desire.*

* Hamley, *Crimea*, p. 242. Established now at last on the shores of the Sea of Azof, the Allies might even at this late period have inflicted a crushing blow on the enemy in the direction of Circassia, and so have brought about the end of the war, and a severe check to Russia's advance through Central Asia and towards India—the objects that Great Britain had in view when she undertook to curb the Tsar's pretensions in the East. It appears that the attention of the Foreign Secretary (Lord Clarendon) was directed at that time to this most important point; but there was a difficulty with the French, who, conceiving that they would be giving assistance to a purely English policy, would not concur in any such scheme (see Rawlinson, *England and Russia in the East*, 272 note). It must not be forgotten that Louis Napoleon disapproved of the expedition to Kertch — the one operation in the war which was

The Allied Commanders now directed their efforts to the Russian advanced works covering the Karabelnaya, and, determining to attack them, they prepared for the assault by a fierce cannonade (the third bombardment), which opened on the 6th of June with tremendous violence and effect, and lasted until the 10th. On the evening of the 7th, the French advanced against the White works (situated on Mount Inkerman, to the east of Careenage Ravine), and the Kamskatka Lunette (on the Mamelon, covering the Malakoff and some 500 yards in front of it); and the English moved against the Quarries (covering the Redan and about 400 yards from it). These attacks were successful, and the enemy, driven from all these outworks, was restricted to his main line of defence. The captured positions were occupied and held by the Allies. Between the 6th and the 10th the Russians lost altogether, in killed, wounded, and prisoners, 8500 men and 73 guns; the Allies nearly 7000 men.

These advantages were now to be pressed home, and a great effort made to assault the main line round the Karabelnaya; the Malakoff and the Redan were to be attacked, and the fortress so long besieged was at last to fall. The final act of

crowned with complete and immediate success, and which cost the Allies nothing,—and that he peremptorily ordered Pélissier to take no part in the attack on Anapa on the Circassian coast (Kinglake viii. 79).

the long drama was fixed for the 18th of June, when the Anglo-French allies, having shared so many dangers and hardships in common, might reap the reward of their arduous labours, and obliterate the memories of the day of Waterloo.

CHAPTER XVII.

END OF THE SIEGE.

Fourth bombardment; assault on Sevastopol—Its failure—Death of Lord Raglan; succeeded by General Simpson—Siege operations continued—Battle of the Tchernaya—Fifth bombardment—Sixth bombardment; the second assault—The Malakoff is captured—Failure of the assault on the Redan—Fall of the south side of Sevastopol—The Russians evacuate the town, and retreat to the north side—State in which the Allies found Sevastopol.

THE fourth bombardment opened on the 17th, and the fleets once more joined their fire to the numerous great siege guns planted before Sevastopol. The devastating force of the artillery soon obtained a mastery over that of the fortress, and the usual results followed: the enemy's works were knocked to pieces, his defences ruined, and he lost 4000 men. Now, therefore, was the time for the assault to take place, and, as we have seen, the Guards Brigade were brought up to the front from Balaklava to participate in the operations about to ensue. But the ardent expectations of the besiegers were not yet to be realized, and the attack

R

ended unfortunately. Neither in the Malakoff nor in the Redan, were the French or ourselves able to effect a lodgment; the only consolation was the capture of a position in front of our Left Attack.

Among the blunders that occurred to account for the failure, perhaps the most unfortunate was that of Pélissier himself. It had been settled that the bombardment was to continue for two hours after dawn on the 18th, so as to shatter the repairs which the Russians invariably made to their works during the night, and that then the assault was to commence at about 5.30 in the morning. But this plan was altered at the last moment, by Pélissier, who wished the advance to begin at dawn, without any previous preparation by artillery fire. Lord Raglan was not consulted, and, when he heard of it, he submitted to the change most reluctantly. The enemy, therefore, was ready, behind parapets hastily renewed and armed with field guns during the night, and thereby he was enabled to repel the attack.

That this was probably the main cause of the failure, may perhaps be inferred from the fact that when, after the assault, the bombardment recommenced, the soldierlike spirit of the Russians gave way, and many of them, unable to stand against the terrific fire poured upon them, fled to the harbour, and endeavoured to escape to the north side of Sevastopol.* The Guards Brigade were not engaged upon this occasion ; they remained in reserve, and were not brought forward. In fact, the attack had failed, and further expenditure of lives had to be avoided. The losses were great on that fatal day ; that of the English amounted to 1500, of the French to 3500, and of the enemy only to 1500.

Two Officers occupying very conspicuous positions in their respective armies disappeared from the scene of their labours about this time. General Todleben was slightly wounded on the 18th, and more gravely hurt a few days later, so that he had to leave Sevastopol, and the Russians lost the services of that master mind to whose conspicuous ability, energy, and courage, the prolonged and successful defence of the fortress was primarily due.

The Allied armies also were plunged into mourning by the unexpected death of Lord Raglan, who never recovered from the grief and disappointment which oppressed his mind after the events of the 18th. This reverse, added to the labours and anxieties of the previous fifteen months, during which time he discharged his high but onerous duties without intermission, undermined his constitution, and he died on the 28th, surrounded by his personal friends and his military staff. He was succeeded by General Simpson.†

* Hamley, *War in the Crimea*, p. 261.
† See Appendix B, containing General Orders on Lord Raglan's death.

His body was removed to England, and was taken to the Bay of Kazatch with full military honours, on the 3rd of July; and, in accordance with General Orders, the troops not engaged in the funeral or on duty in the field, remained in their tents during the afternoon. While the ceremony lasted, the Allied forces before Sevastopol were passive in the trenches, and, whether owing to chance or to a graceful act of courtesy on the part of the Russian Commander, the guns of the garrison also kept silence.*

The siege was pushed forward with great activity after the 18th, and in this portion of the weary operations the Guards Brigade took their full share. Seeing the mistake committed by advancing over open ground for a distance of 400 to 500 yards, against the *enceinte* covering the Karabelnaya, General Pélissier now proposed to sap up close to the fortress. The soil near his own siege-works favoured such an undertaking; but not so that which lay in front of our positions, where a thin layer of earth only covered the solid rock. Thus, while the French were able to get close to the ramparts of the Malakoff, the British were prevented from pushing through the ground much beyond the Quarries, or from lessening to any considerable extent the distance that separated them from their objective—the Redan.

* Kinglake, viii. 299.

END OF THE SIEGE.

These siege operations lasted without intermission until early in September. On the night of June 18th, the Brigade found 30 Officers and 1000 men for the trenches, of which the Coldstream furnished 8 Officers and 263 men ; and so on, from day to day, in varying numbers, according to the requirements of the moment. It was ordered on the 21st, that " in future the proportion of Officers and men in the trenches will be one Captain and one Subaltern to every 100 men ; " and also " should any part of the guard of the trenches be called upon to work, they are positively forbidden to take off their accoutrements or to go far from their arms." * Commencing July 10th, the duties were found by divisions — the First, Second, and Light in the Right, the Third and the Fourth in the Left Attack, —and during that night the Battalion furnished 7 Officers and 312 men, also 21 men more as a special working party.†

* *First Divisional Morning Order*, June 21st.

† Special and other working parties and shot-loading fatigues in the trenches were frequently ordered at this time. The following, relating to the duties in the trenches, may be of interest :—

Head-quarter Memo., July 10th: "General Officers of divisions will be so good as to detail not less than a Brigadier-General, three Field Officers, and two Adjutants for duty in the trenches on the days that their divisions furnish the guard, Right Attack."

Divisional Order, July 12th : " The troops will be told off to their places in the trenches before they leave their camp, and they will move off from the parade in front of the camp, after being so told off, at 6.15, so that they may all be in their places in the trenches and the relief completed by 8 o'clock, according to the General Order on the subject."

It should be noticed here, that the Guards Brigade, on August 31st, exchanged the whole of

Head-quarter Memo., July 24th: "Until further orders the guard in the trenches by night, will be 2400 men, under a General of the day with three Field Officers; of this number 600 men will work if required by the Royal Engineers, from 4 to 8 a.m., and return to their camp at 8 a.m. if it should seem prudent to the senior Officer in the trenches to dispense with them. . . . The remainder of the guard will furnish working parties as usual during the day, when required by the Royal Engineers. . . . There will be a special working party, consisting of 400 men under a Field Officer, independent of the guard of the trenches, except in case of an attack, when they will be available to be called upon by the Officer commanding in the trenches. . . . General Officers of divisions furnishing the guards in the trenches are to consider the remainder of their division as a support ready to reinforce the guard, with which they will proceed in case of alarm, and resume the command of the whole force in the trenches."

Later, in the middle of August, a reserve of 600 men was ordered "to remain in the trenches the twenty-four hours, and will be planted during the day in such spots in the 1st parallel or other places of security as may be pointed out by the Generals of the Attacks. Troops not on duty are to remain in camp till further orders" (*Head-quarter Memo.*, Aug. 16th).

Head-quarter Memo., Aug. 17th: "A steady fire of musketry by riflemen and good shots, must be kept up during the night, from the advanced trenches of both Attacks on the Redan and works in rear and flank. The object being to prevent the enemy from repairing the damage done to their works. The artillery should assist this as much as possible by throwing light balls."

Colonel Tower says that, on August 21st, he was in the 5th parallel, and that he was ordered to keep up a heavy fire all night on the embrasures. 75,000 rounds were fired from the trench in which he was stationed. He also says that the custom in the middle of August, was to withdraw the guards of the trenches to a position in rear, and to leave an Officer and small party in the advanced line to watch the enemy's works, and to fire at the embrasures when any one showed himself (Tower, *Diary*).

Towards the end of August, and during the beginning of September, more men were employed. There was a party for the their arms and ammunition for the new Enfield rifle then introduced, and that, at this time, there were two patterns in use by the troops of the British army standing before Sevastopol.*

Notwithstanding the interest which the operations undertaken between June and September excited, and the high hopes generally entertained that the fortress would soon fall, the little-varying duty in the trenches became monotonous in the extreme, and all wished earnestly that this phase of the war might quickly pass away. Some cricket matches served to while away a few of the weary hours; but the weather was extremely hot and oppressive, and the season was sickly. There was, of course, much to distract the minds of men who, for the first time, found themselves in the presence of an enemy; but it was different for those who had been almost constantly at work for many months on the same spot and at the same object, and thus even these distractions lost much of their novelty and interest.

"The siege was really getting too fearfully tedious now," writes Colonel Tower, about August 28th. "The

trenches 2800 strong, the guard as before 2400, and the special working party, 400 men. During this period, more than one division furnished the necessary daily number required.

* "After 5 p.m. on the 28th inst. the small-arm ammunition magazine on the right of the eight-gun battery in the Right Attack will contain only Enfield rifle ammunition, pattern 1853, bore ·577; the three other magazines will still be supplied with Minié rifle ammunition, pattern 1851, bore ·702."

weather was hot and sultry; our camp was a long way from the works. We used to parade about 5 p.m., having crammed in all the victuals we could get. We toiled down three miles in the sun, carrying great coat, haversack, revolver, and defiled into the zigzags before sundown; all night (if in the advance) we were straining our eyes over the parapet, momentarily expecting a *sortie*, being graped and shelled the whole time, and losing a good many of our party. The sun got up very early, and often a breeze with it, and from sunrise to sunset we had to sit in a dusty ditch, being shelled, our food—salt pork and biscuit—covered with dust and sand. The men could not show their noses over the parapet. . . . The deep blue sea stretching away, dotted with ships coming in and going out, looked so cool and nice in the distance, I used to think of home far away, and long for the siege to be over. It really seemed now as if it were drawing to a close. The bridge across the harbour had been constructed some time, and could be for no other purpose than as a means for the enemy to retire. The French pressed the enemy at the bastion Du Mât [the Flagstaff Battery] and the Malakoff; I used to spend a good deal of time in the French trenches, and knew the whole position as well as any one in the army."

The casualties in the Battalion were not very severe during these three months, and amounted to 47 wounded, of whom 6 died of their injuries. Besides this number, an Officer of the Regiment, Captain Hon. R. Drummond, was wounded, on August 25th, in the trenches, having been shot through the chest; he left the Crimea on September 6th, but died before he reached England, unfortunately, indeed, just before the steamer anchored at Spithead. The general health of the Battalion may be seen from the following table:—

	Admissions into Hospital from		Deaths from	
	Disease.	Wounds.	Disease.	Wounds.
July ..	138	20	8	1
August ..	132	15	5	3
September	65	12	2	2

Between June 20th and September 21st, 78 men returned to duty from the hospital at Balaklava; but, *per contra*, 95 men were sent down from the front for treatment during the same period.*

The Russians could do little to resist the formidable preparations made by the Allies to bring about the capture of Sevastopol. They lost heavily every day, even under the ordinary fire which the besiegers poured upon them, and, perceiving that the end of the long struggle was imminent, they resolved to make one final effort to free themselves from the forces that were closing nearer and nearer to their defences. After much consideration, General Michael Gortchakoff† determined to bring down the field army, which was established

* Wyatt, p. 86.
† General Menshikoff had been replaced in his command in the Crimea by General Gortchakoff in the spring of 1855; the same who fought on the Danube, and whose curious movements, on the day of Inkerman, have already been adverted to.

on the Mackenzie Heights and on the Belbek, into the valley of the Tchernaya, and to attack the French, Sardinians, and Turks holding that portion of the field.

On August 15th, accordingly, a general action took place in that quarter, known as the battle of the Tchernaya, between a Russian army of 48,000 infantry, 10,000 cavalry, and 272 guns, and a somewhat smaller force of the Allies, who, though they massed as many as 60,000 men, did not deploy their whole strength upon that occasion. The enemy displayed much bravery, but showed little skill. He was routed, and fell back slowly towards Mackenzie Farm, losing 69 Officers and 2300 men killed, 160 Officers and 4000 men wounded, and 31 Officers and 1700 men missing—total, 8260. The French had 1500 killed and wounded, and the Sardinians 200.*

The besieging armies expected that this battle would be accompanied by a general *sortie* from Sevastopol; but it did not take place, for the Russians were getting exhausted, and their resources were almost entirely at an end. In order to prevent any such attempt, and also to enable the French to sap up quite close to the defences of the Karabelnaya opposite to them, the Allies opened another, though only a partial, bombardment (the fifth) on August 16th, and continued

* Hamley, *War in the Crimea*, p. 271.

their fire for some days with great violence ; but no assault followed, for they were not yet ready to enact the final scene that was soon to begin.

General Gortchakoff might now have yielded the fortress which had been held so tenaciously and gloriously by the armies of the Tsar ; but, after a full inspection of the town, of its ruins, and of the miseries and horrors it contained, he came to the resolution that it was to be held to the last extremity, and that the honour of his Sovereign prevented him from either evacuating it or capitulating. He determined, therefore, to bring into Sevastopol all he could spare of his field army, and to resist to the end. Hopeless as the outlook was at this moment, he still professed to believe that he could hold out for another month.

The last and sixth bombardment commenced on September 5th, and continued, if possible, with even greater fierceness and intensity than before, till the 8th, the day set apart for the grand assault. Pélissier guarded himself this time against advancing at dawn ; and, having observed that at noon the Malakoff was usually more weakly occupied than at any other hour of the day or night, he resolved to take advantage of this circumstance, and to deliver the attack then. At noon therefore, the French, under Bosquet, were to storm the Malakoff, the Curtain near, and the little Redan ; while the English, under General Codrington, were to attack the Redan. The town defences, moreover, were to be assailed by the French opposite to them, aided by a Sardinian brigade under General Cialdini; but this movement was subject to further orders.

A very fierce fight took place at all these places, of which one alone was successful; for the French, having entered the Malakoff, secured a firm footing there, and gained that important position in the enemy's main line. Their losses were immense, not less than 3087 in killed and wounded out of 7446 men engaged in this portion of the battlefield. Everywhere else the assaults were beaten back, and the Allies could only believe at first that they had but gained an indecisive victory.

The attack on the Redan was made, as has been seen, under very difficult — almost impossible — circumstances; but, if it was only undertaken to relieve the pressure which the enemy brought to bear upon our allies near the Malakoff, our purpose was fulfilled. It is, however, difficult to believe that a diversion was all we intended to effect, since this assault was to be the final act of the great military drama which had been going on for a whole year in the Crimea, and which riveted the eyes of Europe upon Sevastopol.

The troops engaged comprised the Second and Light Divisions, 6200 strong—1700 in the first line, 1500 in support, and 3000 in reserve in the 3rd parallel; the Third and Fourth Divisions formed a main reserve; but neither the Highland nor the First Division, to which the Guards Brigade belonged, was called up to share in the action. The Brigade was posted in rear, about half a mile from the Malakoff, where a splendid view of the fighting was obtained. There was much regret among all ranks composing it that they were not allowed to advance and take part in the attack; more especially since, when the French (according to Colonel Tower) asked General Simpson to send some of his troops to help them to hold the Malakoff, the request was refused, and the First Division, or, at least, the Guards, who were close by, were not told off to perform this duty. If this is more than camp gossip, it is, indeed, to be regretted that no British troops were enabled to participate in the glory of inflicting a final reverse upon the enemy's position in the Karabelnaya.

General Simpson explains that he determined to give the honour of leading the assault to the Second and Light Divisions, because they had defended the trenches and approaches to the Redan for many months, and because of the intimate knowledge they possessed of the ground. Military critics believe that this was a "cruel kindness to the army." The two divisions were exhausted by the siege, and the knowledge of the ground is considered upon this occasion to have been a positive disadvantage, "for, in acquiring it, the troops generally lost the dash which is essential to success." Moreover, these divisions were now filled with young and only partially trained soldiers, "who paid no attention to the orders that were given;" "the companies lost all formation and cohesion from the irregular manner in which they ran forward, and they stood in confused groups behind the parapets;" "the battalions got mixed up;" in fact, "the young, raw recruits failed to follow their leaders in the way in which the soldiers had done at the Alma and Inkerman." * On the other hand, there were fresh troops available; the Guards had only shortly before come up to the front from Balaklava, where they passed three and a half months, and the Highlanders had been there between October and June. Neither, as we know, were employed in the assault, much to their disappointment and chagrin.

All this, however, is only one side of the story. The task before the British was, under any circumstances, most difficult to fulfil. They had to advance over the open for a considerable distance, against a strong work, covered in front by obstacles, whose rear was unenclosed, and whose fire was unsubdued. It had been impossible to construct *places d'armes* in our trenches, owing to the rocky nature of the soil, and hence the

* Wood, *Crimea in 1854 and 1894*, pp. 370-378.

reserves could not be concentrated in suitable positions, whence to push forward at the proper moment, and feed the attack.

Nevertheless, the leading British troops advanced with the utmost gallantry and spirit, notwithstanding the furious fire to which they were exposed; they penetrated into the Redan, and clung to the position they had gained. But they could not maintain themselves there; for the Russians, hurrying up in immense numbers, forced them to retire before the reserves—hampered in the narrow trenches—were able to advance to their support. The French, moreover, having spiked the guns they found in the Malakoff, had none to turn upon the enemy as he entered the Redan in force to drive out our storming parties. After this failure, the attack was put off to the following day; our losses amounted to 2271 Officers and men, those of the French to 7567, and of the Russians to 12,913.*

But there was no necessity to renew the combat; for the enemy, aware of the strength of the Malakoff position, which commanded the whole of the defences of Sevastopol, evacuated the south side during the night of the 8th–9th, and withdrew to the northern bank of the roadstead, blowing up

* Hamley, *War in the Crimea*, pp. 278-285. The 23rd Royal Welsh Fusiliers, in support, lost, in killed and wounded, 15 Officers out of 18, and 197 men out of five companies (Wood, *Crimea*, loc. cit.).

his magazines, and firing the town in several places. The Allies had thus early intimation of the impending fall of the fortress which for so long had withstood their valour; but the full extent of the victory was scarcely appreciated before the morning of the 9th, when the enemy's retreat became known to the armies engaged. The evacuation of the Redan was first ascertained by some Highlanders in the trenches in the night, who, stalking up to the ditch and abatis that was near it, found the work tenanted only by spiked guns and by dead men.

"N——, who knew my wandering tendencies, came to me in the middle of the night before daybreak, and told me to get up at once, that some one had come out of the trenches, and that the Redan was evacuated. I got on Bono Johnnie and galloped off about daylight. I arrived at our trenches, which I found occupied by the Highland Division; they were fast putting out a line of sentries to prevent any one going over to the Russian works. . . . I went across the hill towards the Malakoff, the ground literally paved with iron; the great high parapet was already broken down, and in the afternoon the ditch was filled in with gabions and a regular road made into the work. Dead and dying inside the work; such a scene of devastation and confusion impossible to conceive: guns broken and upset; powder in the embrasures, two or three inches deep, all loose on the ground; wounded men, French and Russians, still crawling about, and the trenches full of Russians who had crept in. . . . From the top of the parapet our trenches were spread out like a map. I was wild with delight at thinking the siege was over, and all the country opened to us. I posted off to the White barracks, and ransacked the whole place, coming back through the Redan." *

The Allies did not enter the town on the 9th, for Sevastopol was a blazing mass of ruins, and the frequent explosions showed the place to be undermined. The garrison having escaped under cover of the night, when we were unaware of their intention, could not be further pressed at that moment, so there was no object to serve by sending the troops into a fire-trap. A terrible conflagration raged, and to this was added the burning and the final destruction of the Russian Black Sea fleet. The minds of our men could be well filled with awe and joy at the wonderful sights that met their gaze—awe at the fiery furnace the enemy kindled to mark his departure from the stronghold he had held so audaciously and bravely, and joy that the protracted siege was at last concluded.†

Early on the 10th, the fires had ceased, and the conquerors, advancing to secure their prize, found one great building intact. Having penetrated into it, they were amazed to discover that it was a hospital containing no less than 2000

* Tower, *Diary*, Sept. 9, 1855.
† The Battalion Order dated the 9th, "The Battalion will parade for inspection of necessaries at 9 a.m. to-morrow, Officers in blue coats, etc.," shows that the ordinary routine of military duty was never relaxed.

dead and dying men, who had been left to their fate without food or treatment for two days and nights, in the midst of the dire confusion and chaos that prevailed in the town; among them were three English Officers.* At midday on the 13th, a fatigue party of 500 men of the First Division, under Major Ponsonby, Grenadier Guards, were ordered into the town to help to cleanse it, and to bury the numerous dead. The duty was a disagreeable one, as may well be imagined; it was well performed, as can be seen from the following Divisional Memorandum, dated September 15th:—

"The General Commanding the Forces expresses, through Lieut.-General Lord Rokeby, his regret at being obliged to employ the Brigade on the disagreeable fatigue duty of Thursday last, but which, for the health of the army, was absolutely necessary; and he was fully satisfied with the manner in which that duty was performed."

The French now occupied the town of Sevastopol, and the English the Karabelnaya, where regular guards were established. The British troops (500 each day from the Brigade) were employed, with a working pay of 1s. 6d. a day, in making a main road from Balaklava to the front, and others in the neighbourhood, under the superintendence of Lieut.-Colonel Hon. A. Hardinge, Coldstream Guards.

* Hamley, *Crimea*, p. 286; Nolan, ii. 473.

It should be stated here, that, on the 27th of August, Lord Stratford de Redcliffe, Ambassador at Constantinople, reached the Crimea for the purpose of investing several Officers with the Order of the Bath. The ceremony took place at the British head-quarters, in the presence of General Pélissier and his Staff. The Guards Brigade furnished a Guard of Honour; the Coldstream, the Queen's Colour, the Ensign and Lieutenant (Lieutenant Whitshed), and 50 men; and the Scots Fusilier Guards, the Captain and Lieutenant-Colonel, the Lieutenant and Captain, and 50 men. Among those on whom the honour was conferred, connected with the Regiment or to be connected with it, were Lieut.-Generals Sir Colin Campbell, Sir H. Bentinck, and Sir W. Codrington.

The Brigade paraded in review order on the 20th of September, for the purpose of receiving medals and clasps, which were distributed to the Officers, Non-commissioned officers, and men, who had landed in the Crimea before the 1st of October, 1854.

Early in October, 1855, new reinforcements reached the Battalion. On the 2nd, 24 convalescents arrived for duty from Balaklava, as against 7 invalids sent to England next day. On the 4th, the fifth draft landed from home, consisting of 8 Officers and 207 men, whose average age was 24 years, and service 15 months. "They were principally volunteers from the Militia, and a remarkably fine body of men, not so tall as the original Guardsmen, but in every way better adapted [than the former drafts had been] for the exigencies of active service." *

* Wyatt, 86.

PART VII.

THE END OF THE RUSSIAN WAR.

CHAPTER XVIII.

HOW THE UNFINISHED WAR LANGUISHED.

Home events during the war—Sympathy of Her Majesty with her Crimean soldiers—Badges of distinction added to the Colours—Inactivity of the Allies after the fall of the south side of Sevastopol—Causes for this—Small expeditions against the Russian coast—The fall of Kars—Sir W. Codrington succeeds as Commander of the Forces—The winter 1855-56—Negotiations for a peace, which is concluded, March 30th, 1856.

THE details of the great struggle in the Crimea have necessarily occupied so much of the space of this volume, that there has been little opportunity to allude to the occurrences connected therewith which took place at home during this eventful period. It will therefore be well to pause in the narrative of the war, and to devote a few lines to that subject.

The principal duty of the home Battalion was naturally at this moment to train and supply men to the 1st Battalion in the Crimea, and we have already seen something of the quality of the drafts that were sent out to the East.* But as the

* See Appendix, C.

ordinary recruiting was not sufficient to maintain the forces at the seat of war in a proper state of efficiency, the militia—the true reserve of the British army at that time—was called upon to perform its functions in the emergency. Not only was a portion of the militia embodied and employed as garrisons in those places where regular troops were not available, but volunteers were obtained from its ranks to fill up the gaps which the war created in the active army fighting before Sevastopol. In this manner men of good physique and trained to military service were obtained, and were drafted into the regular army. In April, 1854, the Non-commissioned officers and men of the Brigade told off to assist in training militia regiments, were ordered to use their best exertions to induce men to volunteer for their Regiments.*
In December, 1854, Officers of the Brigade were employed to superintend recruiting from the militia. Men were also obtained from the Irish Constabulary, and it was settled, December 18, 1855, that volunteers to the Guards from that corps might reckon their previous police service as military service.

It appears that there was an intention to form a Brigade depôt at Malta, in March, 1855, the companies to form which were to be borne on the strength of the Battalions in the East, from

* *Brigade Order*, April 1, 1854.

EVENTS AFTER THE SIEGE. 265

the date of embarkation. But this plan was not carried out, and the home Battalions remained all through the war with twelve companies, as against eight companies belonging to the service Battalions; the drafts to the latter were always furnished direct from London.

It is well known to all her subjects that Her Majesty the Queen followed the varying fortunes of the Russian war with the utmost attention, interest, and concern; and that to none was her warm sympathy more heartily and graciously expressed than to her gallant army, who, amid unparalleled privations and difficulties, maintained intact the glory of the British Crown and of the country. Frequently did Her Majesty, surrounded by the Royal Family at Buckingham Palace, personally see such of her wounded soldiers as were able to be brought into the presence of their Sovereign, and there praise them for their merit, and condole with them on their sufferings. This honour was freely bestowed on the men of the Brigade, and on many occasions the Commanding Officers of Regiments were ordered to furnish lists of Guardsmen who were well enough to participate in it.

In 1855, the Queen's birthday was celebrated on the 18th of May, and on the Horse Guards parade, Her Majesty presented medals for service in the Crimea to all Officers and to three Non-commissioned officers and twenty privates per Regiment of the Brigade, entitled to receive them. Next day the following Order was published:—

"The Field Officer in Brigade Waiting is commanded to express to the Officers and soldiers of the Brigade of Guards who were present yesterday at the ceremony of the presentation of medals, Her Majesty's solicitude as to whether they have suffered from the effort which evidently many of them made, at the cost of much suffering and inconvenience, and requests that Officers Commanding Battalions will make the necessary inquiries, and forward the result of them to him with as little delay as possible."

When the fall of Sevastopol was known in England, there was much rejoicing that the Allied arms had captured the enemy's stronghold and great naval arsenal in the Black Sea. But hostilities were not at an end, nor was an immediate peace in prospect. Nevertheless, certain distinct stages in the war were concluded, and victory had more than once smiled upon our standards. A General Order, therefore, was issued on the 16th of October, 1855, giving authority to inscribe the words "Alma," "Inkerman," "Balaklava," and "Sevastopol" upon the Colours of the regiments taking part in these actions and in the siege. On the following December 28th the three badges of distinction, "Alma," "Inkerman," and "Sevastopol," were inscribed upon the Colours of the Regiments of Foot Guards.

EVENTS AFTER THE SIEGE. 267

The Allied armies, having captured the south side of the fortress that so long resisted their skill and courage, found themselves placed in considerable embarrassment. The question naturally arose as to what should now be done. But that question was not readily answered, because no steps had been taken beforehand to decide it. The northern side was still held by the Russians, and their forces there were closely united to their field army, which occupied defensive positions on the Mackenzie Heights. The undertaking to clear the two banks of the Sevastopol roadstead of the enemy, and to drive him out of the peninsula had the outward appearance of a difficult operation, and no measures had been concerted to proceed with it.* The Anglo-French armies made no attempt to follow up the victory of the 8th of September, but hung listlessly on the ground they had won, deliberating as to their future movements, and doing nothing to secure success. In short, though the capture effected brought prestige to the besiegers, and placed in their power the fleet, the docks, and most of the forts at Sevastopol, no further advantage seemed likely to accrue, and we found ourselves almost as far as ever from exercising a coercive control over the councils of the Tsar.

* It will be remembered that the north side of Sevastopol commands the south side. The capture of the former would have jeopardized the latter; but the fall of the south side left the other intact.

As a matter of fact, General Gortchakoff was by no means as strong as he was supposed to be, and could scarcely have maintained himself in the Crimea had he been vigorously attacked by the brave forces that had invariably beaten his troops whenever they met them in the field. His position, indeed, was very precarious—so precarious was it, in the opinion of his own Government, that he had the fullest liberty given him to evacuate the peninsula if he found it necessary to do so. But he was not obliged to resort to this painful and humiliating measure; for the Allies never pressed him. Far from making any effort to dislodge him, or from even manœuvring against him to ascertain how he was circumstanced, they kept almost entirely aloof, and they left him alone in peace.

The British Government, sincerely desirous to achieve a more important success than had been gained, urged that the war should be vigorously prosecuted. They poured troops into the Crimea, so that our army there in November numbered as much as 51,000 men, of whom 4000 were cavalry, and 96 guns, besides a Turkish legion, raised by England, of 20,000, and a German legion of 10,000. The transport was now completely re-organized, and the medical service in good working order; and, added to this, the fleet, always overwhelmingly strong, was more powerful than it had been before.*

* Hamley, *War in the Crimea*, p. 296. These forces continued to increase, and by Christmas, 1855, the British army in the Crimea

A campaign was now at last possible against an enfeebled enemy under far better conditions than had been the case in the same season of the previous year, when we invaded Russia, whose resources then were practically unimpaired. The English people, also, were at one with their Government, and were anxious for a vigorous prosecution of hostilities, if the enemy could not be otherwise subjugated.

But they and their rulers could effect nothing, for our allies would not move, and above all things was it necessary that the alliance should be cordially maintained. Hence, our political relations with the French interfered with our national interests, and controlled our military operations against the enemy: and, as has happened in the past, and will again happen, in wars conducted by several nations, the common foe reaped no inconsiderable benefit by having a confederation of Powers ranged against him.

In short, the fall of a part of Sevastopol practically brought the drama to a close. The efforts of the besiegers to take the town, after they had allowed it to grow into military importance, seemed to exhaust the further zeal and ardour of the Emperor

was still more numerous than is stated in the text, and there were 120 guns; besides, a reserve force was collected at Aldershot, and amounted to over 18,000 men in April, 1856; at which time it appears we had in the East about 60,000 men (excluding transport, etc.).

Napoleon. It was impossible for us to re-kindle them into activity. Nor could Marshal Pélissier be roused to action; his enthusiasm for the success of the struggle had now grown cold, and his former energy had evaporated. His troops had taken the Malakoff, the key of the fortress, and, proud of their victory over the enemy, the French were content with the glory their army had achieved. So, also, had the Emperor gained all he wanted to secure; and, the war having established him firmly on the throne, he was anxious for peace with Russia, and for some new and more profitable adventure.

And yet something had to be done to preserve the semblance of war. The Turks, already at Eupatoria, were therefore reinforced, and some successful reconnaissances were effected in that important quarter: operations were, moreover, continued on the shores of the Sea of Azof, with advantage to the Allies; and lastly, after threatening Odessa, a descent was made upon Kinburn and its neighbourhood. These desultory expeditions served to keep up the illusion that the fight was still earnestly maintained. But they led to no permanent results, and they need not be further described; because, under the circumstances and conditions in which they were undertaken, they only exercised, and could only exercise, a very minor influence on the war.

Omar Pasha had at last (end of September) been allowed to take a portion of his hitherto inactive army—chained for no useful purpose in the Crimea — to attempt the relief of Kars, a Turkish stronghold in Armenia, then besieged by the Russians. He was only barely supported by the Allies, if indeed he was not hampered by them, and he failed to accomplish his object. Kars fell on the 28th of November, and the victory gained there by the enemy compensated him not a little for the reverse he sustained at Sevastopol. The French might view the incident with unconcern ; but to England, having vital interests in Asia, the loss of this place was of far greater moment.*

The Brigade remained on the upland of the Chersonese, with the bulk of the British army, guarding the Karabelnaya, constructing roads, drilling, practising musketry, and performing the ordinary duties of camp life.† A tent had been

* While this important event was taking place, the bulk of the British army was engaged in improving the communications of the Chersonese—a work which cost us much labour and was of little use to us, though shortly afterwards, when the peace was signed, it was of great value to the Russians.

† The duties in the Karabelnaya district were composed of seven guards, amounting all told to 2 Captains, 4 Subalterns, 12 sergeants, 2 drummers, 12 corporals, and 249 privates.

At first the Brigade supplied 500 men daily for road-making ; but later in the year these parties were frequently double that strength. It also furnished large fatigue-parties of several hundred men to bring up huts from Balaklava, wherein to lodge the troops. Musketry, converted into a Crimean Guards Club, "where we used all to meet, read the newspapers, talk, and smoke," and there the first anniversary of the battle of the Alma was duly celebrated by a dinner. There were races at Kamara on the 17th of October, shooting expeditions, and other expedients to pass away the time. Occasionally an interchange of shots took place across the roadstead that divided the hostile armies; but they were rather signals to show that the war had not yet officially come to an end than anything else, and they never produced any important results.

The monotony of these proceedings during an inactive campaign, and in the presence of an unsubdued enemy, was one day electrified into new life by a terrible explosion that occurred in the lines of our allies. On the 15th of November, 100,000 lbs. of powder blew up in the French artillery park, and kindled a fire that placed one of the principal English magazines in imminent danger. Looking from the British camp, a huge column of smoke was seen to ascend high in the air; it then spread out like a tree,[*] broke, and sent down a shower of iron, stones, rubbish, broken

---

moreover, was carried out with considerable energy during the winter months, and special orders on the subject were issued by the Commander of the Forces.

[*] Pliny describes the great eruption of Vesuvius which overwhelmed Pompeii, as having at first the appearance of a gigantic pine tree emerging from the volcano.

side arms, guns, gun carriages, and every conceivable appurtenance of war; shells burst in all directions, and other combustibles added their flames to the conflagration. Happily the fire was got under without further mishap, but many Officers and men, mostly French, were killed and wounded.*

On the 11th of November, a few days before the accident just mentioned, General Sir James Simpson having resigned, Lieut.-General Sir William Codrington was appointed by Her Majesty the Queen to the chief command of the British army in the Crimea. This Officer, a Coldstreamer, served in the Regiment from 1823 until July, 1854, when,

* Nolan, ii. 638.
It appears that our troops had cause to be somewhat accustomed to this class of misadventure. Under date Nov. 14th, Colonel Tower writes, "On guard in the Redan; as I was walking about inside the works, I met two of my men who were off duty, with pipes in their mouths, wandering about. I cautioned them, and told them there had been many accidents. A short time afterwards my sergeant came rushing up to me with all his eyebrows singed off, to tell me Goodram and Bates (the two men) were buried alive in a Russian magazine. I got Engineers, and we dug for a long time in smoking ruins; at last we came upon them, burnt to cinders, and hardly a bone in either of their bodies that was not broken. . . . They died soon after we got them out. Goodram was a most gallant fellow, and would have got the V.C. for going into the Redan with the assaulting party on the 8th of September. They had trodden on a fougasse left, probably on purpose, by the enemy when he evacuated."

Private Goodram, it appears, slipped out of camp at night, September 7th–8th, crept close to the Redan in the dark, and joined the leading files of the storming party. He greatly distinguished himself during the assault, and is said to have been the first man to reach the parapet of the work.

T

as junior Acting-Major of the 1st Battalion, and present with it in Bulgaria, he was promoted Major-General. Remaining at the seat of war, he very soon obtained the command of a brigade in the Light Division, as has been previously recorded. At the head of this gallant brigade he greatly distinguished himself at the battle of the Alma by his cool and intrepid bearing. The part he played at Inkerman has already been mentioned. He was with the army from start to finish of the war against Russia, being present on the upland before Sevastopol throughout the whole of the first severe winter (except once for the space of a very few days, when on the sick list), and engaged in all the fights (usually in executive command) that took place round and in the Redan. Few Officers in the British army were more exposed to the dangers and the privations of this war than Sir W. Codrington, and he survived both without a scratch and without even a temporary illness of a serious nature.

The second winter was now approaching, and hostilities, while they showed no sign of coming to an end, still languished. But it was passed under very different conditions to those which prevailed during the terrible season that overtook us in 1854–55. The autumn was fine and enjoyable, and the real cold weather was not felt until the end of November. We were then quite prepared for it, so that the army did not suffer. The health of the troops was excellent, and for some time prior to the end of 1855 there was such an abundance of every kind of supply, that scarcely any requirement remained for the Medical Officer in charge to suggest.

"During the six months which ensued from the commencement of January, 1856, until the period of embarkation from the Crimea to England, the condition of the men, in every respect, both as regards amount of sickness and duties performed, was so much allied to a similar period passed in any garrison, that a detailed notice would be useless, except so far as it would display an almost unprecedented amount of good health, compared with a period passed at any of the out-quarters at which the Guards are stationed in England, and far better than obtains in the close and confined barracks of the Metropolis." *

Both in respect to the comfort and the good administration which our men now enjoyed, we contrasted very favourably with the French, who, though they were better off than we had been in the winter 1854-55, did not improve their services as we had done; they consequently fared worse than the British army in the cold season of 1855-56, and suffered considerably in the spring of 1856.

When Sevastopol was in the power of the Allies,

---

* Wyatt, 91. Written in 1858, before the small London barracks in Portman Street and St. George's ceased each to contain the headquarters and the main portion of a Guards Battalion.

they destroyed its value, as much as they could, as a naval arsenal, and thus the docks, all the forts in their possession, the barracks, and the aqueducts that led into the town were demolished. These tasks were accomplished in the mid-winter.

On the 1st of March the sixth and last draft reached the 1st Battalion, consisting of 8 Officers and 263 men, whose average age and service amounted to 23½ years and 18 months respectively. The men were stout and robust, and, like the preceding draft, well adapted for all the possible requirements of active service.*

Ever since the capture of Sevastopol, the work of diplomacy had again been active at Vienna; and with some additional advantage this time to the Russians, for it succeeded in partially alienating the Emperor Napoleon from the alliance. In form that Sovereign remained true to Great Britain; but it was clear that, as far as he was concerned, the war was at an end, and that the Tsar had no more to fear from his animosity. This facilitated the action of Austria, and under her mediation a project of peace was accepted by the Russians on the 16th of January, 1856. A month later a Conference sat in Paris to settle an immediate armistice and to conclude a general peace.

The Treaty of Paris was accordingly signed on the 30th of March, and it put an end finally to

* Wyatt, p. 91.

the war that had lasted two years. By the terms of this agreement, which yielded back to their original Sovereigns all territories in possession of either of the combatants, an important article was included, viz. the Black Sea was neutralized, its waters and ports were "formally and in perpetuity interdicted to the flag of war," naval arsenals on its shores were not to be maintained, and ships of war were forbidden to enter or pass through the Dardanelles and the Bosphorus.

It is of interest to record the fact that this article, to gain which England had expended so much blood and treasure, was infringed by Russia in 1859, who, with no one to interfere in the neutralized sea, blockaded the Circassian coast, and at last overcame the stubborn resistance of the liberty-loving tribes of the Caucasus that for so long checked her progress in Central Asia. Having accomplished this work she then boldly repudiated the article, with scarcely a protest on our part, in the beginning of 1871, when we were at peace with her, just fifteen years after the conclusion of the Crimean war; and again she prepared her forces to effect another development of the Eastern Question.

On the 2nd of April official tidings of peace were communicated to the several armies engaged in the struggle, by a salute fired upon the upland. Thenceforward the contending forces, drawn together by that mutual respect and esteem with which brave men regard one another, looked upon each other as friends, and all traces of hostility vanished as if by magic. British and Russian soldiers were to be seen in scores on their respective sides of the Tchernaya, conversing as best as they could, and exchanging presents. The thoughts of our men, however, were now naturally turned towards home; but two months were still to elapse before the Coldstream quitted the soil on which they had for so long lived and suffered, and where their military virtues had been so conspicuously displayed.

About this time the French appointed a special mission to inquire into the relative sanitary conditions of the English and French field hospitals in the East, and Assistant-Surgeon Wyatt was sent to aid in the investigation made.

"The whole of the Field hospitals," says Dr. Wyatt, "were inspected, and the most satisfactory conclusions drawn by the Inspector in favour of the detached system of Regimental hospitals in the English army, compared with the congregated ambulance arrangements of the French; he was very favourably impressed with the Field hospitals of the Guards, which he examined most minutely in all their details."

Added to this, British Sanitary Commissioners made an inspection of the hospitals in the Crimea, and it is with satisfaction that portions of two paragraphs of the report are recorded here.

"The best example of a marquee hospital was that belonging to the Guards, after they went to the front in June, 1855. . . . Among the best examples of a winter camp which came under the notice of the Commission during the winter of 1855, was that of the Brigade of Guards on the plateau, in laying out of which great care and intelligence had evidently been bestowed. There was plenty of space for allowing the air to circulate; the arrangement of the huts was good, the ground was well trenched and drained, and many of the huts were raised on stone foundations."*

Shortly before the conclusion of the peace an event of great interest to our allies took place (March 16, 1856)—the birth of a son to the French Emperor, an heir destined, it was confidently hoped, to preserve the Napoleonic dynasty, and to hand down to posterity the glory of the great founder of the Imperial House. Rejoicings were unstinted in Paris and in London; and in the former place, where the peace Conference was sitting, the representatives of all the Powers, not excluding Russia, added their congratulations to the happy Emperor. Nor was the auspicious occasion forgotten in the Crimea, where it was celebrated by a ball on the 1st of April.† And yet how fickle is Fortune, and

* Wyatt, 92, 93.
† "A ball will be given to-morrow, in honour of the birth of the Imperial Prince, by the Officers of the 1st Division of the Corps of Reserve French army, in their camp on the Woronzoff road, near the Sardinian army, to which all the English ladies and the Officers of the English army are invited. Officers attending the ball will appear in full dress uniform, but without swords and spurs" (*Head-Quarter Memo.*, March 31, 1856).

how cruelly she decided against this unfortunate prince! He did not ascend the French throne, and was but a lad of fourteen years of age when he was condemned to fly from his native land, never to return to it. Napoleon III., overwhelmed by the united might of Germany, was driven from his capital in 1870, and a few years later he ended his days an exile in England. Living in our midst, his son, the Prince Imperial, served in the British army, and lost his life, when only twenty-three years of age, in a small skirmish in South Africa; and thus he died before any new phase among his unstable countrymen, could recall him in the character of a pretender to the French Imperial Crown. *Sic transit gloria mundi.*

CHAPTER XIX.

RETURN OF THE TROOPS, AND SUMMARY.

Events after the cessation of hostilities—A British cemetery in the Crimea—Embarkation and return home—Regimental Crimean statistics—British losses during the war—Computation of Russian losses—The Crimean Guards Brigade at Aldershot; visit of Her Majesty the Queen—Move to London, and cordial reception there—Distribution of the Victoria Cross—Summary of events connected with the war.

THE interval between the conclusion of hostilities and the departure from the Crimea was eagerly seized by many to visit their late enemy and the places of interest to be found in the peninsula. A few extracts from the diary of Colonel Tower will perhaps give a fair example of these experiences.

"*April 8th.*—Rode to Mackenzie Farm to visit the Russian camp; the Russian Officers were extremely civil, and showed us all round their camp. The men lived in excavations in the ground, like cellars, two or three steps down, with a roof of branches or anything to make it waterproof; fusty little holes, and the usual Russian soldier's smell. This is very peculiar, the tan of the leather is the chief ingredient, and the sour smell of the black bread is another powerful ingredient. They are decidedly unclean in their persons, and never appear without their long brown coats and high boots. . . . They seem to be always fetching water in their tins. The Officers seemed as pleased as we were that the war was over, and regaled us with whatever liquor they had, generally champagne.

"*April* 13*th*.—We all went in a body to the Mackenzie heights [*i.e.* with Sir W. Codrington and his Staff], and were received by Luders [the Russian General then in command] and his Staff. A capital luncheon with every sort of delicacy was prepared for us, Pélissier and his Staff also being there. About 10,000 Ruskis passed us in review, as they were being sent away northwards. It was very interesting, as we saw specimens of almost every branch of the Russian service. . . . A great many Officers of the Guards who had volunteered for service in the Crimea, marched past with the regiments to which they were attached; also cavalry Officers with their sabres and spurs in the infantry. They point their toes as they march past, like the Prussians.

"*April* 17*th*.—Luders returned Codrington's and Pélissier's visit, and came down to have an exhibition of the English and French armies. We were in line of contiguous columns, nearly 30,000 strong and 86 guns (no cavalry), all in the most perfect order; I never saw anything so well as our troops looked. The men had their best clothing on; regiments all made up to their full strength; artillery with new harness, horses in first-rate condition. I saw one of the Russian Generals separate himself from the Staff, and ride down between the Grenadiers and our Battalion, to see the size of the men and depth of the column; he kept muttering exclamations of surprise and admiration, and well he might. I think 30,000 puts it under the mark. The French were in line with big intervals between their regiments, which made a line extending almost to Kamiesh, and it must have been very tiring riding all along such a line, but I suppose they thought it would make them appear stronger. It would have looked much better if they had also been in contiguous columns.

"*April 25th.*—Rode with General Craufurd [Commanding Guards Brigade] and Percy Feilding to the Alma; we got there easily in the mid-day, and spent all the afternoon stepping the distance from the river to the epaulment, clambering up where the French ascended the steep bank, looking for Horace Cust's grave. We found the field of battle exactly as we left it, not a spade was put into the ground in the valley, not a vine cultivated or a house rebuilt. It had quite the appearance of a 'Field of blood.'

"Next day, off at daybreak to Bakshiserai—a good big town, full of soldiers and Officers who were quartered there. We went by appointment to our friend Trubetskoi, who had a very good house and put us up famously; he introduced us to a set of Ruski Officers, who were the most rollicking and debauched set I ever came across. They had a tremendous orgie in our honour, drinking, singing, etc.; they mix every liquor they can get together. . . . Percy and I rode back to our camp that evening (the 27th), after taking leave of Trubetskoi, who really did all he could to make our expedition pleasant."

So the days passed on, varied, besides duty, by *fêtes* of pleasure, excursions, cricket matches, and races, until the embarkation took place, and the Battalion returned to England. But, prior to this event, a solemn duty was performed, and a resting-place for the dead was prepared, where the remains of those who had fallen in the war might be laid. A site selected on Cathcart's Hill was enclosed, and a portion of it was devoted as a burial place for the Brigade. A number of masons from the Guards were employed, early in April, to build a suitable wall, and fatigue parties were furnished to finish the work. The bodies of most of the Officers and others, killed at Inkerman and elsewhere in the vicinity, were exhumed, and reverently interred in the new cemetery.

The masses of the dead, however, could not then be removed there, so, instead, the places where they lay were carefully fenced in. But this arrangement did not last, because the enclosures became dilapidated through time, and the graves were liable to be desecrated.

A few years ago this was remedied, and the bones of the departed, together with the monuments erected by the care of their comrades, were taken to Cathcart's Hill, and are there preserved in perpetuity within the cemetery which had been first laid out in the spring of 1856.

The welcome news that the Battalion was to be sent back home, published on the 3rd of June, was preceded by a Divisional Order of Lieut.-General Lord Rokeby, commanding the First Division, dated the 2nd :—

"As the embarkation of the various regiments will shortly cause the dissolution of the First Division, Lieut.-

General Lord Rokeby wishes to permit himself the pleasure of expressing the grateful thanks he entertains of the support he has received from all ranks during the period he has had the honour of being in command. Every one has at all times endeavoured to meet his wishes, and the Lieut.-General confidently believes that the record of the army will afford proof of the good results which have emanated from the cheerful spirit of obedience which has characterized the conduct of the noble regiments and corps of which it was formed. The state of the hospitals and the general health of the regiments, under God's blessing, speaks for and forms the best reward of the Divisional and Regimental Medical Staff, and the Lieut.-General requests Dr. Williams, and all junior to him in that Department, to accept their full share of the thanks he presumes to offer to all ranks, and the wishes he forms for their prosperity and happiness."

On the 4th of June, the Battalion embarked at Kamiesh Bay, and sailed from the Crimea in H.M.S. *Agamemnon*, arriving at Spithead on the 28th, whence they were sent by train to Aldershot camp.

They had been absent on foreign service for 2 years and 126 days (856 days), which time was passed in the following places: Malta, 48 days; Scutari, 45 days; Bulgaria, 75 days; Crimea, 627 days; and at sea 61 days.

The strength on embarkation from England (February, 1854) had been 35 Officers and 919 Non-commissioned officers and men, and during the period of duty in the East, reinforcements amounting to 1141 men were sent out in six drafts, making a total of 2060 men who served in the war.

The number of primary admissions from all causes into the Regimental and general hospitals was 3101, of which 2785 were from disease, 243 from wounds, and 73 from accidental injuries. Death reduced the Battalion by 699 men, of whom 81 were killed in action, 54 died from wounds, and 564 from disease. Sixty-five men were invalided home by wounds, and 187 by disease; and 111 men were finally discharged the army on account of disabilities contracted during active service— 59 from the effects of wounds, and 52 from those of disease.* Total loss of Non-commissioned officers and men, 810.

Ninety-one Coldstream Officers were employed in the Russian war. Of these, nine were killed in action, viz. Lieut.-Colonels Hon. T. Vesey Dawson and J. C. Cowell; Captains L. D. MacKinnon, H. M. Bouverie, Hon. G. Eliot, Horace Cust, and F. Ramsden; and Lieutenants E. A. Disbrowe and C. H. Greville. One died of wounds, viz. Captain Hon. R. Drummond. Three died of disease, viz. Lieut.-Colonel Hon. R. Boyle, Colonel Trevelyan, and Captain Hylton Jolliffe. Total loss of Officers, thirteen. Seven were wounded, viz. Major-General Sir H. Bentinck, Colonel Hon. G.

* Wyatt, 97; see Appendix D.

Upton, Lieut.-Colonels J. Halkett, Lord C. Fitz-Roy, Hon. P. Feilding, and C. Baring, and Captain Hon. W. Amherst. Seventeen were invalided on account of illness, of whom seven were unable to return to the Crimea. Several were obliged to leave the seat of war on promotion, and altogether twenty-two seem to have done duty at least twice before Sevastopol.

The results of the war were indeed dearly purchased. According to a return presented to Parliament, 390 Officers and 20,425 Non-commissioned officers and men of the British army were killed or died of wounds or of disease in the Crimea, and 14,718 men were invalided at the conclusion of the war, bringing the total casualties up to 35,533 of all ranks. But this return omits to include casualties in the Naval brigade and in the Marines (doing duty on land), and in the Commissariat, Transport, and Hospital departments; nor does it seem to give our losses incurred during the disastrous stay in Bulgaria, etc.: so that the figures do not represent the entire losses to which even our Land forces were subjected.*

* Appendix E. It will be observed that the losses mentioned in the text do not take into account those of the Navy incurred on board ship. On the 8th of May, 1856, Lord Panmure made a statement in the House of Lords, to the effect that from the 19th of September, 1854 (that is, the day before the battle of the Alma), 270 Officers and 19,314 men were killed, or died of wounds or of disease, and that 2873 men were discharged the service as incapacitated for further service by war; total, 22,457 casualties,—excluding,

On the other hand, it was computed that the Russians lost as many as half a million men. But this is a surmise, and the facts have never been known. The estimate is probably exaggerated, though it is certain that the enemy's casualties were exceedingly great; but loss of men is not the greatest calamity that could befall an Empire like Russia.

The Crimean Guards Brigade, concentrated at Aldershot, remained there a few days, and during that time the Battalion was inspected by the Colonel of the Regiment, Field-Marshal Earl of Strafford, whose presence, as a Coldstream Officer, formed a connecting link between the glories of Waterloo and those achieved in the Russian war.

On the 8th July, Her Majesty the Queen appeared at the camp, and was received by the troops quartered there who had lately come back from the East. After the march past, a representative body of Officers and men, who had been under fire, from each regiment, was formed up in a hollow square round Her Majesty's carriage, to listen to the gracious address of welcome pronounced by the Queen herself to her brave men just returned

apparently, soldiers who died on board ship, sailors and marines serving on shore, and departmental troops. It seems strange that this imperfect statement should be sometimes quoted, instead of the return above mentioned, even though the latter is far from being satisfactory, and does not complete the tale of the losses to the Naval and Military Forces of the Crown during the war with Russia.

from an arduous and protracted war. The address was thus published in Orders :—

"Officers, Non-commissioned officers, and soldiers, I wish personally to convey through you, to the regiments assembled here this day, my hearty welcome on their return to England in health and full efficiency. Say to them, that I have watched anxiously over the difficulties and hardships which they have so nobly borne, that I have mourned with deep sorrow for the brave men who have fallen for their country, and that I have felt proud of that valour which with their gallant allies they have displayed on every field. I thank God that your dangers are over, whilst the glory of your deeds remains. But I know that, should your services be again required, you will be animated by the same devotion which in the Crimea has rendered you invincible."

Colonel Tower, who was present upon this interesting occasion, throws light upon it by recording in his diary that Her Majesty "made us a capital speech, full of gratitude and good feeling, and got quite eloquent; at last she quite broke down, and burst into tears when she talked of the poor fellows that were not there to receive her thanks." He adds, "If she had seen us in the trenches in July, 1855, or in Bulgaria in July, 1854, she would not have recognized her Brigade; we were now [July, 1856] all so nice and smart."

Next day the Crimean Battalions of the Brigade, 3200 strong, left Aldershot to make their public entry into London. Parading at 5.30 in the morning, they were conveyed to Nine Elms Station by train, where the three bands met them. The day was observed as a general holiday; the route taken was densely thronged by an enthusiastic crowd; the houses were decorated with flags; and the church bells rang out a joyous peal of welcome. On passing the Horse Guards, H.R.H. the Duke of Cambridge met the column, and as soon as the men perceived their former Commander, who had been with them at the hard-fought battle of Inkerman, "their stern gravity gave way, and they honoured him with the heartiest cheers." As they defiled past Buckingham Palace, the Queen accompanied by the Royal children, by her mother the Duchess of Kent, her uncle the King of the Belgians, and by other illustrious persons, came to the balcony to greet her gallant troops with her gracious presence.

Arrived in Hyde Park, they found the other four Guards Battalions, with the Colonels at the head of their respective Regiments, formed up in a line of quarter columns, facing Park Lane, with sufficient interval between them to receive the Crimean Battalions in their proper places on parade; and while the latter marched into their positions under the orders of Generals Lord Rokeby and Craufurd, their comrades presented arms. The three Regiments, now complete, were then handed over to their respective Colonels, to H.R.H. the Prince

Consort, Field-Marshal Earl of Strafford (seated in a carriage, because he was too infirm to head his Regiment on horseback), and H.R.H. the Duke of Cambridge. The Prince Consort having proceeded to join Her Majesty, the Duke of Cambridge assumed command of the whole. On the arrival of the Queen the bands played the national anthem, and the seven Battalions marched past Her Majesty, to the air, "See, the Conquering Hero comes." The Brigade then advanced in Review order to the flagstaff; another Royal salute was given ; and the pageant came to an end.

Where four allies were conducting a war in common, it was only natural that there should be an interchange of medals and of decorations, and this was done with no ungenerous hand. A new medal, more coveted than any other by soldiers and sailors, was established early in 1856, both for Officers and men in the Naval and Military services, who had distinguished themselves before the enemy "for valour." The distribution of the Victoria Cross did not, however, take place until the 26th of June, 1857, when all the claims for that most conspicuous honour had been fully investigated. The day appointed for the ceremony was observed as a general holiday, and a review was held in Hyde Park before Her Majesty the Queen, who affixed to the breast of each man entitled to it, the bronze cross he had won in the field by his personal bravery. In the Coldstream the recipients of this proud distinction were Majors Goodlake and Conolly, and Privates Strong and Stanlock.

This event, though it took place more than a year after the conclusion of peace, is connected with the Crimean struggle, and may be said to terminate the history of the protracted hostilities that troubled our relations with Russia. Thenceforward the war became a thing of the past, and its memories were merged into or overshadowed by other events which occurred elsewhere.

We have seen how the struggle shaped itself; how disastrously it was directed; and how devotedly our army maintained it, under very adverse and wholly exceptional circumstances. We allied ourselves to a Potentate whose tenure of power was precarious, whose interests were not our interests, and who only wished to adopt a foreign policy of adventure to reconcile his new subjects to his rule. His armies loyally supported ours in the field, and there we happily formed a sincere respect for the brave French troops who fought by our side. But the Government of Paris,—objecting always to transfer the theatre of war to Asia, where the enemy was really vulnerable,—restricted our field of operations to Europe ; and as Austria protected the Russians on the Bessarabian frontier, after their defeat, we were forced at a late period of the year to make a descent upon the Crimea.

Unhappily we had made no preparations for such an expedition, and had formed no plan for carrying it out ; in fact, such an invasion had not seriously entered into our calculations when we declared war against the Tsar.

Thus, we landed fortuitously at a point where the road led to the north side of Sevastopol, but where no harbours near that town were at hand to form a base of operations. Hence, without a base, we advanced to our objective, and, in due course, and after a successful battle, we arrived before it. But, on reaching this point, the Commander of our allies was indisposed to carry out the plan to which we had committed ourselves.

We therefore shifted our forces by a strange flank march to the south side, in the hope that we might there at least be enabled to bring the campaign to a speedy conclusion.

Sevastopol was at that time guarded by a small garrison, composed of a medley of indifferent and badly armed troops ; it was imperfectly defended towards the land, and in this direction it was an insignificant stronghold. Still, as long as it remained in that state, we hesitated to make any or even the least move against it ; we preferred to wait to bring up our siege-train, and to open regular approaches, with the expectation that the town would fall before the cold weather should set in, and put an end to all field operations.

But we had miscalculated. We did not take into account what a patriotic and energetic garrison might achieve during the unexpected respite granted them; nor did we perceive that we were altering, just as winter was approaching, the whole plan of invasion from an expedition of surprise to the more lengthened process of a regular siege. Thus, under the direction of an Engineer Officer of genius, did Sevastopol assume the proportions of a fortress, while the English and the French were looking idly on. And before they could batter down simultaneously the new works in front of each (which they allowed the enemy to construct), the Russian forces,—drawn from the Danubian Principalities, and set free to move against us by the unfortunate action of Austria—were hurried by forced marches into the Crimea, to the support of the scanty troops that were then to be found there.

The very moment we had meant to deliver our final blow, the enemy's arrangements were complete, and we had to fight the unequal battle of Inkerman. Although we were victorious there against tremendous odds, the result obliged us to spend the winter on the barren and snow-swept plain of the Chersonese.

For this emergency we were entirely unprepared, and an intensely cold season having begun early, our troops, as we have seen, suffered in consequence. We then hung on to our positions before Sevastopol with strong tenacity of purpose, and with a resolution which is above all praise. But we could not resume the siege till the spring of 1855, and it was early in September before the south side fell.

Taught by disaster, we then made every arrangement to continue the struggle with the best prospects of success. But the French, having gained the objects they had in view, became inactive; they clamoured for a cessation of hostilities; and thus, to preserve an alliance into which we had permitted ourselves to be drawn, we signed a peace of little value, and so put an end to the war.

The successes gained were not due to the skill of the Government that directed the struggle. On the contrary, our statesmanship had little or no claim upon our regard on that occasion. And yet, notwithstanding, the war brought many compensations to the nation, to make up for the lack of political forethought then disclosed. For, the military achievements, under disastrous conditions, were justly a cause of pride to the country, and were worthy of the best traditions of a glorious past. These achievements were solely brought about by that indomitable bravery, discipline, and power of endurance that have ever characterized our soldiers, as well as by the admirable system which made the British regimental Officers and men second to none that existed, at that time, in any other European army. To the rank and file, and to those who led them in the field, is all the merit to be ascribed, and not to any other body of Englishmen.

APPENDIX A.

GENERAL ORDER, No. 1, CONSTANTINOPLE, APRIL 30, 1854.

"THE Queen having been graciously pleased to appoint General Lord Raglan, G.C.B., to be Commander of the Forces to be employed in Turkey in support of Her Ally, His Imperial Majesty the Sultan, and His Lordship having arrived, all reports, etc., are to be made to him through the channels prescribed by Her Majesty's Regulations.

" The Commander of the Forces avails himself of the earliest opportunity to impress upon the Army the necessity of maintaining the strictest discipline, of respecting persons and property and the laws and usages of the country they have been sent to aid and defend, and particularly of avoiding to enter Mosques, Churches, and private dwellings of a people whose habits are peculiar and unlike those of the other nations of Europe.

" Lord Raglan fully relies upon the General and other Officers of the Army to afford him their support in the repression of disorder, and he confidently hopes that the troops themselves, anxious to maintain the character they have acquired elsewhere, will endeavour to become the example of obedience to orders and of attention to discipline, without which success is impossible, and their presence would be an evil instead of an advantage to those whose cause their Sovereign has deemed it proper to espouse.

"The Army will for the first time be associated with an Ally to whom it has been the lot of the British nation to be opposed in the field for many centuries.

"The gallantry and high military qualities of the French Army are matters of history, and the alliance which has now been formed, will, the Commander of the Forces trusts, be of long duration, as well as productive of the most important and the happiest consequences.

"Lord Raglan is aware, from personal communication with the distinguished Officer who is appointed to command the French Army, Marshal St. Arnaud, and many of the Superior Officers, that every disposition exists throughout their ranks to cultivate the best understanding with the British Army, and to co-operate most warmly with it, and he entertains no doubt that Her Majesty's troops are animated by the same spirit, and that the first ambition of each Army will be, to acquire the confidence and good opinion of the other.

"By Command,
"(Signed)   J. BUCKNALL B. ESTCOURT,
"Brigadier-General and D. A. General."

APPENDIX B.

DEATH OF FIELD-MARSHAL LORD RAGLAN, G.C.B.

I.

GENERAL ORDER, HORSE GUARDS, JULY 4, 1855.*

"THE General Commanding-in-Chief has received Her Majesty's most gracious Commands to express to the Army the deep regret with which Her Majesty has to deplore the loss of a most devoted and able Officer by the death of Field-Marshal Lord Raglan, the Commander of the Forces in the Crimea.

"Her Majesty has been pleased to command that her sentiments shall be communicated to the Army, in order that the military career of so illustrious an Officer shall be recorded, not only as an honourable testimony of Her Majesty's sense of his eminent services, and the respect due to his memory, but as an example worthy of imitation by all ranks of her Army.

"Selected by the Duke of Wellington to be his Military Secretary and Aide-de-camp, he took part, nearly fifty years ago, in all the military achievements of our greatest Commander. From him Lord Raglan adopted, as the

* Kinglake, *Invasion of the Crimea*, viii. 283.

guiding principle of his life, a constant, undeviating obedience to the call of duty.

"During a long peace, his life was most usefully employed in those unwearied attentions to the interests and welfare of the Army, shown by the kindness, the impartiality, and justice, with which he transacted all his duties.

"When war broke out last year, he was selected by his Sovereign to take command of the Army proceeding to the East; he never hesitated—he obeyed the summons, although he had reached an age when an Officer may be disposed to retire from active duties in the field.

"At the head of the troops during the arduous operations of the campaign, he resumed the early habits of his life; by his calmness in the hottest moments of the battle, and by his quick perception in taking advantage of the ground, or the movements of the enemy, he won the confidence of his Army and performed great and brilliant services.

"In the midst of a winter's campaign, in a severe climate, and surrounded by difficulties, he never despaired.

"The heroic Army, whose fortitude amidst the severest privations is recognized by Her Majesty as beyond all praise, have shown their attachment to their Commander by the deep regrets with which they now mourn his loss.

"Her Majesty is confident that the talents and virtues which distinguished Lord Raglan throughout the whole of his valuable life, will for ever endear his memory to the British Army.

"By Command of General the Right Hon. Viscount
"Hardinge, Commanding-in-Chief.
"(Signed)   G. A. WETHERALL,
"Adjutant-General."

2.

FRENCH ARMY OF THE EAST, NO. 15 GENERAL ORDER.*

"Death has suddenly taken away, while in full exercise of his command, the Field-Marshal Lord Raglan, and has plunged the British in mourning.

"We all share the sorrow of our brave Allies. Those who knew Lord Raglan, who knew the history of his life —so noble, so pure, so replete with service rendered to his country—those who witnessed his fearless demeanour at Alma and Inkerman, who recall the calm and stoic greatness of his character throughout this rude and memorable campaign, every generous heart indeed, will deplore the loss of such a man. The sentiments here expressed by the General-in-chief, are those of the whole Army. He has himself been cruelly struck by this unlooked-for blow.

"The public grief only increases his sorrow at being for ever separated from a companion-in-arms, whose genial spirit he loved, whose virtues he admired, and from whom he has always received the most loyal and hearty co-operation.

"(Signed)   A. PÉLISSIER,
                "Commander-in-Chief.

"Head-Quarters before Sevastopol; June 29, 1855."

---

* Kinglake, *Invasion of the Crimea*, viii. 291.

APPENDIX C.

I.

RETURN SHOWING THE AGES OF THE NON-COMMISSIONED OFFICERS AND MEN COMPOSING THE 1ST BATTALION COLDSTREAM GUARDS WHICH PROCEEDED TO THE EAST IN FEBRUARY, 1854, AND OF THE DRAFTS SENT OUT DURING THE WAR WITH RUSSIA.

Battalion and Drafts.	Strength.	Date of Departure from England.	Under 20 years of age.	20 and under 25.	25 and under 30.	30 and under 35.	35 and under 40.	Over 40 years of age.	Age of the Oldest Soldier.
									Years.
1st Battalion	919	23-2-54	42	300	286	165	110	16	43
1st Draft	153	28-6-54	48	86	10	6	1	2	40
2nd ,,	58	27-10-54	26	26	2	3	1	—	36
3rd ,,	153	25-11-54	45	93	14	—	1	—	35
4th ,,	307	13-4-55	54	198	50	3	2	—	36
5th ,,	207	16-9-55	4	108	76	16	2	1	44
6th ,,	263	14-2-56	13	182	51	16	1	—	35
Total ..	2060		232	993	489	209	118	19	

2.

RETURN SHOWING THE PREVIOUS OCCUPATIONS OF THE NON-COMMISSIONED OFFICERS AND MEN COMPOSING THE 1ST BATTALION, AND THE DRAFTS THAT WERE ENGAGED IN THE WAR WITH RUSSIA.

Battalion and Drafts.	Agricultural Labourers.	Manufacturing Mechanics, Cloth Weavers, etc.	Mechanics in occupations favourable to physical development, as Masons, etc.	Shopmen and Clerks.	Professional occupations.	No previous occupation, as boys, etc.	Total.
1st Battalion	694	103	83	13	1	25	919
1st Draft ..	128	10	14	—	—	1	153
2nd ,, ..	44	2	4	1	1	6	58
3rd ,, ..	121	14	15	1	1	1	153
4th ,, ..	240	23	43	1	—	—	307
5th ,, ..	122	40	42	3	—	—	207
6th ,, ..	174	46	39	1	—	3	263
Total ..	1523	238	240	20	3	36	2060

APPENDIX D.

RETURN SHOWING BY MONTHS THE NUMBER OF NON-COMMISSIONED OFFICERS AND MEN OF THE 1st BATTALION COLDSTREAM GUARDS WHO LOST THEIR LIVES DURING THE WAR WITH RUSSIA, BETWEEN FEBRUARY 23, 1854, AND JUNE 30, 1856, AND THE CAUSE OF DEATH.*

	Killed in Action or in the Trenches.	Died of Wounds.	Total Deaths by the Enemy.	Died of Disease.					Total.	Grand Total.
				Cholera.	Dysentery.	Fevers.	Diarrhœa.	Miscellaneous.		
1854.										
March	—	—	—	—	—	—	—	1	1	1
April	—	—	—	—	—	—	—	1	1	1
July	—	—	—	2	—	6	—	1	9	9
August	—	—	—	28	—	22	2	1	53	53
September	—	2	2	5	—	12	2	—	19	21
October	1	2	3	14	—	10	11	1	36	39
November	67	22	89	9	4	4	13	2	32	121
December	—	6	6	7	11	9	45	6	78	84

* This table is not absolutely correct, as it accounts only for 691 instead of 699 Non-commissioned officers and men, who fell in the war, either killed, or wounded, or by disease. According to Dr. Wyatt, who does not classify the casualties by months, the total losses were 81 killed in action, 54 died of wounds, and 564 died by disease, or 699 men. But the above return has been given, as it indicates sufficiently the months during which the bulk of the men lost their lives.

APPENDIX.

	Killed in Action or in the Trenches.	Died of Wounds.	Total Deaths by the Enemy.	Died of Disease.					Total.	Grand Total.
				Cholera.	Dysentery.	Fevers.	Diarrhœa.	Miscellaneous.		
1855.										
January ..	2	3	5	2	12	14	61	13	102	107
February ..	—	4	4	—	11	16	42	14	83	87
March ..	—	2	2	—	4	8	15	2	29	31
April ..	—	—	—	—	3	8	6	1	18	18
May ..	—	—	—	3	2	5	2	1	13	13
June ..	—	—	—	25	—	10	4	2	41	41
July ..	—	1	1	—	—	9	1	1	11	12
August ..	4	5	9	2	—	6	1	—	9	18
September	—	—	—	1	—	2	1	—	4	4
October ..	—	2	2	1	—	4	1	1	7	9
November	—	2	2	1	—	5	2	2	10	12
December	—	—	—	—	—	1	—	2	3	3
1856.										
January ..	—	—	—	—	2	4	—	—	6	6
March ..	—	—	—	—	—	—	1	—	1	1
Total ..	74	51	125	100	49	155	210	52	566	691

APPENDIX E.

1.

RETURN OF THE TOTAL NUMBER OF OFFICERS AND MEN IN THE ARMY WHO HAVE BEEN KILLED IN THE CRIMEA, UP TO JUNE 1, 1856.*

	Officers.	Non-Com. Officers.	Men.	Total.
Cavalry	8	10	104	122
Artillery	10	10	111	131
Sappers and Miners	9	1	31	41
Infantry	119	140	2191	2450
Staff	11	—	—	11
Total	157	161	2437	2755

* *Annual Register*, 1856, "Public Documents," p. 347.

2.

RETURN OF TOTAL NUMBER OF OFFICERS AND MEN IN THE ARMY WHO HAVE BEEN WOUNDED IN THE CRIMEA; OF THE WOUNDED WHO HAVE SINCE DIED; OF THOSE WHO HAVE RECOVERED AND HAVE RETURNED TO THEIR DUTY; OF THOSE WHO HAVE DIED OF SICKNESS; AND OF THOSE INVALIDED, UP TO JUNE 1, 1856.*

	NUMBER WOUNDED.				NUMBER WOUNDED SINCE DIED.				NUMBER RECOVERED AND RETURNED TO DUTY.†		
	Officers.	N.-C. Offs.	Men.	Total.	Officers.	N.-C. Offs.	Men.	Total.	N.-C. Offs.	Men.	Total.
Cavalry	22	21	216	259	4	1	25	30	38	585	623
Artillery	30	37	595	662	1	4	48	53	98	1171	1269
Sappers and Miners	12	7	79	98	6	1	22	29	18	154	172
Infantry	422	514	9892	10828	73	79	1753	1905	528	8920	9448
Staff ..	29	—	—	29	2	—	—	2	—	—	—
Total	515	579	10782	11876	86	85	1848	2019	682	10830	11512

[*Continued on next page.*

* *Annual Register*, 1856, "Public Documents," p. 347.

† The columns marked with † are published with the following remark: " There are no documents in the Adjutant-General's Office which will afford the information specified in the above columns, and the same can only be obtained (and probably then only imperfectly) from the Officers Commanding in the Crimea."

	Number Died from Sickness.*				Number Invalided End of War.*		
	Officers	Non-Com. Officers	Men	Total	Non-Com. Officers	Men	Total
Cavalry	23	53	954	1030	70	850	920
Artillery	10	35	1263	1308	164	1953	2117
Sappers and Miners	5	7	168	180	41	176	217
Infantry	104	479	12935	13518	862	10602	11464
Staff ..	5	—	—	5	—	—	—
Total	147	574	15320	16041	1137	13581	14718

* The columns marked with * are published with the following remark: "There are no documents in the Adjutant-General's Office which will afford the information specified in the above columns, and the same can only be obtained (and probably then only imperfectly) from the Officers Commanding in the Crimea."

INDEX.

Adams, Gen :, 46, 156, 158, 161
Aladyn, camp at, 29, 39, 42
Aldershot camp, 269, 285, 288
Alexander II., Tsar of Russia, 234
Alma, the, 72, 76
Armament of the British Infantry, 22, 190, 191, 221, 247
Austria, 9, 10, 36, 52, 56, 59, 276, 292, 294
Azof, Sea of, 60, 61, 209, 220, 236, 238, 270

Balaklava, 64, 97, 103, 110, 111, 113, 129, 146, 202, 206, 209, 211, 215, 225
Baltic Sea, the, 55
Bath, Order of, investiture of, in the Crimea, 259
Bentinck, Gen : Sir H., 21, 41, 46, 80, 165, 185, 198, 232, 259
Black Sea, the, 15, 17, 55, 57, 277
Bombardments of Sevastopol, 122, 234, 239, 241, 250, 251
Bosphorus, the, 16, 277
Bosquet, Gen :, 48, 76, 111, 113, 134, 149, 175, 179, 251

Brigade of Guards, 19, 23, 39, 45, 67, 79, 82, 113, 118, 134, 149, 150, 159, 161, 163, 164, 166, 182, 185, 197, 220, 222, 224, 232, 241, 243, 244, 253, 258, 264, 265, 266, 271, 278, 288, 289
British army in the East, 21, 25, 46, 63, 65, 69, 77, 87, 98, 111, 113, 120, 123, 133, 137, 145, 149, 190, 199, 209, 212, 216, 237, 252, 258, 268, 275, 287, 296
Brown, Gen : Sir G., 23, 27, 47
Bulgaria, 27, 31, 64, 285
Buller, Gen :, 47, 155, 157
Butler, Maj : J. A., 33, 35

Cambridge, H.R.H. Duke of, 46, 67, 79, 165, 197, 198, 202, 290
Campbell, Gen : Sir Colin [Lord Clyde], 46, 83, 112, 232, 259
Canrobert, Gen :, 29, 48, 76, 103, 105, 150, 209, 233, 236
Cardigan, Gen : Earl of, 39, 47, 69, 130

INDEX.

Carleton, Col: Dudley [Lord Dorchester], 223
Casualties, 85, 125, 127, 131, 134, 136, 185, 186, 220, 235, 239, 241, 243, 250, 252, 255, 286, 287
Cathcart, Gen: Hon: Sir G., 47, 102, 105, 163, 175, 176, 177
Caucasus, the, 57
Cemetery, a British, in the Crimea, 284
Cholera. *See* Sickness among the troops.
Circassians, the, 58, 59, 238, 277
Citate, defeat of the Russians at, 13
Clarendon, Earl of, 17, 238
Codrington, Gen: Sir W., 41, 47, 78, 80, 148, 154, 162, 232, 251, 259, 273, 282
Coldstream Guards, the, 19, 29, 41, 42, 45, 65, 79, 80, 82, 83, 86, 114, 116, 125, 126, 127, 132, 137, 149, 151, 152, 159, 160, 165, 166, 178, 181, 186, 198, 199, 210, 213, 221, 223, 225, 229, 230, 231, 232, 245, 248, 259, 263, 276, 284, 285, 286, 292
Conolly, Maj:, 136, 292
Craufurd, Gen:, 232, 283, 290
Crimea, the, 38, 45, 55, 60, 62, 71, 80, 110, 143, 196, 200, 209, 215, 268, 281, 285, 293, 294

Dannenberg, Gen:, 144, 154, 159, 174, 185
Danube, the, 11, 12, 31, 39
Danubian Principalities, the, 11, 12, 16, 38, 294

Dawson, Lt:·Col: Hon. T. Vesey, 151, 160, 169, 187
Devna, the Lake of, 42
Dobrudsha, the, 32
Drummond, Col: Gordon, 40, 223, 231

Eupatoria, 64, 65, 219, 237, 270
Evans, Gen: Sir de L., 46, 78, 154, 155

Flank march round Sevastopol, 97
Fleet, the British, in the East, 16, 17, 38, 46, 64, 69, 122, 241
Forey, Gen :, 48, 111, 150, 184
French army, the, in the East, 22, 29, 39, 48, 54, 69, 76, 86, 101, 106, 111, 123, 139, 145, 170, 180, 200, 206, 209, 219, 234, 252, 258, 275, 292

Gevreklek, camp at, 42
Goodlake, Maj:, 120, 135, 292
Gordon, Col:, R.E., 119
Gortchakoff, Gen: Prince Michael, 11, 32, 36, 145, 159, 177, 179, 184, 249, 251, 268
Grenadier Guards, the, 19, 45, 79, 82, 86, 127, 159, 160, 165, 168, 221, 225
Guards, the. *See* Brigade of Guards.

Hamley, Capt: [Gen: Sir E.], 161
Hardinge, Lord, 22
Hay, Col:, 41
Highlanders, the, 27, 46, 79, 83, 111, 120, 134, 232, 253, 254

INDEX.

Hospitals, the military, 43, 70, 211, 212, 223, 278

Inkerman, 112, 144, 146

Kars, fall of, 271
Kertch, 61, 220, 236
Kitspur, the, 148, 166, 175, 179

La Marmora, Gen :, 237
Lindsay, Lt : R. [Lord Wantage], 82
Liprandi, Gen :, 129, 133, 136, 145
Lucan, Gen : Earl of, 47, 112
Luders, Gen :, 32, 282
Lyons, Adm : Sir E. [Lord Lyons], 93, 105, 107

Mackenzie heights, 99, 101, 128, 250, 267, 281
Malakoff, the, 107, 108, 115, 123, 239, 252
Malta, 19, 24, 264, 285
Menshikoff, Gen : Prince, 71, 73, 92, 99, 102, 110, 121, 128, 144, 195, 197, 220, 249
Minié rifle, the. *See* Armament of the British Infantry.
Mussa Pasha, 34, 35

Napoleon III., Emperor of the French, 7, 233, 235, 238, 269, 276, 280
Napoleon, Gen : Prince, 48, 76
Newton, Col :, 151, 222
Nicholas I., Tsar of Russia, 6, 10, 14, 18, 54, 234
Nightingale, Miss, 212

Omar Pasha, 12, 27, 31, 34, 40, 146, 207, 219, 237, 271

Paris, Treaty of, (1856), 276
Paulet, Col : Lord F., 45, 151, 198, 223, 231
Pavloff, Gen :, 145, 157, 172
Pélisser, Marshal, 236, 242, 259, 270, 282
Pennefather, Gen :, 46, 155, 157
Perekop, isthmus of, 60, 220
Prince Consort, H.R.H. the, 291
Prince Imperial, the, 279

Queen Victoria, Her Majesty, 265, 288, 289, 290, 291

Raglan, F.-M. Lord, 23, 46, 71, 74, 77, 85, 87, 93, 104, 146, 150, 183, 210, 236, 243
Redan, the, 107, 123, 239, 252, 256
Rokeby, Gen : Lord, 222, 224, 232, 284, 290
Roumania. *See* Danubian Principalities.
Russian army, the, 11, 32, 57, 59, 71, 73, 84, 91, 111, 128, 143, 145, 154, 163, 166, 183, 189, 190, 209, 218, 237, 249, 267, 268, 282, 294. *See also* Sevastopol.
Russian empire, the, 3, 55, 58, 292

St. Arnaud, Marshal, 29, 48, 74, 77, 85, 88, 103
Sandbag battery, the, 113, 126, 148, 156, 160, 165, 168, 189
Sardinian army, the, 237
Scarlett, Gen : Hon : Sir J., 47, 232

Scots Fusilier Guards, the, 19, 79, 81, 82, 159, 160, 165, 221, 225
Scots Guards. *See* Scots Fusilier Guards.
Scutari, 23, 28, 203, 212, 285
Sevastopol, 52, 54, 56, 60, 62, 88, 91, 92, 93, 98, 102, 105, 110, 113, 121, 128, 135, 139, 144, 183, 190, 200, 202, 217, 218, 219, 232, 233, 249, 251, 255, 257, 267, 269, 275, 293
Sickness among the troops, 29, 39, 42, 44, 65, 70, 102, 104, 114, 199, 211, 212, 225, 229, 231, 286, 287
Silistria, siege of, 32
Simpson, Gen : Sir J., 243, 253, 273
Sinope, battle of, 13
Soimonoff, Gen :, 144, 154, 157, 158
Stanlock, Private, 292
Steele, Col : [Gen : Sir T.], 23, 79, 211
Strafford, F.-M. Earl of, 288, 291
Stratford de Redcliffe, Lord, 17, 259
Strong, Private, 292
Suleiman Pasha, 48
Sultan of Turkey, 10, 25

Tchernaya, the, 101, 109, 128, 148, 177, 203, 217, 230, 250
Timofeyeff, Gen :, 184.
Todleben, Gen :, 93, 108, 189, 233, 238, 243
Torrens, Gen :, 47, 176, 177
Tower, Col :, 171, 281, 289
Transport, the army, 25, 66, 69, 114, 207, 216, 268
Turkish army, the, 12, 31, 48, 56, 65, 69, 76, 130, 145, 200, 207, 219, 237, 270

Upton, Col : Hon : G. [Viscount Templetown], 41, 80, 151, 160, 176, 182, 186, 198, 221, 223

Varna, 27, 29, 43, 45
Victoria Cross, the, 291
Vienna Note, the, 11

Wilson, Col :, 117, 171, 177, 181
Women at the seat of war, 27
Woronzoff road, the, 110, 133, 134, 206
Wyatt, Dr :, 211, 278

www.ingramcontent.com/pod-product-compliance
Lightning Source LLC
Chambersburg PA
CBHW030014240426
43672CB00007B/944